MY
SILK ROAD

MY
SILK ROAD

The Adventures & Struggles
of a British Asian Refugee

RAM GIDOOMAL CBE

Foreword by Dame Prue Leith DBE

Pippa Rann
books & media

An imprint of
Salt Desert Media Group Limited,
7 Mulgrave Chambers, 26 Mulgrave Rd,
Sutton SM2 6LE, England, UK.
Email: publisher@pipparannbooks.com
Website: www.pipparannbooks.com

ISBN 978-1-913738-60-0

Designed and typeset by Raghav Khattar

Printed and bound by CPI Group (UK) Ltd, Croydon, CR0 4YY

These memoirs are dedicated to *Daddy*.

Naraindas Dayaram Gidoomal
1925–1969

I owe him a huge debt of gratitude,
as do so many others,
for his willingness to accept hardship
in order to support and care sacrificially
for dependents from the extended family.

Contents

Glossary

Ama – an endearing and respectful term for a grandmother or an older relative (sometimes used as an honorific)

Baba – An endearing and respectful term for a grandfather or an older relative (sometimes used as an honorific)

Bhajias – South Asian savoury dishes made of chopped vegetables, whether presented as a dry vegetable curry, or mixed in a spiced batter before being lightly deep-fried. The latter, whether by themselves or with the former sort of bhajia, can be included in the more encompassing term "bhajia", but are accurately called "pakoras".

BNP – The British National Party is a far-right, fascist political party in the United Kingdom

BSE – Bovine spongiform encephalopathy, commonly known as "mad cow disease", is an incurable and inevitably fatal neurodegenerative disease of cattle.

D'Hondt Rule – Named after a Belgian lawyer and mathematician, the d'Hondt system is a form of proportional representation widely used in continental Europe.

Dada – A term of respect for an older brother or male relative (sometimes used as an honorific)

Dadi – A term of respect for an elder sister or female relative (sometimes used as an honorific)

Dogo – A Swahili word meaning 'the younger'.

Gulaab jamun: Indian sweet made of dried (or, nowadays, often, powdered) milk, garnished with dried nuts such as almonds and cashews, slow-cooked at a low temperature in oil or ghee (clarified butter) until it reaches a golden brown color; then soaked in a light sugar or other sweet syrup flavoured with green cardamom and either rose water or kewra, and sometimes enhanced with saffron. There are innumerable varieties of *gulaab jamun*, just as there are innumerable varieties of cake.

Kuba – A Swahili word meaning 'the elder'.

Lambeth Partner – A partnership of donors supporting the Archbishop of Canterbury's personal ministry priorities

Lausanne – the Lausanne Movement; a global movement founded by Billy Graham and by Dr John Stott that mobilizes evangelical leaders to collaborate for world evangelization. The stated vision is "the whole church taking the whole gospel to the whole world".

LGB/ LGBT/ LGBTQ, etc. – acronyms indicating lesbian, gay, bisexual, and other minorities who are not simply heterosexual. In other words, LGB (and variations on that) are shorthand for non-mainstream sexual orientations.

NASDAQ – The Nasdaq Stock Market (National Association of Securities Dealers Automated Quotations Stock Market) is an American stock exchange based in New York City.

The New Statesman – a British political and cultural magazine published from London.

NGO – Non-Governmental Organization, such as Oxfam and Tearfund

NHS – The National Health Service of the UK

Pakoras – South Asian savoury dishes made of chopped vegetables, mixed in a spiced batter before being lightly deep-fried.

Panorama broadcast – a British current affairs documentary programme aired on BBC Television.

Rai Bahadur: (or *Rao Bahadur* in South India), abbreviated R.B., was a title of honour bestowed during British rule in India to individuals for faithful service to the Empire or for acts of public service. From 1911, the title was accompanied by a medal called a Title Badge. Translated, "*Rao*" means "prince", and "*Bahadur*" means "brave" or "most honourable". Bestowed mainly on Hindus, the equivalent title for Muslim and Parsi subjects was *Khan Bahadur*. For Sikhs, it was *Sardar Bahadur*.

Foreword

For more than one reason this book is aptly named.

Ram Gidoomal's path appears to have indeed been silken, but behind that illusion, the real cause of Ram's success lies in his character and his determination to overcome the potholes and dead ends.

The first bump in the road was a veritable crater: the expulsion of his successful and wealthy family from Kenya and the confiscation of their business. The 17-year-old Ram found himself running a corner shop in Shepherd's bush, living above the shop with his parents and gaggle of siblings. But the young Ram was clever and had his father's head for business. He worked hard, studied hard and did well.

Ram's progress in all fields: academic; business; love and marriage seem now to have been on a continuous upward path to glory, but it wasn't quite like that. His and Sunita's constancy and determination to marry, finally overcame her high caste parent's horror at the prospect of a low-caste son in law: his diligence and cleverness reaped an enviable crop of scholarships, degrees and awards. His business acumen led to a life of wealth so beyond his needs that it troubled his conscience – and Sunita and he decided to step off the gravy train.

The most successful biographies are generally ones where the subject's life is tragic and where there is plenty of scandal. But Ram has no skeletons in his cupboard, has behaved honourably in business, and is an all-round good egg. His primary motive in writing is to leave his story for his grandchildren. Yet I find that story full of interest, particularly the early chapters about life in Mombasa, the tale of his conversion to Christ in a pub, the endless discrimination when applying for government appointments traditionally dished out to public school toffs, and the deep breath he and Sunita had to take when opting to work exclusively for charities doing good.

I've known Ram a long time and I am not surprised that the threads that run through the book are so constant and strong. The importance of family, hard work, constant learning, moral decency, and prayer matter deeply to him. His motto is *Never Let What Cant be Done Stop You Doing What Can Be Done*. It's a mantra he has followed all his life.

The result is a book that is deeply stimulating and challenging, but also riveting, witty, and humorous – and therefore inspiring.

– **Dame Prue Leith DBE**

Author's Note

The idea for this book was sparked following my 70th birthday celebrations when the children and grandchildren went out of their way to prepare a surprise birthday party for me. That was in December 2020 at the height of the lockdown when it was not possible to meet indoors. The children contacted a lot of my family, extended family, and friends across the world, inviting them to send their birthday messages for me which they then put together in a surprise video.

I was, of course, overwhelmed by the video and the very special virtual celebration that followed which naturally led on to many questions from the children and, especially, the grandchildren. They wanted to know who the various contributors were and to learn about the different family members who they had never met or even known about, and how we were all connected.

I decided to draw up a family tree – with a lot of help from my wife, Sunita, and from the family graphic design expert, Ricki. I managed to contact many of my extended family spread all over the globe, and the full tree, complete with photos, was circulated to the whole family. A small portion of that family tree, which relates to my immediate family can be seen in the photo inserts in the middle of this book. The full family tree extends beyond my grandfather's lineage to include his two younger brothers and their children. The total number on the tree is nearly 200 and it was wonderful to be able to connect with many relatives across the globe to get the full names, confirm the relevant dates of birth, and catch up on their news.

With each name, memories and stories came flooding back, and I was keen to share some of these with the children and grandchildren, and so came the idea to write these down. The outcome of that exercise is now in your hands.

Some names have had to be changed and some removed to protect the privacy of the individuals who have requested this. One name that is missing in my memoirs is that of my mother's sister, Aunty Hari. I never had the joy and privilege of meeting Dr Hari Sen. She was, however, always held up to me as the example of someone to emulate. My mother would often recount with great pride how her sister had to fight against all odds, as a single woman, in pre-independence India (in fact, in the 1930s!) to earn a PhD from the University of California, Berkeley – and then willingly return to India for the purpose of wrestling with the challenges of establishing a school in Delhi – Tagore International School. You can read more about Dr Hari Sen at https://www.vv.tagoreint.com/about-us/introduction/

I am grateful to Helen Barker for introducing me to Clare O'Driscoll with whom I have worked closely in writing these memoirs. Clare not only listened to my memories and wrote them up, but also shaped and structured them into the words of this book, though I wanted to make sure that the final style and voice is mine. Without her wordsmithery, however, I greatly doubt that the book would have got done – at least, not within the timeframe set by the publisher. Clare and I communicated mostly virtually, and we did not in fact meet face to face until the first draft of the book was completed a year after our first phone call to discuss my project.

I could not have even begun the construction of the family tree or writing my stories themselves without the support and encouragement of my wife, Sunita, to whom I owe a huge debt of gratitude. I would like to thank my children, as well, for their helpful feedback and comments on the manuscript.

Chapter One
The Silence

There arc places where you can not only see the stars, you feel like you could touch them.

On the night my life changed forever, the view from my uncle's rooftop was bathed in moonlight stretching for miles. It was a warm Mombasa evening but, despite the sticky humidity that sometimes hung at the heart of our densely built-up little island, we were cooled by the gentle brush of sea breeze.

I looked down at the jumble of colourful neon lights, dotted along streets all the way from the port to the centre of Mombasa. They flashed from bars, restaurants, and hotels – all vying for the custom of sailors or other travellers from recently docked ships. A cacophony of shouts, chatter and blaring music drifted up to us. On the rooftop terrace however, our own noise levels were beginning to compete, the volume rising with every new arrival. Women and children always turned up first, laden with flavoursome dishes for the buffet and already swapping notes on recipes. There was Aunty Kamla with her special chicken curry, Aunty Janki and her macaroni cheese, my mum's amazing fragrant curried lamb, and my favourite, sweet *gulaab jamuns*, made by my father's eldest sister, Dadi Kala.

The men, dependent on the comings and goings of cargo ships at the port for goods to buy and sell, would join the party later, always muttering about bad business, despite having pulled up in flash cars that told quite another story. It was all part of the happy banter that would go on long into the night. Later, the adults would probably move indoors, where family members would sing while local amateur musicians might play traditional music on the sitar, tabla, and harmonium.

Was it a special occasion? Even at the time I don't think I knew. Our family thrived on parties so there could have been any number of excuses. I simply knew it as an opportunity to stay up late with my brothers, sisters, and cousins. We played chase around the rooftop, screaming with laughter as we weaved in and out of the crowd of at least a hundred family members and friends from the local Sindhi community. The buffet table was filling up now, creaking under the weight of the shared feast which, in true Asian style, would have catered for numbers far exceeding those present. In anticipation, I breathed in the fragrant aromas of cumin, coriander, ginger, and garlic.

Our family lives were those of hard work but also of idyllic beauty, rich with friendship, music, and food. A life of pleasure and play, afternoon swims and evening strolls, lively family meals and parties, just like this one.

I had no idea that our perfect island life was about to be upended.

A sudden hushed silence fell upon the crowd, conversations breaking off mid-sentence. Instinctively I followed the collective gaze. My father, Daddy, had just walked in. Why was everyone staring? Normally, each new arrival was met with a burst of noisy excited greetings but, like a moment suspended in time, no one seemed able to say a word. Then, in a beat, with a touch of embarrassment, the murmur of chat started up again. It was too late. No amount of new noise could smother the roar of that silence for me. What had just happened? I knew something was amiss as I watched my uncles and aunts gathering around Daddy, huddled together in urgent but muted discussions.

As the evening wore on, sadness spread across the faces of those present. Our immediate family looked shocked and fearful, my mother and aunts failing to fight back tears. I tried to get closer, but the crowd around Daddy was growing and anyway, at 16, I was considered a child. I would be told nothing.

Finally, one of my older sisters rushed over and whispered to me, "You are not going to believe this!"

It was her standard conversation starter and, I must admit, my reply was normally, "I don't", but for once I could tell this was not for dramatic effect. Something was seriously wrong.

"Daddy's been given a deportation order," she blurted out, "He has 24 hours to leave the country!"

"24 hours? But that means...tomorrow? He can't...Where will he go?" My mind was racing with panic.

"Well, London I suppose. We're British."

We. This wasn't just about Daddy. We were all dependent on him. What would happen to us once he went?

I wasn't naïve. I knew about the deportations. I'd been following them in our local paper, The Mombasa Times. Every day, another story, another life thrown into disarray. The owner of the Rex Hotel, just across the street from us? Gone overnight for refusing to replace the Queen's portrait with the President's. And that was just one.

The gathering was becoming quieter now, eerily so. The buffet table sat mostly untouched. We children were given food, but the adults had lost their appetites and anyway, everyone seemed in a rush to leave.

We drove home in silence, so many unanswered questions on the tips of our tongues. Who would run the business? None of the children were old enough and all the other uncles had enough work and responsibilities of their own. What about school? Exams? What about friends? What about our life?

It all felt like some terrible mistake. Deportations happened yes, but to other people. Not us. Never us, with our 15-bedroomed apartment in the heart of Mombasa tended by a string of domestic helpers: a cook, driver, and servants. Not us, with our hard earned, thriving business. Us, who had sunk our roots deep into the African soil. Us who belonged here.

And, not us, who had seen all this before.

Because, while it was new to me, the older generation of my family had already been here, fleeing my grandfather's palace in Hyderabad when they found themselves on the wrong side of the border during the Partition of British India in 1947, some short years before I was born. Surely such an upheaval shouldn't happen to anyone more than once in a lifetime?

Back in British India, despite being from the lowest of the low in terms of caste, my family had hauled themselves up to success and wealth, mostly through my grandfather's hard work in Hyderabad, Sindh, where he had bought the exquisite Moti Mahal, a palace in which my father and his six siblings grew up and wed.

However, Partition meant that, as Hindus, they were no longer safe there. They had a choice: move over the border into the new India, or make their way to East Africa where the family had established trading links. We supplied silk procured from Japan in the east, to ports in East and South Africa. In those days, young Sindhi men were expected to travel in order to develop the family's business interests, so my grandfather Baba Dayaram, the eldest male, and therefore head of the family, was already living and working overseas, having moved to South Africa with his uncle in 1907. Grandfather had opened his silk business, Japan Bazaar, in Johannesburg before later settling in Cape Town where he sadly died in 1936. It was this same silk business that employed his two brothers. Dada Hiranand was based in Kenya, while the youngest, Dada Jethanand, was stationed in Japan.

Such was the level of affluence the brothers achieved, that they were able to travel First Class long distances, and stay at Five Star hotels in expensive destinations. That is attested by documents, discovered by my cousin Hashu while searching the internet, which show his father Dada Jethanand, my grandfather's youngest brother, travelling from Kobe in Japan via the Panama Canal to New York. And, there, he stayed at the five-star Knickerbocker Hotel – which still exists in Manhattan!

It was decided that my parents, their siblings and extended family should make the long journey, leaving the subcontinent on a ship docked in Karachi and destined for Mombasa port. They packed up their life and left their homeland. They left their beloved India, but bundled what remnants they could carry onto the boat with them: a stone milling grinder to make flour for chapattis; a silver jug inscribed with their wedding date; their icons and idols and cooking utensils, plus an old trumpet-style gramophone and a pile of 78 records of their favourite Sindhi songs. This was how they carried their heritage with them, in their hearts and in their arms, even as they tore themselves away.

One final thing my father could not leave behind was his precious stamp collection, built up lovingly since childhood. Using his privileged position as eldest son and head of the family, he made sure his stamps were not forgotten and packed them up with great care, taking time to protect them from travel damage, even as the family rushed to leave with their lives.

Starting from scratch, they built a new life here in Mombasa. My father and uncles worked with Dada Hiranand, adding their astute commercial acumen and experience to build on the business already established by their father, Baba Dayaram, in Cape Town, selling silk procured by Dada Jethanand in Japan. To ensure the efficiency of these international transactions, telegrams were used, but also a coded language to protect confidentiality. When making an order, essential details such as design, quantity, colour, delivery time and price needed to be communicated discreetly.

For pricing, we used the word "LordShivaj" to represent the digits from 0 to 9. For example, DS would be 34 and OJ, 19. We would write the customer sale price on one side of the label and the actual cost, in code, on the other. This enabled shop assistants to haggle and negotiate with all the information they needed. Of course, knowing how these codes worked also meant we could cheekily visit other shops and decipher their codes to work out their pricing systems!

The business was founded in 1918 and World War Two had meant that the price of any goods arriving in East Africa could be multiplied by a factor of tens or even hundreds, depending on the products. The family, quickly grasping this, made their fortunes, importing even more swathes of exquisite Japanese silk in every shade, which they then cut to order from large reels at the customer's request. We mostly sold to the railway workers and other Indian immigrants, buying sari material for their wives and daughters, with the high point for sales being Diwali. As well as silk, the brothers soon added any other products that Dada Jethanand could source from Japan and the Far East. Mombasa Port was an important stopover and we quickly discovered that, in addition to those railway workers for whom we had first set up shop, the passing trade of sailors and tourists in transit would also give a huge boost to business.

The family flagship shop, J.H. Gidoomal, was housed in a grand corner building with arched windows, quickly becoming a landmark and meeting point in the city. Daddy's own shop, Mombasa Silk Emporium on the Salim Road, was smaller but, selling imported Van Heusen shirts from Britain and suitcases from Hong Kong along with the finest silk, he made a very lucrative living and gained the respect of his community.

Home was three large apartments, converted and joined together. With five bedrooms in each, the buildings formed a square around a courtyard. I grew up there, one of 15 children, never wanting for company. Besides my ten siblings, there were Dada Roopa's four children, Meera, Anita, Chandru and Renu. Our other cousins, Chandra, Daya and Dogo Lachu only lived a stone's throw away, and often joined us too, and then there was the constant flow of extended family from all over the world. We loved it when Daddy's youngest sister, Ishwari, and her husband, Uncle Sunder, visited from across the border in Tanganyika. Their son, Shyam, was our youngest cousin, and gave us lots of joy. Anyone who came would be roped into the games and we whiled away our days playing on the large veranda, climbing on the roof, and jumping from balconies as a short cut to the neighbouring flats.

Fifteen children playing under the African sun was a dream, but trying to get everyone out of the house in time for school? Not so much. Three crammed cars would file out of the property every morning: the driver took one, my mum drove another and my aunt the third. It was chaos. There was always someone who hadn't had breakfast, had forgotten something or who was "just coming in a minute!" Getting to school on time was almost impossible.

After accepting two canings for late arrival, I took it upon myself to walk to school. The alternative punishment for tardiness was a fine, which meant giving up my break-time tuck – a far worse ordeal in my book. Every break, I would meet up with my younger cousin, Dogo Lachu, and his best friend, Bharat Desai, in the playground. Realising I was given significantly more tuck money than the others and having had ideas of equality drummed into me from an early age, it seemed only fair to pool our resources and split the plunder three ways. It was a small act of generosity. So small I never thought twice about it, but decades later I would learn how much it had meant to the others.

So, it was to avoid losing this treat or getting any more canings that I began leaving the house very early in the morning to walk across our tiny island to school every day, despite the 35° heat and 100% humidity. On the way home, we picked mangoes straight from trees and, depending on pocket money or the generosity of friends, bought grilled *mohogo* (cassava), and *mabungo* fruits which were so sharp they made your teeth grate, or maize cobs with salt, red chilli and lemon. We sucked the nectar out of life like we sucked the juice from those mango stones, drawing out every drop of goodness, getting the best from everything.

Although we were immigrants, Mombasa was my home. I was born there. True, I knew very few Kenyans: just our much-loved domestic helpers and one Kenyan student – Habili Musundi – who appeared at school during my final year. Yet, I belonged there, in that noisy, lovingly chaotic 15 bedroomed home near the Tusks on the Kilindini Road. There we lived a life full of family, friends, music, and books. It was my life, and I thought it would be forever.

On school days, my eldest sister, Dhaneshwari, who we fondly still call Babu, and I would wake up at around 4.00 am to study in the cool tranquillity of dawn. Usually, I was the one to greet the milkman at six, collecting our delivery in a large saucepan ready for boiling in time for breakfast once the domestic helpers arrived. School started and finished relatively early in order to avoid the heat, meaning that every afternoon, if we could get to Uncle Motiram's office quickly enough, he would drive us across the old Nyali floating bridge down to an almost deserted Bamburi beach. Running past the palm trees across the powdery white sands, we would dive into the warm turquoise waters of the Indian Ocean. I swam like a fish and loved it. I had learnt the typical way for Sindhis and other Asian youngsters – every Saturday morning being thrown out of a creaky wooden fishing boat into the depths of the sea just off the Old Port. It was sink or swim and, luckily for me, I quickly did the latter and never stopped enjoying it.

Later in the afternoon, my best friend Jacky would call up to our first floor flat. After finishing off any homework, we would escape to our favourite café, The Blue Room, for a daily dose of Aloo Bondas, delicious fried potato cakes, before going on for ice creams together. At the Aga Khan Ismaili school where we were in a class together, Jacky and I were Sindhis within the Hindu minority. The other students were Asian, like us, but most of them were Ismaili Muslims. So we were a minority within a minority.

It was very rarely a problem. Occasionally there was playground bullying but having Lachu Kuba, my six-foot-tall older brother around was normally a good safeguard against that. The 'Kuba' part of his name affectionately described him as the older of the two Lachus, distinguishing him from 'Dogo' (the respective word in the Swahili language for 'older' and 'younger') Lachu. We loved and respected the Muslim students, and they us – maybe surprisingly so, given all the horrific stories we heard about animosity between Hindus and Muslims. Interestingly in East Africa, relationships were very cordial and friendly between the Asian communities. I suppose we all realised we were minorities in a British colony.

Despite our friendships with the Muslim students and the way they embraced our otherness, we knew we could never be at the heart of their community. There were threads spooling around them, intricately tied to their specific situation, which were impossible for them to extend to us – the Mosque, their daily bus ride to school and even the compound of flats, built by the Aga Khan for Ismaili families, where most of them lived. Looking back, I realise my closest friends were, like me, not Ismaili. Jacky and I, in particular, both came from Sindhi trading families, but our friendship went deeper than that and has lasted a lifetime.

Being good Hindus, our family dutifully attended the Shiva temple every Monday and then, because we were brought up in the Sikh faith too (given the proximity of Sindh to the Punjab), we would also go to the Gurdwara on a Saturday. Sundays, however, were kept for family. Often, we would make for the Drive-in cinema – cramming as many as possible into one car as tickets were sold per vehicle; or we would gather at the Lighthouse, a popular meeting point in Mombasa. Each family group would sit on their own bench, always in the same places. We used these times to catch up on news, deepening our bonds of family and community friendships – bonds that remain strong to this day.

We relished any excuse to visit our cousins Rupi and Veena in Nairobi, along with their older brothers, Prem, Chandu, Chimu, Hashu, and Nini, but on 12th December 1963, we had a particularly good reason to be there. That was the day we witnessed the handing over of power to the Kenyan people. There were around ten of us in our party, setting off from my cousins' house early in the evening. We parked a good distance away and then walked to the Donholm Road Stadium. It was approaching sunset and not yet dark. My cousin Chimu drew a lot of attention from passers-by, who smiled at this flamboyantly dressed Asian boy, disguised as a tribal warrior with an animal skin jacket over his shirt, a tall lion skin hat and a whip – a handle with long strands of hair attached – just like the one President Jomo Kenyatta carried.

Once we reached the floodlit stadium, the air was electric with anticipation, the mood full of festivity with an estimated quarter of a million people there to witness the ceremony of independence and enjoy the festivities. We sang, screamed like Masai warriors and waved our Kenyan flags crazily. There was a feeling of solemnity as Prince Philip handed over the instruments of independence to General Jomo Kenyatta in the presence of Churchill's son in law, Duncan Sandys, who was then Secretary of State for the Colonies and Commonwealth Relations. We gazed transfixed at the exactness of soldiers marching in perfect formation contrasting with the wild freedom of the tribal dancers. Later as the British flag was lowered and the Kenyan one raised at midnight, we all sang the new national anthem with great gusto, fireworks adding to the sense of celebration. We would have a long walk back to the car and a battle with crammed streets and hooting traffic before we could fall into bed in the early hours of the morning, but we didn't care. This was history in the making, and we were there, caught up in the frenzy of excitement and optimism. As I cheered and clapped and waved my Kenyan flag, I had no idea that a new path was being forged in the country.

One on which I would not be welcome to walk. One that would change everything.

All I knew was the sense of fun and adventure that ran through our life, and the fullness of our hearts. Thinking back on all this, it seemed impossible that it could be coming to an end, but that night in 1966, Daddy's bags were packed hurriedly, and the next day he was gone. The hush, that desolate silence which began at my uncle's party, never really left us for the rest of our time in Kenya.

Some cultures mourn with anguished wails, noisy and cathartic, others mourn in quiet. When Daddy left that day, it was as if our world had ended. A numb silence descended upon the family and rested there, like a sheet covering us, touching everything we did. We functioned, we existed, but all the colour and flavour had gone from our lives. Gone were the treats, outings, and visits to restaurants. Now everything was focused on essentials, on our future survival.

Perhaps we were not completely blameless. We had amassed wealth in a place of poverty and flashed our not insignificant riches around. We had never truly made an effort to mix with Kenyans. Our own Sindhi community was large and vibrant – we had simply never felt the need to be with anyone else. We were not irreproachable; but still, we had not expected the price of our come-uppance to be quite so high.

Even as Daddy packed up a few scant belongings, we had to make hurried plans for how we would manage in his absence and when we would join him in England. None of the children were brought into the loop as the adults were keen not to scare us, wanting us to continue working hard for our exams. The decision was taken to send the children to London in twos and threes depending on each one's individual circumstances. Duru and Pushpa accompanied my mother to London with Usha joining them in London from Bombay. I was doing my O-levels the following year, in December 1967, and it was decided I should stay in Kenya until these were finished.

My family had enjoyed the pleasures of a life that was rich in every way, but they had also worked hard for it. Now they were facing another journey, another resettlement, another culture to learn, with all the personal, emotional, and financial implications of that. This is the experience of the refugee: not a lovingly planned trip, made in excited anticipation, but a harsh tearing away from everything you know and value: comfort, wealth, education, friends, home.

And so, I left that home, with my brother Lachu, taking the overnight train for Nairobi right after my O-levels to catch a flight arriving in London on 2nd January 1968, wondering all the time what would be waiting for us there.

Chapter Two
Aliens

Aliens.

I stared at the sign at the front of the queue I'd been sent to. I had never thought of myself as an alien before, but standing in that line, I began to wonder. It certainly felt like I had landed on another planet.

Waiting gave me ample time to observe the comings and goings of other travellers. What were they wearing? Come to think of it, what was I wearing? In Mombasa I lived in shorts and t-shirts, but had had a suit and waistcoat tailor-made so that I would 'fit in' here in London. I now had the sinking realisation that these were only going to make me stand out more. It was the late sixties and I had completely missed the fact that the British fashion scene was undergoing a revolution, with bright patterns and flower-power. I had been in the country mere hours, and already I was aware how different I was.

It felt like an age had passed since my brother had disappeared through the door to the terminal, to freedom, shooting me one last worried glance. He had been in another queue, of course, the kind of queue where you are waved through without questions. Despite our shared genes, he was not an alien.

I and a couple of my sisters Nirmala (Nimu) and Durga (Duru) were the only ones in the family who did not hold a full British passport, due to a quirk of birthplace and timing. Having taken my first breath on the island of Mombasa, at that time a protectorate under the Heligoland agreement, I was considered a British Protected Person.

That sounds quite reassuring. Surely, if you are British protected, you are fine. Protected means 'looked after', doesn't it? However, it soon became clear that this stood for very little. I had no right to be there. I had no right to be anywhere. Before the trip my family had talked it through with me, warning that I might end up as part of 'the shuttle'.

'British protected' passport holders were being shuttled from one country to another and back again, never finding acceptance anywhere. There was a notorious tale of one Alitalia flight which left Nairobi for London via Rome. London would not accept the passengers who were then shuttled back to Rome... who, in turn, shuttled them back to London and so on, up to 15 times with neither country willing to take them. Therefore, to give me a fighting chance, they booked me onto a British Overseas Airways Corporation (BOAC) flight, direct to London Heathrow. At least that way I would be on British soil before the problem arose. No one checked citizenship when you booked the flights – they would only find out at Immigration. And they did.

On landing at Heathrow, while my brother was sent off to one queue, I had to follow the other unfortunate 'aliens' to an unknown fate. I had just turned 17. I was still a minor, and probably shouldn't have been separated from my family. We didn't know that though. We didn't know anything.

Finally reaching the front of the queue, I tried to stay calm. The official held my passport – and my life – in his hands. Taking one look at me, he asked,

"So, where's your family? Are you on your own?"

"No, no…. my brother's just gone through, but the rest of the family is on the other side waiting for us."

He looked at my passport, then at me, then back at my passport. I held my breath. What was he going to do? This man had the power to let me stay or send me away. But where would I go?

On my uncle Dev's advice, I had started reading the London broadsheets some years earlier. Once a week, when I had saved enough pocket money, I would run down to the shop below our apartment to buy *The Times*, printed on the thinnest onion paper to save air freight costs. I always read it from cover to cover, column by column, so I knew the mood was changing here towards immigrants. I wished I could explain that we did not pick out this place from a holiday brochure. We literally had nowhere else to go. We couldn't stay in Mombasa because we were not Kenyans. India would not have us because the family as a whole had kept British citizenship. Britain was our only logical choice, but for me, even that was looking a little shaky now.

With hindsight, I now know that other African countries had offered asylum for people like us. But with my entire family already in England, I would have been completely alone if I had chosen one of these.

While these thoughts churned over in my mind, the official seemed to come to a decision. He took a piece of white paper and stuck it in my passport. I couldn't see it clearly, but it seemed to feature the word "No".

I was not used to this. Normally I loved travelling. Normally there was no question as to whether I would be allowed to do anything or go anywhere. Some of my happiest childhood memories were of the long train journeys between Mombasa and Nairobi. With family and businesses in both cities, travelling between the two was second nature to us. Sometimes I would travel with Uncle Lachmandas Kimatrai, discussing politics as we watched the landscape rushing by. In fact, I honed my debating skills by deliberately disagreeing with all his views. Another time, the whole family travelled together for Uncle Dev's wedding. Taking over an entire carriage meant the party began even as we journeyed.

Then there was my first trip to India in 1964 with my older brothers, making the unforgettable journey from what was then Bombay to Poona by train, on the iconic Deccan Queen Express. Dashing through built up towns and lush green valleys, through tunnels and over viaducts, it felt like a whistle-stop tour of my vast and diverse motherland.

It was also a rite of passage at school to attend the Royal Agricultural Show in Nairobi. We were all bundled into third class and then, on arrival in Nairobi, slept on the school floor. Returning to Mombasa, every single one of us was caned by the Headmaster as a punishment for our raucous behaviour on the trip. But for us that was simply a badge of honour.

Occasionally we made the journey by car, me staring out of the window as my uncle's car-lights shone on passing elephants. The road between Mombasa and Nairobi was infamously dangerous, much of the 300 miles being a mere dust track with the risk of wild animals suddenly appearing in your path. As such, it went without saying we would stop at Makindu Sikh Gurdwara Temple to pray for safety.

My family were dedicated Hindus with Sikh influences and, although I no longer follow this path myself, I can see the roots of my lifelong commitment to equality and care for others in the things I learned during my childhood.

As a wealthy family, we supported both the Hindu priests and the Sikh Gurdwara. We held Satsangs (Hindu worship services), where the priest, along with other leaders from the temple, would come to our home and sing late into the night. With the Gurdwara, we had the great privilege of hosting a three-day reading event.

This was a non-stop reading of the Guru Granth Sahib – the Sikh Holy Scriptures - which would go on all day and night for those three days, with people being collected on a rota basis through the early hours of the morning to take the different reading slots. My eldest brother Kanu would let me know in advance which early morning pickup slot he was scheduled for, and I had the privilege of accompanying him, even if it was at 3.00am.

Our regular worship time at home involved opening the holy book every morning – that was considered the act of waking God up. Then in the evening we would close the holy book, putting God to sleep. Sunrise and sunset. Prayer was a daily occurrence. For me, I would pray in English in my own heart. There was one Indian private prayer we were taught, a Sindhi prayer which we all said. If you translated it, it was almost like the Lord's Prayer, not mentioning any of the Hindu gods, but rather speaking of one God. That was the prayer I would say whenever I was in distress or difficulty. Of course, I also learnt all the Hindu and Sikh songs and recited them by rote. Then there were other prayers which were just like Psalms, with words like "Oh Lord the Almighty God, we worship you".

Added to all this, I attended the Aga Khan school, which was, of course, Muslim. Every day there was an Islamic assembly, and then a class on religious education too. Being Hindus, we were exempt and sat on the back benches while the others continued their studies. But of course, the words floated over to me and so I came to know everything about Islam too. I could recite chunks of the Quran and the lineage of the Imams to the extent that I often helped my Muslim classmates escape punishment by whispering the answers to them. The teachers could be quite tough in those days, and if you didn't do your work, you could expect what we called a *thappat* or *chammat* which was a fairly violent slap. So, my knowledge of the Muslim faith kept my classmates from this fate and, as a result, probably increased my popularity with them.

However, I didn't always escape *thappats* myself. On one occasion, when my older brother was not around to protect me, I found myself at the mercy of another student. As he approached me in the playground, I saw trouble in his eyes. He said something deeply offensive to me and, in the heat of the moment, I retorted with something equally unpleasant. It seemed a fair exchange to me, but quickly escalated into a fight. What I hadn't considered was that the other student had the privilege of access to the religious instruction teacher in our Muslim school.

"You won't believe what Ram said to me!"

The teacher was irate and dragged me to the front of the class.

"What is this I hear you said in the playground?"

I hardly dared speak, but wanted to give my side of the story. Surely he would see then that I had been provoked. I began, "Sir, he…"

"I don't care what he said!" his thunderous reply cut in. "Don't you ever dare repeat those words or I will have you expelled."

Then he gave me a thappat on the face, not one but two hard smacks.

One! Two!

The pain coursed through me, and I just stood there, shocked. There had been no chance for me to explain what had really happened. No checking whether it was true. There was no trial, no hope of me standing up for myself.

Finally, I sat down, shell shocked and bruised. In the car on the way home, I didn't say a word, still petrified of repercussions. I walked into the house in fear, wondering if a phone call had been made.

Thankfully the teacher did not pursue it any further. Maybe he could see by my reaction that I was genuinely terrified. Or maybe he discussed it with others who spoke more rationally, pointing out that he had only half the story. Either way, to my huge relief, it was never spoken of again.

In fact, I myself had forgotten about those two stinging smacks on the face until I was reminded about it 50 years later, by a classmate, Ikbal Rahemtulla. At the time he had watched with indignation that I had not been given the right to defend myself. He saw the injustice of it, that the boy concerned could say something so hideous to me, but when I responded, I got all the blame. All the power was on his side. It was one of the very few times I felt the vulnerability of being in the minority there.

And this classmate came to me recently saying, "I will never forget that day and I'm really ashamed, as a leader in my community today, at what happened. Forgive us, forgive me."

Of course I told him that I had forgotten all about it, but it was gracious of him to raise the matter now - and since he had done so, I assured him that it was also now forgiven.

However, that was a rare blip in a mostly harmonious experience. I got on well at school with the students as well as with all the teachers there. Along with three others, I was appointed a class librarian, and during one holiday we were entrusted with the job of cataloguing the school library in the decimal system. I loved books, and this gave me a chance to pick out a few to read. I stumbled upon one book which was about all the 'isms' – Hinduism, Sikhism, Buddhism, Taoism, even Confucianism. I read it from cover to cover, drinking in all the information. Philosophy and religion fascinated me, and I wanted to be aware of all the different religious ideas.

If it was books I wanted, one place I was sure to find them was at Dada Lekhraj's house. He and Dadi Kala lived a stone's throw away and it was a standing joke that I would make a beeline for his bookshelf anytime I visited. Law was Dada Lekhraj's training, despite the fact that he never actually practiced it. His books added a new element to my education and his knowledgeable legal advice was often sought by the wider family.

Back at home, our own library shelves were packed with English Penguin books, their spines shouting out our colonial heritage. English was always my language of instruction. However, at home my mother spoke Sindhi to me: it was the language the old men swore in, and the language I was scolded in. I also needed Gujarati because my Ismaili classmates spoke it (though we were fined if we spoke anything other than English in class). Films were in Hindi with no subtitles, and our domestic helpers spoke Swahili, so we quickly learnt we needed those languages too. I still speak Swahili to this day, remembering with fondness the friendships I'd built with our beloved cooks, domestic helpers, and drivers.

Life had been a melting pot of cultures for me and one of those cultures was British. Its influence had always been there in my schooling and in the books I read. As one of the family 'brainboxes', it was expected that I would finish my A-levels in Mombasa and then attend a top UK university as a wealthy international student before returning to Kenya to get a high-level job as a doctor, lawyer or engineer – my mind was an open book. That was the plan. Now I was right here in England, though under rather different circumstances, standing in the airport as an unwanted refugee.

I looked again at the official, wondering what would be waiting for me in this new world if he did let me pass. I knew Daddy had been able to get a little established in those months of head start he'd had in London. When he was first deported in 1966, Daddy went to India on a tourist visa to explore business opportunities there, but decided it would be difficult as a British subject, given his deportation from Kenya. He returned to London where, despite not understanding the system or knowing how to get help from the government, he had received invaluable support from the local Asian community. In particular, our good family friend Harkishan Gopaldas had put him up and pointed him in the right direction, helping him with the mechanics of buying a corner shop which had a flat above it, in Shepherd's Bush.

Realising he couldn't do it alone, Daddy asked my older brother Bharat to take on responsibility for the corner shop, instead of pursuing a career in accounting. A telegram was sent to Aunty Ishwari, Daddy's sister who had recently moved to Bombay, asking her to arrange for Bharat to fly to London as soon as he could. Bharat arrived on 12th December 1966 and began running the shop which had been appropriately named 'G. Bharat'. He had just turned 17 and was given a one-third share in the business, with Aunty Janki and my mother also receiving a third each. The shop sold sweets and newspapers, a far cry from our prestigious silk business in Mombasa, but at least it was a roof over our heads and a way of surviving.

This fall from grace for the family didn't really worry my siblings and me. Despite our deep sadness at leaving Mombasa, we held a certain nervous excitement about this future, full of unknowns and, we hoped, opportunities. We were just starting out. We could make something new of our lives. For Daddy however, it felt too late. He had been through this before, starting from nothing when he had had everything, decades of hard work and success wiped out. I knew it was an unbearable blow for him, and the strength of character that had always seen him through seemed to be dented.

My thoughts were interrupted by the official. Relief flooded through me as he stamped the piece of paper, handed me my passport and said, "Go!"

Later, I had a chance to read that paper in my passport. It began with 'No right to work' and continued to list all the other things I couldn't do. I had no rights, but I was able to go through that door to my family. I had no rights, but I would be with them, and that was all I needed in that moment.

However, my happiness at being allowed to enter was soon overtaken by the sheer enormity of what faced me. This was a different world, and the stamp in my passport had done little to diminish my feelings of being an alien.

My alien status was something that would affect my freedom for many years to come. Sometime later, as a student making a trip around Europe with my friends Jack and Ashok, it seemed like I spent more time visiting embassies to get visas for the next steps of our trip, than actually seeing the countries involved. I was turned back at almost every border because of my British Protected passport.

But that was later. Right now, on my first arrival in England, as we drove to our new home, I looked out of the window at my surroundings: the houses, the people, the grey January sky. A family friend had driven Daddy to the airport to collect us, public transport being a step too far from his previous experiences. Although he had begun to build a life here, to survive, it was clear he had not really adapted. He especially struggled with the cold. Not understanding the need for proper shoes, he had already slipped in the snow and ice several times. My mother was the same, for a very long time insisting on wearing her traditional slippers everywhere, because 'that's what you wear with saris'.

My life as I knew it, my whole childhood that had seemed so permanent, had turned out to be nothing more than a short episode sandwiched between my family history in India on the one hand, and my family future in the UK on the other.

A future that would begin with 15 of us living above the shop in a four bedroomed flat.

Chapter Three

The Last Room

I was eleven when I learned that the man I'd always called 'Daddy' was not in fact my father. As is often the way with these things, I found out by accident, during one of those moments of candour that children excel in.

We were playing out on the veranda as usual when I got into a teasing match with one of my siblings. Perhaps it went too far. Perhaps I said something upsetting, because, before anyone could intervene, they turned to me and said,

"Well, you know, my daddy is not your daddy!"

"Oh yeah?" I replied playfully, "Tell me about it."

As far as I was concerned, we were still teasing, but one of the others agreed.

"Yep. Your daddy died."

"Really?" I stopped still for a moment.

Perhaps the most surprising thing about the discovery was that it wasn't really a surprise. By this, I don't mean that I had

had any suspicion. No, I'd never questioned the fact that my mother slept in one room and my 'Daddy' in another with his wife, who was of course my aunt – Aunty Janki. It was all I'd ever known. I simply mean that it was not a shocking, life changing revelation. Just another fact to store up in my mind. Daddy, my uncle, had treated us like his own. Better in some ways, perhaps to compensate for our lack of a natural father. He always went above and beyond in his love for us. This new knowledge would never change that for me.

The pause was only momentary before I added, "Alright, he died. Fine. Let's keep playing."

Over time I did ask more questions and learnt that my biological father, Gagandas Dayaram Gidoomal, died in Nairobi in tragic circumstances on 15th February 1951. I was just seven weeks old. The pressure of Partition, leaving India, and setting up a new life in Kenya as the eldest son of the family, had all taken a toll on him. He began to find success, but after taking one business gamble too many, everything came crashing down on him. Life felt too big a burden to bear.

I was not my father's only child. My mother, Vasanti, had two other sons, aged one and two years old when our father died, and a daughter who was three. My siblings. Mother was widowed at 21. Who would want to marry someone with four children and no inheritance? So it was that she stayed widowed until she passed away in December 1999.

She was not left alone of course. The next eldest brother in line – Naraindas Dayaram Gidoomal – known as Dada Nari by his siblings and for me, simply Daddy, immediately took responsibility for all of us. This is how the Indian extended family works. This is the example of caring for one another that I received, from a younger age than I even knew. This Daddy who raised me was dedicated and loving. I could not have wished for a better father figure or a more caring start in life. Other uncles and family friends stepped in too, giving me advice, taking me on outings, teaching me new things. So, within this sad situation which, in some families might result in a disastrous lack of male role models, I had more than my fair share of mentors and help. Meanwhile, Aunty Janki, Daddy's wife, was always on the lookout for times when I needed a father figure, when I was ill for example, making sure I had time with him.

My father's youngest brother, Dada Roopa, taught me chess and was good-naturedly disgruntled when I started beating him within a few days of learning. Eventually he was so impressed he took me to the Indian Consul's house, to play against him. Walking into the grand colonial home was nerve wracking – I was in my early teens and not yet in senior school – how could I even consider playing this man of such great brilliance? But I did. Of course, I didn't win, but I put up enough of a fight to make him sweat, at one point coming within three moves of checkmating him.

Gradually more stories came out about my father, stories that painted a picture of someone I could be proud of, a man of character, with a strong sense of justice and equality. He didn't only work hard for his own community of Sindhis but also organised charitable events for the Kathiyawadi community, among whom he was treated as an honorary member. His acts of kindness were recognised and appreciated to such an extent that, after he died, they had a bust made of him and put it in the Kathiyawadi Club in Nairobi in his memory.

Although only 14 when his own father died in 1936, my father was the eldest son. Therefore, he took on the role of the head of his family at a very young age. The others adored him. Exuberant, but always a proper gentleman; self-assured but without being full of himself, he was determined to do what was right in every situation, even at the expense of social norms. Once, at a fayre he had organised in Nairobi to raise funds for the Kathiyawadi community, he noticed that a young boy had won a bicycle but had been denied his prize by the stall holder. There was a general acceptance that adults were always right, children did not have a voice. Although this was intended to breed a healthy respect for the wisdom of the older generation, at times it could be misused. He recognised this as one of those times and stopped at nothing to ensure the boy received the bicycle which was rightly his.

He was also an extremely sharp businessman, at one stage having anything up to eleven ships' worth of cargo on order from Japan to make the most of the fact that any goods which made it across the seas in wartime would multiply in value ten, or even a hundredfold. This scheme did eventually backfire on him once the war was over and he failed to cancel pre-ordered cargo in good time. However, for a long time my father made a huge success from this business.

Later, I would notice his initials, GDG, flamboyantly inscribed on the inside covers of his old encyclopaedia Britannica set which I stumbled upon at Uncle Dev's home in Nairobi. It was there that I also found a copy of the 1936 South Africa 'Who's Who' which, I was delighted to note, listed my grandfather as a prominent local businessman.

I saw those same initials, GDG, again in his handwriting on the stamp collection that I worked on with my uncle, Dada Roopa. Suddenly these initials I'd probably seen countless times before, took on a deeply moving significance for me.

It turned out that stamp collecting had been one of my biological father's passions and somehow this great love was passed down to me too. My uncle showed me my father's old albums – that same precious stamp collection he had very carefully packed and carried from Hyderabad Sindh following the Partition – and urged me to continue building on them. I started trading stamps at school and, most Saturdays, that same uncle would take me to the shop so that Daddy could give me money to buy more. I'd then spend all afternoon, or whatever free time I had on it – marvelling at the intricacy of these miniature works of art as I turned the pages carefully and lovingly. Although I no longer have these precious albums, later in life, all the love I had put into stamp collecting would be given back to me in a way I couldn't have dreamed of.

The time spent with these numerous uncles and family friends was invaluable, but it was Daddy who truly took us all under his wing, along with the seven biological children of his own: two boys and five girls. Both before and since the revelation about my father, I have never once considered them as anything other than my true brothers and sisters. Family.

Mostly I loved being in the hub of that family, but occasionally I needed peace and quiet, and when those moments hit, I would steal away to 'The Last Room'. Situated right at the end of the corridor, beyond the temple room where we would open and close the Holy Book at sunrise and sunset daily, the Last Room had many different purposes. Sometimes it was used for homework, or tuition for those who needed it. We played games there but equally you might be sent there as a punishment. Then, when we had a houseful, it became emergency accommodation for long or short-term guests. For me, however, it was somewhere to hide away, to think and read to my heart's content.

There I would devour books, losing myself in 'Just William', 'Les Misérables' and, later, 'War and Peace'. Reading the final chapter of this, I stumbled upon a reference to a super force, a power above all powers. I stared at the page, something stirring deep within me. What was this? A longing for something? A recognition of a depth I was missing, maybe even yearning for? There in Mombasa we had everything we needed and more, but these words, this image of a higher power, it triggered something profound in me.

As a Hindu I had been taught about hundreds of gods of course, each one with their own unique powers, but here was Tolstoy, talking about an ultimate super force. I pondered the idea, this thought of one higher God. At the time, Christ did not cross my mind because, for me, He was the white man's God, a colonial God from London, blue eyed and blond haired, with a bowler hat and pin striped suit. What interest could a God like that possibly have in me, or I in him?

The Last Room became for me a place to mull things over. It was also where I studied. Perhaps it was this combination that put me in such good standing with the family. I was always in the top three in my class, and Daddy loved that. My eldest sister Babu and I were known as the family brainboxes.

I didn't sail through everything, however. I was hopeless at sports. I played football and broke my toe; played cricket and broke my finger; my running was equally disastrous. After several attempts to find a sport I could enjoy, I decided that what I did best was being a spectator. All my true efforts went into academia. It made Daddy proud, and any potential for jealousy from other siblings was quashed by the fact that I often stepped in to help them with homework. In fact, Daddy even appointed me as a guardian of the youngest two – Vinod and Sheila – to ensure they did their homework and studied for exams.

One day, just as I was leaving school, somebody called me over to look at the notice board. I couldn't believe my eyes when I saw that the position of Head Boy for the following year had my name next to it. It was the last thing I'd expected. Admittedly it was a shock to the Ismaili community too – it was the first time a Hindu boy had ever been appointed to this position and, as such, was perhaps my first experience of breaking cultural barriers. What was particularly special to me was the fact that nobody seemed to begrudge it, despite me not being Muslim. To this day, over fifty years later, my alumni classmates tell me I was the right man for the job, although at the time I confess I was very nervous and wasn't convinced that was the case. I had not received any preparation and didn't really have a clue as to what I was taking on.

Of course, this made Daddy prouder than ever. On my very first day in the role, the Headmaster gave me the task of reorganising the chaos that ensued every day when the entire school population crowded out of the assembly hall at once. Liaising with prefects and drawing up complicated maps and flow charts I came up with a successful working system. I still think of this as my first foray into management consultancy, albeit an unpaid one!

Being head boy didn't exempt me from punishment of course. I got on well with the teachers and generally toed the line, but I also felt a loyalty to my classmates. One day, some misdemeanour took place, and it was that loyalty that prevented me from divulging the culprit. In keeping that code of honour, I was sent out of class and made to stand on a desk where the entire school could see me – the revered head boy – being punished. What the teacher didn't seem to realise was that it simply added to my prestige and kudos with the other students, who now knew for certain 'the head boy is one of us'.

This was my school community, one where I was known, respected, and accepted by teachers and classmates alike. Leaving the honour of my role and my academic place in the class to start afresh in a completely new country was a little intimidating. My new London school was just a stone's throw from Wormwood Scrubs and, sadly, it became clear that some of the boys had relatives there. On top of this, because the African school year runs from January to December, when I joined the Lower Sixth Form in January 1968, all my English classmates had already done a full term's work. Not wanting to wait another year, I assured them I would catch up. So it was that I began at the Christopher Wren school, alone, culture-shocked, and with a double workload.

I had promised I would study twice as hard, but there was no 'Last Room' in the flat in Shepherd's Bush; very little peace and quiet at all in fact. Instead, I did my homework on a makeshift table by the window in the room I shared with my brothers. Studying there, my eyes would be drawn to the glow of floodlights from QPR's stadium, my studies interrupted by victory roars each time a goal was scored. Back in Mombasa the sights and sounds from my bedroom window had been rather different. There it was the Rainbow Club's neon lights and loud music that blared out nightly – always Tequila, Helen Shapiro and 'Cherry Pink and Apple Blossom White'. Such different lights, different sounds, different places! All signs of the journey I had travelled, from one country to another.

All these years later as we've watched fraught families trying to home-school their children during lockdown with little or no workspace, I am reminded of that tiny, improvised table and how hard it was to find a place to breathe and think. l knew nothing about local libraries – and, in any case, I needed to be on standby to do my bit in the shop – although my family, still recognising me as 'the brainy one', gave me extra study time and required less of me than my brothers.

Daddy held his head high in England, refusing to accept any help from the State at all, declaring, "We have not paid into this system, and it would not be right to take such money!" He instilled in us the importance of self-reliance. However, despite this, the family still struggled with the loss of status that came with this new situation – no longer the owners of a flourishing prestigious business in Mombasa but now running a small shop selling sweets and cigarettes. Because of this, Daddy wasn't keen for his sister to visit from Jamaica. Of course, eventually she and the family did come, but that was afterwards. After Daddy had returned to Mombasa. After everything changed again. The irony is, they didn't care what our shop was like. They just wanted to see us. When Aunty Mohini, Uncle Nari Vaswani and their children finally made the long journey to London, it was a wonderful time of catching up. I remember being put in charge of their London sightseeing tour and still recall their daughters Asha and Rosa desperately pleading outside the shoe shop in Oxford Circus for Gogo boots! Their sons Deepak, Prakash and Lalu had also visited London on a school trip and we, the cousins, all got on like a house on fire.

For my brothers and I the corner shop was a huge novelty, the edible merchandise being far more interesting for teenage boys than the silk and saris Daddy used to sell. In the evenings we would smuggle sweets and large bottles of Tizer up to our room, pushing threepenny bits into the meter to ensure that we wouldn't freeze as we fell asleep. And when the threepenny bits ran out, hot-water bottles came into their own.

While there was no 'Last Room' in our Shepherd's Bush flat, the shop took on a character of its own. It was there that we began to understand the loneliness and isolation of people here, when many customers, having made their purchases, seemed to want to hang on in the shop for a lengthy chat. It quickly became apparent that, for some, it was the only conversation they had all day, maybe even all week. We happily took time to talk with them, not rushing them on, realising that while our home was sometimes uncomfortably cramped, it was also full in more positive ways, ways that some people were missing.

Not everyone was quite so friendly though. We occasionally struggled with post-match hooliganism during football season and got into the habit of shutting up shop early on those days. This became a serious problem when my team, Queens Park Rangers, was promoted to the top division. Eventually, many shops were forced to install metal shutters to prevent the shop windows being smashed every time a match was played, and the visiting team lost. When my elder brother Bharat, known as Barry, proudly brought home a brand-new mustard coloured Rover 2.2, with luxurious off-white leather seats, it wasn't long before someone keyed it, leaving long ugly scratches down the side. Mostly, however, racism was rare within the shop itself. Our biggest problems seemed to come when we set off from the flat to go to school, but after a while we learnt that this could be lessened by investing in QPR colours for our much-needed scarves, hats and gloves. It was part of taking on the local identity, finding ways to blend in.

Gradually we got to know the area and sought to meet more of the needs of our regulars. My brother Barry, as the working partner, took on the day to day running of the shop. Realising there was an Irish community in the neighbourhood, he started importing newspapers from Ireland and even learnt a few words of Irish to banter around with them. Barry also became aware of the power of TV advertising campaigns and how he needed to be prepared with extra stocks of certain chocolates when these were advertised. Next, we spotted the Bingo halls spilling out their customers late at night. Discussing this strange phenomenon, Barry and I agreed to experiment, amending our opening hours to allow them to pop in for any essentials on their way home. It was a great success, upping our turnover considerably. And so, our humble little corner shop, in its own way, became a kind of community hub.

Rather like those Saturday mornings in Mombasa, being thrown into the Indian Ocean, we had to learn to swim in these new waters quickly. The shop was one of the places I learnt business skills, helping my brother – especially when he went on a six-week holiday leaving me in charge of the shop. But really my apprenticeship had begun far earlier, back in Kenya sitting around the lunch table with my uncles. As they discussed currency exchanges that they had made that morning, stories flowed about customers wanting to change say, Rhodesian pounds into sterling. With their hard-earned knowledge and expertise in the mechanics of foreign exchange my uncles were able to provide this service and make thousands of pounds' profit in a matter of hours.

My learning curve steepened further when Daddy introduced me to the *hawala* system that was used to transfer funds between trusted parties either in the same geographic location or across borders. By now, he had returned to Mombasa but would call every day, or sometimes send telegrams, with instructions to keep his foreign exchange business ticking over.

At that time, standard calls were expensive and only lasted three minutes, after which the operator would interrupt to ask if we needed more time. Of course, we always did. Daddy and I would speak in our own language on those calls, not just Sindhi, but also in code. When people wanted different currencies exchanged in London, he would tell me, "Look Ram, you'll be getting 7000 yards of Italian silk and 2000 yards of French chiffon.

A customer from Mombasa is sending their agent to come and collect it." or, "This time it's German nylon..." all code for which currency would be arriving at the shop for me to deal with: Italian Lira, French Francs or German Deutschmarks.

I would then expect to receive these notes or Travellers Cheques either through a personal courier who had travelled from Mombasa or maybe by Registered Mail. I would deal with these as Daddy had instructed by phone, which normally meant ensuring the money was converted to Sterling at the local bank. He fixed his rate of exchange for the purchase of foreign currency (with a lucrative margin added) based on the rates quoted in the daily telegram he received from Brown Shipley Bank in London which gave him the closing rates for key currencies there.

Daddy used the *hawala* system as a way of establishing legitimacy. To ensure I was passing on the requested currency to the correct person, Daddy would first give me the name over the phone, maybe also a password, then sometimes, as added security, the person whose money it was, would cut in half a currency note which of course showed the serial number on both halves. Usually this would be a low denomination note in Kenyan shillings. Daddy would send me one half and, when the other person turned up at the shop with the matching half, I knew I had the right person.

Another thing I quickly became adept at dealing with was *hoondees*. These are bills of exchange (like IOU notes) which allow you to raise working capital from your network of relationships without relying on banks – who would never lend to us anyway, or only with great difficulty and at enormous cost. With *hoondees*, you borrow money on the strength of a promise to pay it back on an agreed date. And that promise is everything. In the community, one's reputation speaks for itself, the only security required being integrity, protecting the family name. No one wants their reputation sullied because they all have daughters to marry. Who will accept your daughters into their family if you don't honour an agreement to pay back your dues?

The *hoondee* system bypasses the traditional banking system, legal jurisdictions, and foreign exchange restrictions and is therefore frowned upon by the authorities given the risks it poses for liquidity in the markets as amounts can be very large. The reason that many people struggle to understand these systems is because they rely heavily on trust and relationship rather than formal rules. I, however, had seen them in action all my life and learnt about them from Daddy and my uncles. We had even needed to use loans backed up by *hoondees* ourselves, to finance all those new initiatives at the shop when we first arrived in London. No bank would lend to us, so Daddy got in touch with his contacts in Hong Kong who had agents in Manchester. Secured with a *hoondee*, they were happy to lend Daddy the money we needed, confident that he would repay – with interest – in a timely fashion.

I was just a child really, especially in Asian terms, still in my teens at the time, trying to understand the system and work it all out. Daddy entrusted me with huge levels of financial responsibility, dealing with accounts and ensuring that capital was preserved. He seemed to want me to know everything. While my older brothers took on more of the practical work, I was carrying out financial transactions which, looking back, were richly fertile soil for the growth of my later career. I was also the one given charge of the bank account and, every Saturday morning, I would wander a few doors along the Uxbridge Road to Barclays Bank to queue up and sort out cash deposits, the foreign exchanges we'd discussed in our coded phone calls and whatever other banking needed doing. After my first Saturday morning visit, the cashiers asked that I go straight to the branch manager's office given the amounts, different currencies and mix of cash, travellers cheques and bankers drafts I brought with me! I still remember the manager smiling, not quite believing the complexity or the amount of money coming in with a 17-year-old schoolboy.

Meanwhile, although we couldn't recreate the huge family parties and lunches of Mombasa, we did our best to welcome any local extended family and Sindhi friends into the fold, all squashing up as they crowded into our tiny above-the-shop living space for dinner. When I recently made contact with a second cousin, Nina Jani, she described me to her mother saying, "You know – the Gidoomals who lived in Shepherd's Bush where Dad used to go for free food when he was a student."

However, while we loved these community times together, we were all too aware of the antagonistic sentiments rising in the country. London in 1968 did not feel a safe place to be an immigrant. We cowered around our black-and-white television set while Enoch Powell warned the good people of Britain about the risk of racial conflict which would soon topple the comfortable status quo, causing 'rivers of blood' to flow. It seemed there were some pretty dangerous people out there. They were ready and waiting to overthrow British culture, we heard. We trembled in disbelief as it dawned on us that, apparently, we were those people. In reality, all our energies were focused on mere survival, gathering around the fire, shivering despite our extra layers, trying to stave off the flu and winter bugs. We felt powerless. It was hard to think of ourselves as a threat to anyone.

Maybe it was because of all this that we also huddled closer together metaphorically, sheltering in the safety of our traditions and exclusive gatherings. This is the vicious cycle faced by new immigrant communities. The lack of welcome, sometimes extending to violence, makes it feel far easier for them to just stay in their own little cluster, but this keeps them confined, hindering opportunities for valuable connections to be made. Arriving in Britain, we wanted to integrate but, being abused and feeling unwelcome, we began to question whether this place could ever feel like home.

Decades after our arrival here, I was made a trustee of the Institute for Citizenship. We had been working on some materials and happened to have a meeting the day after the Bradford riots broke out in July 2001. Several of my fellow trustees commented that our citizenship material would be helpful for the rioters, to which I replied, "As it will be for the residents of Bradford, because they also haven't understood citizenship." Citizenship is a two-way street: those arriving and those welcoming. It is about that welcome as much as about the effort to integrate and, without that, we will never get very far.

As the years unfold of course, it gets easier, with second and third generations fitting in more naturally, albeit still facing discrimination. Growing up here, they know this place is home. For us, however, no matter what our passports said, we sensed we were aliens, different and not particularly wanted.

Despite having always been educated in English, one thing I was always conscious of was my 'alien' accent and its constant potential for ridicule. Although I took on a leadership role within my community, helping other families enrol their children in local schools by taking them to the town council, in my own school life I had no desire to draw attention to myself. Even if I knew the answer in class, I would never put my hand up for fear of the other students' barely smothered sniggers at the way I spoke.

We made the best of things but the excitement and optimism of living in a buzzing new city was always slightly tinged with fear and insecurity. Even at night with the doors locked, our minds never quite rested.

In Kenya, 'being different' was a garment we wore with pride, its rich colours and textures standing out and adding interest to life. Here however, we would have sometimes preferred to cover it up, to hide. At first glance, it was impossible to know who were our friends, and who saw us as a threat to their livelihood. Safer simply to keep ourselves to ourselves.

It was even tougher out on the street, where shouts of 'Paki' or worse taught me to keep my head down as I walked, knowing better than to look anyone in the eye, constantly wondering if the same thing that happened in Kenya might happen here. Might we be rejected again? It was hard to imagine truly belonging.

Would we ever live here without fear?

Chapter Four
Homesick

As I walked from the ramp onto solid ground, it was as if my feet were standing on a lifetime of stories: my heritage, the soil in which my family tree had taken root and grown.

It was 1964, three years before our move to London, and I had just made a very different journey; stepping off a ship into another world. Back then, Mumbai was still Bombay, a bustling port full of noise and energy. I gazed wide-eyed at the magnificent Gateway of India near the famous Taj Hotel, places I had only heard of or seen in photos. But the thing which made me audibly gasp was greater than the splendour of any bricks and mortar.

The people. The people all looked like me.

The feeling of belonging was overwhelming. So, this is how it feels to fit in! I'd had no idea. It is still difficult to put it into words, the intense emotion of those first steps, entering my country of origin, the sense of coming home. No longer did I feel different. Instead, I felt I could walk freely without fear. To this day, every visit to India makes the same unique and dramatic impression on me.

However, for my 14-year-old self it was something completely new and, ironically, the difference was in the similarity. The difference was that I was the same as everyone else. In this place – unlike any other I'd known – I felt a deep recognition. Any one of these people could be passed off as my brother, my sister, my uncle. It was the first time in my life that I didn't stand out. I was flooded with relief and confidence, as if I'd found a lost piece of myself I had not even known was missing.

My family had of course told me countless tales of Mother India, waxing lyrical and oozing idealism. Now I was here and, within that one moment, every word they had told me became real around me. Stories and histories seemed even to float on the breeze along with a good helping of second-hand nostalgia. All I could think was 'India, India. This is my country.'

* * *

The whole adventure had begun some months previously, with a simple conversation:

"If you really want the best for Ram, you need to send him to boarding school. And I know just the one."

Mr Cameron, my teacher, was talking Daddy round, dropping into the conversation irresistible morsels about Bishop Cotton's School in Bangalore: the perfect place apparently, for me to fulfil both my senior education and my potential. It was his alma mater – and, with his recommendation, the Headmaster would be certain to accept me. There was an element of persuasion, but to be honest, not much was needed. Daddy always wanted the best for me, and was quickly convinced.

They would not send me alone however. My older brothers, Bharat, Lachu and Kanu were to travel with me in the hope that we would all get a place at the school together.

We left the family nest and set sail on the SS Safina ul Hujaj, proud to be on the then-fastest ship from Mombasa to Bombay, crossing the seas in a mere ten days as opposed to the usual two weeks. And thank goodness for that because, being confined to bunk beds in third class, with military style food, I'm not sure we could have handled much longer. I looked up to my savvier big brothers for survival, especially the eldest who somehow managed to smuggle food from the first-class section of the ship to keep us all going.

Now finally we were coming into dock, watching sharks gliding territorially through the harbour waters; the Gateway of India in the distance, calling us home. We disembarked and within seconds seemed to be surrounded by coolies all fighting for the chance to take our luggage to Customs.

Admittedly, my dreamy idealism took a sharp knock with the fearful immigration and customs experience at Bombay Port. Our bags were crammed full of presents and foodstuffs that family and friends in India had requested: tins upon tins of South African Kraft Cheese: a common request for anyone making this voyage. Finally, however, we made it through in one piece and were free to explore our motherland.

On landing, we were met by the driver of Rai Bahadur Lalchand Watanmal Boolchand who took us straight to Rai Bahadur's office where we formally shook hands, although first all four of us had to touch his feet as a sign of respect to him – a senior friend of the family. He had a very imperious presence and seemed almost more British than the British in his mannerisms and attitudes. The first thing he did was take us to the photographer who had a studio in the same building. "Dear boys," he said, "The photographs will follow in due course. Now follow me and let's go to my flat".

With that he swept us off to his home, opposite the Cricket Club of India (CCI) premises, housing the prestigious Brabourne Stadium where Test Matches are played. As we gazed up at his beautiful ceilings, painted with scenes from Mogul times, he entertained us by recounting our family history. Even his servant remembered our grandfather, Baba Dayaram, and joined in, telling eloquent tales of his achievements and escapades and describing the family palace, Moti Mahal in Hyderabad, Sindh.

Rai Bahadur wore a ring with an exquisite blue-white diamond, sourced in Durban, a gift from our grandfather to him and a symbol of their deep friendship. Grandfather made a tradition of giving diamonds to his children and grandchildren on their marriages – rings for the sons, and other jewellery for the daughters-in-law, and had extended this special gift to his friend too. Although Rai Bahadur came from a higher caste, the Bhaibands, Grandfather's wealth and business success gave him access to, and acceptance from, those who would normally be considered his social superiors.

Our grandfather was ahead of his time. The money he'd made from the silk trade meant that not only could he afford a palace, but he could also improve the marriageability of future generations, buying his descendants a route into higher castes. Under normal circumstances, nobody from a higher caste would want to marry into our family – we were funeral singers by tradition – the lowest of the low. However, he dared to ask girls from the Bhaiband merchant caste, higher than ours, to marry his sons – my father and uncle – because he could afford to take them without demanding any dowry. These were known as 'sari weddings' because the brides could literally just turn up in their saris. Nothing was expected from them. In fact, if anything, their families received gifts from ours. No expense was spared as my grandfather had the town lit up and sent horse drawn carriages to pick up the girls – who were of course my mother and aunt – for a double wedding which was, by all accounts, spectacular.

As we listened enthralled to the stories, we realised our family had a legacy here, and had left strong memories in the hearts and minds of those they left behind. Eventually though, we said goodbye to Bombay and family friends, taking the Deccan Queen Express to Poona, more coolies rushing ahead to throw crisp white sheets onto our places and colonise our seats which, although booked, were never guaranteed.

Aunty Kishu chaperoned us for this part of the journey. She and Uncle Tahilram lived in Poona with their four children, Ram, Nanik, Pushpa and Mana. We were delighted to be able to stay a couple of nights with them. Then came the final leg of our journey, the overnight train to Bangalore, complete with gauge changes – a relic from the Raj – meaning we had to change trains part-way. As we surfaced the following morning, we blinked sleepily out at the station where we'd stopped.

Up and down the length of the train stood a line of waiters, not only on the platform side but also along the tracks on the outer edge. Through the windows they handed us huge banana leaves holding tantalising breakfasts of spiced omelettes, idli, sambar, dosas, papadum, yogurt and rice in a range of glorious colours and variety. The bright green of the leaves contrasted with the yellows and reds of papadums and chutneys like a work of art. They tasted as delicious as they looked and, even now when I return to South India for business, my breakfast order never changes.

As it was still the school holidays when we arrived in Bangalore, we stayed with our uncles Vashi and Dayaram Chatlani, owners of the 'Favourite Shop' chain there. At first, the excitement of the trip and the newness of discovering my homeland carried me through. But it was not enough.

In the light of my powerful eureka moment disembarking in Bombay, it is perhaps surprising to learn that I longed for home from day one. Despite feeling that I had found my place, I still missed Mombasa. I missed my mother, Daddy, my Aunty Janki, Ama (my grandmother), my other siblings. I missed, dare I say it, my home. Because Mombasa was all I'd ever known.

In short, I was homesick. Although I knew the school was of the highest calibre, an outstanding opportunity, my fears grew daily. The more I heard how much I would need to adapt and adjust, the more nervous I became. Some of this was exaggerated by the boys in the house where we were staying, who relished telling me, "You will have to learn at least two more languages: Telugu and Kannada… and be fluent in them just to survive in the playground!" It scared the life out of me! When I asked to see the Chemistry and Physics textbooks, I was shocked at how different they were from the ones I'd seen in Mombasa. The thought of studying my favourite subjects in such a new way, not to mention a new language, stripped away any last shred of joy.

We lasted a mere two weeks in Bangalore, not even staying for the start of term despite all my uncles' efforts to keep me there. One of them even tried to trick me by calling the house where we were staying from his shop, pretending to be Daddy and begging me to at least stay a few more weeks and give the school a try. By then, however, I was too concerned about missing the start of the new academic year in my own school in Mombasa to be taken in.

Finally, they could ignore my unhappiness no longer. As I wept down the phone, really to Daddy this time, his soft spot for me came good. "It's all right," he said eventually, "Come home. Bharat has a place and will stay. We haven't lost anything."

And so, despite the offer of a place at this prestigious school, I cried my way back to Mombasa, arriving home just in time for the start of senior school in 1964. Bharat was excited at the opportunity to stay in the school, and Lachu, Kanu and I made our way back to Poona, then to Bombay for our flight to Nairobi. Stopping over in Aden, Lachu fulfilled his ambition of buying a Parker ink pen with the pocket money he had saved. Meanwhile Kanu, like many family members before him, bought a bottle of Johnny Walker Red Label Whisky and 200 Benson and Hedges cigarettes for our Ama in duty free.

Although it may have seemed like a wasted journey, for me it was nonetheless the start of a love affair, tying me with an unbreakable thread to my mother country, a thread that has been woven through my life's story, pulling me back time and again, inspiring decisions that would change my life.

For now, however, I was heading back to Mombasa, where I belonged. The place where I fit in despite standing out.

This is the paradox of the immigrant: a constant homesickness wherever you are. There's a craving for your country of origin with its powerful sense of cultural belonging and allies in appearance, not to mention the freedom from fear this entails. However, there are also cords of belonging intricately tying you to your birthplace and family, the place you grew up, albeit as a sometimes-anxious immigrant.

For a short while there, I had these two options, two ideals, but of course, when Daddy's deportation order came, I ended up with neither. Kenya no longer wanted us and, while India was our cultural home, the message was clear, "You chose to be British, let the Queen look after you!"

Some homesickness is just too much to bear. A tree ripped up from solid ground can be hard to replant. The older the tree, the stronger the roots, tangling outwards in every direction. And the stronger those roots, the harder for them to curl down into new terrain. My siblings and I were young so, while the later uprooting to London was painful and frightening, after a couple of years the slender fibres of our roots found their way into English ground. Daddy, however, was a different story.

Was it the cold that he found so difficult? Not directly, but certainly it played its part. He never really adapted to the British climate, the different clothes and sensible shoes required to walk this life he had not chosen. He regularly slipped in the snow and ice or simply resigned himself to being housebound. After running a successful, high-end business in Mombasa, it was devastating for him to take on a corner shop. Loss of status made him shrink back into himself, keeping the family at arm's length. This loss of prestige and social status went hand in hand with the pressure of responsibility for the one-hundred-strong extended family he headed up. But it wasn't only that. Having been uprooted twice already, the constant unspoken question hanging in the air of our Shepherd's Bush home was 'could it happen a third time?'

Shortly after my arrival in London, Daddy was granted a dispensation to return to Kenya to settle his affairs. On deportation, he had only been allowed to bring £3000 to England, foreign exchange regulations preventing large sums of money from being taken out of Kenya during the years around Independence (it would have devastated the Kenyan economy if Asians had all taken their millions away). Now he was hoping to bring back to England some much needed extra funds.

Before he made that trip back to Mombasa, while I was still scrambling my way through those early culture-shocked months in London, Daddy seemed eager, desperate almost, to teach me everything about his personal financial affairs as they related to his assets in the UK – his various bank accounts, his contacts, loans he had given secured by *hoondees*, and arrangements for the foreign exchange transactions he would be conducting from Mombasa. It was endless. At the time, I never questioned why, but in retrospect I wonder if at some level he already sensed he would never make it back to London.

The bright African sun welcomed him home and fed his soul, but the system there was not so kind. He soon discovered that the business had been mismanaged in his absence and some of our assets purloined. Meanwhile, tax laws made it difficult to gather up many of our other assets. Without an accountant nearby to bring his books up to date, much of our wealth in Kenya was simply written off, lost forever. What had once been rightfully ours, toiled for over decades, had now been appropriated by others.

Back in London, waiting for news of him, waiting for him to return home, we had no idea of the struggles he was facing there. Meanwhile, an overzealous police officer, noting that Daddy was back in Kenya, had decided to open a case on him, adding further to his pressures and despair. Between this and the constant reminders all around him of what he had lost, the burdens became too much to take. Already at the age of 42, he had suffered a stroke from the stress of his double immigration.

Now everything was crashing down on him again. It was too much. My Daddy, this man of such great strength and character, whose broad shoulders had carried our family across continents and through every challenge of life, died tragically in Mombasa in April 1969.

The grief we'd felt at his deportation came flooding back, multiplied a hundredfold. We were lost, heartbroken. But we also kept going. While family, friends and neighbours queued outside our corner shop in Shepherd's Bush and packed into our tiny front room to pay their respects, my brothers and I kept working in Daddy's honour, breaking the Asian tradition of an official mourning time because we knew he would want this. We knew him.

Even in death he had taken care of the family, ensuring that the dowries of each of his daughters was protected in his will and that my mother and Aunty Janki were also looked after. As for us boys, we were expected to find our own way. And we began immediately.

At the time I didn't put it into words but perhaps even back then, I was developing what would become my lifetime's maxim: *Never let what you can't do stop you from doing what you can.* Despite our deep sadness, my brothers and I saw potential for our lives. We knew that together we could do this, make something of ourselves.

Later, our humble little corner shop would fly, expanding to several branches, with Barry, Lachu and Kanu at the helm, genes and family tradition spurring them on in honest hard work. While the shop 'G. Bharat' did help feed the family in the early days of survival, as the boys got married, they moved out and bought their own shops with accommodation included. Lachman and Meena moved to the flat above their shop in Chiswick, and Kanaya and his wife Asha moved to the flat above their shop on Askew Road. Daddy would never have the joy of seeing us settling properly in London, allowing our roots to reach deeper into the soil as we married and had families of our own.

Because for me that time did come. Although nowhere in the world has ever made me feel quite like I had felt in India, and nothing can replace my idyllic Mombasa childhood, gradually I did come to a time when, despite struggles, discrimination, and ongoing challenges, I could say of London "This is my home".

Chapter Five
Jesus at the Pub

Margarita Ucker put down her pen and smiled at the visitor. The small village of Fraubrunnen, Switzerland where she lived didn't see too many international travellers, but Mr Roopchand Gidoomal (Dada Roopa) came quite regularly from Kenya to meet with her boss in Basle, trading Kenyan wood carvings and other traditional crafts. She had come to think of him warmly, considering him more a friend than a business acquaintance.

She loved hearing stories about his huge extended family: his wife Kamla, his children Meera, Anita, Chandru and Renu, and all his brothers and sisters, not to mention those countless nieces and nephews. His life sounded like an endless criss-crossing stream of family, and she felt almost like she knew them. He knew about her family too, but one thing he didn't know was this:

Margarita Ucker was praying for him.

Praying for him and his family. She started sometime in the late 1950s and she just didn't stop. She prayed over the decades for this huge extended family. She prayed on through the 60s and 70s. She prayed even after Mr Gidoomal stopped trading and no longer visited. She never knew if her prayers were doing any good, but she prayed anyway.

So, in the early 1970s, as I sat in a in a study room in a London Halls of Residence feeling confused and more than a little lost, 600 miles away Margarita Ucker was still praying.

My own journey to this place had not been easy. A bureaucratic side effect of Daddy's death was that the bank letter he'd arranged guaranteeing my university funding was no longer worth a penny. I had been offered a place at Imperial College, so close to home, and yet it seemed impossible that I would ever get there. Unlike my contemporaries, my alien status meant I had no automatic right to a grant for university. I was treated as a foreign student, with the fees bill to match – something I clearly couldn't afford.

I had always prided myself on overcoming obstacles, but here I needed help, and thankfully it came, most notably through Mr Hooton, my Headmaster at Christopher Wren School writing to the Inner London Education Authority (ILEA), appealing for a scholarship. Without such support, all the brains in the world might not have been enough to bring university within my reach. Eventually, I was interviewed by a very tall Jamaican ILEA official with such a warm smile that, despite the rigorous questioning, I felt at ease. I was awarded the scholarship and, much relieved, pressed on with my studies.

When I held that first grant cheque in my hands, it was Dada Roopa who took me aside and asked, "Are you going to start supporting your mother now?" I took his advice and began with a small amount, £25 a month. In our culture, widows must be cared for and I was moved when, many years later, it was also one of the first questions my future father-in-law asked me.

During the first two years I rented a room in Ingersoll Road, a stone's throw from the family shop, which meant that I could still muck in and do my bit. After all, one of the reasons I chose Imperial was because it was just a 5p bus ride from home on the number 49. In my third year however, the College rule was that students had to live in, and I was allocated a room in Linstead Hall, one of the university's Halls of Residence.

I was grateful for the opportunity I'd been given. I was grateful for education and the chance to better myself, but there was one problem.

I was lonely.

I knew several people, but I was similar to exactly none of them. I craved connection but when I tried to socialise, my differences seemed all the more pronounced. Discussions only served to highlight cultural clashes. I had managed to close the education gap caused by starting my A-levels late but the social gulf between me and the other students was still enormous, even after a couple of years in the country. It felt as if there was a secret code to fitting in and I'd somehow missed the briefing. Everything felt hostile. Even the television lounge was a sea of unwelcoming faces – I didn't dare venture there. Easier to fill the empty hours alone in my room reading and working. I was studious but had somehow missed out on the experience of being a student. It felt just beyond my grasp.

I longed to talk to someone about the things that worried me: family expectations, the pressure to agree to an arranged marriage, but who among my contemporaries would have understood?

I had one friend, a study partner who was a Muslim from Trinidad. We got on and worked well together, but a few days beforehand, he had told me he was backing out of the Practical Physics option we had been planning to work on together during the final year. Brains was one thing, hard work another, but a third requirement for success was becoming apparent - mutual support. I needed others. Already I'd missed the chance of taking Theoretical Physics because it was reserved for the brainiest of the brainy and, unbeknown to me, everyone who was interested had been pre-reading for at least a year. Between dashing to and from the shop to help out, and not being in the loop with my classmates, I hadn't heard about this and now it was too late.

That was bad enough, but without a study partner, even the more straightforward, Practical Physics option would feel tough.

I sighed and looked at the book in my lap again. After being born a Hindu, brought up with Sikh influences and educated with Muslims, it seemed strange that my current choice of reading matter was the Bible.

I thought back to the night I'd been given it by a group of musicians I'd met at the pub. In the mix of loneliness and longing to fit in, somehow, I discovered that if you sat in a pub with half a pint of bitter for long enough, someone would come and talk to you. After a few beers I felt less conscious of my accent, less embarrassed to speak to strangers. I gained enough artificial confidence to make conversation. It was not the meaningful connection I craved, but it was something.

That particular night, as I drank my half pint, I heard music. A group of young people, around my age, started singing Gene MacLellan's "Put your hands in the hands of the man from Galilee" in Bob Dylan's rendering of it. Then they began to talk. Apparently, this man's hands could calm rocky waters and change outlooks. Apparently, their God held everything in his hands. Who was this God? My own travels had covered a good chunk of the world, between Africa, India, and Europe. My upbringing and schooling had eloquently versed me in Hinduism, Sikhism, and Islam, yet I had never known of a God who held all things together, everywhere. A niggling memory was surfacing though. Hadn't I read once, many years ago sitting in the 'last room' in my Mombasa home, that there was a power above all powers, one Supreme Being? At the time it had sparked intrigue and excitement in my heart but, not knowing where to take that curiosity, I had let it go.

As they sang more songs, I turned my chair to really listen. Afterwards, I approached them, wanting to know more. They told me about this Jesus, Son of the one true God, who had given his life for us. It was all new to me, and I had endless questions. I invited them back to my Halls for a longer discussion, and we talked for hours, as they gallantly attempted to keep up with my tidal wave of curiosity.

Some of the texts they quoted that evening sounded very familiar. I couldn't work it out until I finally twigged that I'd read them before, in a Scripture Gift Mission booklet called *Daily Strength* which someone had given my family. Unaware that these daily readings were taken from the Christian Scriptures, the Holy Bible, I'd read it right through several times. The ideas sparked by all the quotes had enthralled me, and I had learnt large chunks off by heart for the ongoing encouragement it gave me.

Over the following weeks one of them came back several times. Each time I would treat him to a heated debate! I was hungry for answers, for details, for some kind of clarity. I wanted to believe it all, but I wasn't quite there. They had given me this Bible, which I'd read very selectively, but that only triggered more questions. Having started with the Gospels I was puzzled at the way the story kept repeating itself. I decided instead to flip through some other bits, with equal bewilderment. In lectures I had always sat between the same two students, David Goldsmith and Peter Clayton. At first, I hadn't realised I was hemmed in by Christians, but it gradually became obvious. So, when my Bible reading continued to baffle me, I turned to these friends and told them I was struggling. I had no idea what I should be reading.

"Corinthians!" they both said immediately. "Read Corinthians, that should make it clear."

I decided anything was worth a try, so went back to my room and began to read. My mouth dropped open in amazement as I came across themes and concepts that were both current and relevant. Here was a book that could have been written for the people of today – the sheer currency of the ideas and thoughts there was astounding. For me, Christianity had always been the white man's faith, and something alien to me. But as I read, I found all kinds of resonances with my life. It could have been 'Paul's letter to the people of London'.

However, I still wasn't quite there. My constant "whys?" wore my friends down a bit and, eventually, they concluded I wasn't really interested. The one who had been visiting, stopped. I was left with my Bible and my questions. For the next three months I struggled on alone. I dug deeper with my research, even going to the British Museum to cross-check various references. I found, in the writings of Josephus, a Jewish historian, that Jesus Christ, really had existed. He was a real person with historical records to prove it. A real person, offering me life. I kept coming back to John 14:6 where Jesus describes himself as the only way to God: "I am the way and the truth and the life. No one comes to the Father except through me." Could this really be the one Supreme Power, the only way, that I had read about all those years beforehand?

I was hugely intrigued, but just couldn't take the final step of giving my life over to this Jesus. That would be admitting I was a failure. I had always managed to sort out my own problems, in my own strength. However, I also knew that my own strength would get me nowhere in terms of escaping the trap of sin, or 'karma' as I knew it. All the other religions with which I was acquainted offered self-abnegation or repentance, yes, but no assurance of real escape from eternal consequences. Here was Jesus offering to wipe it all out and give me a fresh start. I knew I needed it – I felt spiritually bankrupt and deadened by loneliness – but the deal seemed too one-sided for someone who'd grown up in a family of negotiators. What was the catch? The more I read the more it seemed there genuinely wasn't one. This was generosity beyond imagination.

Flicking through the pages of my Bible again, my eyes fell upon Revelation 3:20, the same verse I had repeatedly read in the Scripture Gift Mission booklet yet understanding neither where it came from nor what the reference meant. I read it once more. "Here I am! I stand at the door and knock. If anyone hears my voice and opens the door, I will come in and eat with them, and they with me."

I knew I had a choice, to open that door, to do things differently. Finally, with many questions still hanging in the air, I said "Ok, I can give this deal a shot." I'm embarrassed to say I was still viewing it as a business transaction. I say sorry, and he forgives my sins. Job done. It was a little arrogant of me but, even though my attitude may not have been flawless, I did it. I decided to invite Jesus into my life and see what difference it made. With that, I opened the door to Christ, asked him to come in.

Immediately I was filled with a huge sense of relief. I'd been battling for such a long time and suddenly here was this overwhelming peace, a peace I had never known before. God felt so imminent, so near to me. My prayers changed from being something slightly superficial to a profoundly meaningful conversation with someone real; someone who loved me and was listening; someone who cared about the details of my life. Here was someone vast and omnipotent but whom I could truly know. Here was my deep connection. I was not 'admitting defeat'. I was finding the solution to all my loneliness and anxiety.

The following day, my study partner came to find me. "You know what Ram. I think I'll do Practical Physics with you after all." Again, relief flooded through me. It was no doubt a small thing, but it made a huge difference to me. It was my first experience of answered prayer.

Conversing with God was natural and real, but fitting into Christian culture felt quite the opposite. I knew Christians went to church, but how on earth did that work? To begin with I didn't know which church to go to. Could anyone just walk in? Did you need a ticket? An invitation? Did you need permission?

Then one day, my Sri Lankan friend, Ranil Perera, asked me "Which church do you go to?"

I gave a wry laugh. "I don't! It's just me, the Bible and Jesus!"

I explained that I wouldn't know where to start with church. I had walked around the vicinity of the college and Halls to see which churches were nearby, laboriously scribbling down their names. The musicians who had first sparked faith in me had clearly told me I should be careful and only do what's in the Bible. Taking this advice rather literally, I checked my list of church names against the Bible and found that none of them were mentioned there. Evidently, I couldn't risk going to any of these apparently unbiblical places! I decided to avoid making a decision. It would just be me, the Bible and Jesus.

My friend responded by inviting me along to the Christian Union. I started attending their regular meetings and was pleasantly surprised when a vicar turned up free from his robes, wearing a normal suit instead. Finally, someone said, "Look, why don't you come with us to church? Don't be afraid."

Proving my point about the confusion of churches, there then followed a lot of deliberation about which one to choose. Finally, I opted for my local one, St Paul's Onslow Square, but told them I could only go to the evening service. I was still on the College's India Society committee and didn't want my Indian friends seeing me set off on Sunday morning with a bunch of Christians.

Before my first visit I made sure I put on a good pair of socks, certain that these would be on display when I took off my shoes. But when I got there, the shoe rack was nowhere in sight. Hurriedly I checked with my friends who assured me that here, everyone just keeps their shoes on. I then looked for a space on the floor where I could sit, respectfully. But instead, they gently guided me to the pews. I was sitting down gingerly, trying to assimilate this strange situation, when suddenly the organ blasted out. In shock, I turned to my friends again "You didn't tell me it was a funeral! Who's died?" They laughed, "Nobody's dead! This is the normal music!"

The whole set up felt alien and removed from everything I'd ever known, and I was pretty sure it wasn't for me…until I heard the sermon. The text for the day was "You are the salt of the earth". I had read it in a flash that morning, but here was someone actually explaining it. He spoke for 20 minutes, and I was gripped for every second of it. At that moment I knew I needed to go back, if only for the teaching. Here I could finally find out the deeper meaning of all those things I was reading.

It was enough to make me go every week, even if that was all I went for. I would turn up, listen to the sermon, and then run to the Sikh Gurdwara in Shepherd's Bush for free food (my friend and classmate Bipin Desai still teases me that if I ever offered to 'treat' him to dinner I would simply take him to the gurdwara!). It became my Sunday routine.

It took a while for some things to fall into place. At first, I struggled with the idea of the resurrection. I had taken my step of faith without fully believing or even knowing every aspect but trusting that God would make these things clear to me. And he did.

Looking back, I realised that many things had contributed to my faith journey. It helped that, from a very early age, I had been cultivating a spiritual mindset. Prayer was a part of life, as was the desire for humility, faithfulness, and honesty. When I finally grasped the message of Jesus, everything came together. It all made sense.

I also loved to think that as a Sindhi I had a direct connection with the Gospel of Jesus. In Matthew chapter 27 verse 59 the text speaks of Joseph of Arimathea wrapping the body of Jesus in a cloth. The Greek word for this cloth is Sindon, a cloth from the Sindh. A cloth created in my homeland, holding the body of Christ.

I will always be grateful for the Christians who made contact with me in the pub that night, and especially for the one who persevered in visiting me, listening patiently to my arguments and trying to help. When he finally gave up on me, I thought I would never see him again and later told people that the first person I'd want to see in heaven would be him, so that I could thank him for introducing me to Jesus. Many years later, during the mayoral race, a vicar who happened to be the Chairman of Campus Crusade UK (Agape Ministries UK) heard that one of their university workers had helped me meet Jesus. With a little information on dates and locations, he was able to track down John Volland, who was now working amongst students at Reading University. We met and rejoiced together over dinner with our spouses.

I always knew what his role was in my journey. Sometimes, however, we simply don't know all the threads of the story until later. Decades after that experience in the Halls of Residence, we were travelling through Switzerland and decided to contact a lady who had been friends with Dada Roopa, my uncle Roopchand. He had often travelled there and always talked of her kindness and welcome, so I was keen to meet her.

We booked into a hotel and stopped at her home for dinner. After her son Tomas gave thanks for the meal, something on a bookcase across the room caught my eye. It was the German version of a book we had at home, *Good News for Modern Man*, a version of the New Testament.

"Who reads that book?" I asked.

"Oh, all of us do!"

"Really? We read it too, in English."

She stared at me, her mouth became a surprised 'o' as the penny dropped. "So… you're a believer?"

"Not just me, but my wife, her brother, others in the family too…"

Margarita Ucker then told me the story of how she had met my uncle when he visited to trade in African crafts, how she had prayed for him, for me, for my whole family for decade after decade. Praying without ceasing. And I was able to tell her about the fruits of that prayer.

And so, my story is far more than me sitting in a university room on my own with the Bible in 1973.

My story is a woman in Switzerland praying faithfully for my family for decades.

My story is a group of young musicians brave enough to sing Christian songs in a pub.

My story is a little booklet given to a family who had no apparent interest in this 'colonial' religion.

My story is also of a God who works in the dark, in the hidden places, but also in the pain. Because, without that intense loneliness, would I have gone to the pub that night? Would I have longed for connection enough to seek out the greatest connection of all? In the isolation and misery, God was at work, guiding me towards him, impelled by the prayers of a faithful woman in Switzerland who had never even met me.

Chapter Six

Rolls Royce at the Corner Shop

Down, down I descended into the depths of the earth, the escalator creaking ominously beneath my feet. In the distance I could hear the clackety rumble and screech of an approaching tube. The pace of those around me sped up a little with their eagerness to catch the next train. I too was hurrying, holding my ticket and briskly overtaking any dawdlers. Nearly there, not much longer.

I had no interest in catching the train, however. I was there for something quite different. I turned the corner onto the Central Line platform of Shepherd's Bush station and, while the other travellers criss-crossed in and out of the doors, my eyes frantically scanned the platform, waiting for the crowd to clear.

There she was. The girl I loved but was forbidden to see.

There, deep underground, we could meet and talk, torrents of pent-up words finally released as we caught up on each other's news and plotted new ways to be together. It was the deepest station we knew of, burrowing down through two long escalator tunnels to reach the platform. Somehow it felt safe and hidden, but we also knew it would be easy to explain a coincidental meeting should anyone spot us. Faced with the disapproval of my family and a complete veto from hers, these subterranean trysts were our lifeline, our one chance to steal a little time.

Sitting there together we agonised over our situation and tried to come up with ideas to convince our families that our friendship, our relationship, was not the tragedy they feared. It would not bring doom on the family and destroy our reputations. It could even be a good thing. But would they ever accept that?

* * *

The first time I saw Sunita, I didn't speak to her, but I certainly noticed her. My sister Pushpa had persuaded me to attend a Diwali event at a Bayswater hotel – they were short of Sindhi boys. It wasn't difficult for her to lure me in with the promise of free food. Early in the evening, I began dancing with one girl and, being too shy to do anything else, I stuck with her all evening. But even as I danced and chatted to my companion, my eyes kept sneaking glances across the room where another girl was being swept around the floor by her father. Their dancing was incredible; it was hard not to stare.

Soon afterwards, the Imperial College Indian Society of which I was a committee member was organising its own Diwali event. At the time, Imperial had 16 boys to every one girl, and any college in the area with a higher percentage of female students enjoyed honorary status, as if they were part of Imperial, and were offered free tickets.

Even after scouring the area, we were still short on girls. I talked to Pushpa and she agreed to invite some others, one of whom was her friend, Celia. Celia couldn't make it but asked her sister, Sunita, if she would be interested.

This time, I made sure I spoke to her. We chatted for hours, getting to know a little about each other. She had recently finished her A-levels and was now at the French Institute, which happened to be – most conveniently – just down the road from Imperial. It seemed too good to be true.

Even from those very first conversations, our meeting felt significant. For a long time, I had been struggling with the idea of an arranged marriage, much to my family's dismay. My academic success and business skills apparently made me an attractive prospect and I was already being offered premium rates for my potential partnership. Huge sums, ridiculous amounts, had been mentioned, including one family offering an annuity for life if I married their daughter. If I accepted, I would never need to work again. But I did not accept – neither the offer nor the concept. I was not for sale.

I wrestled with my feelings on this. It was the family tradition, and I loved my family. I didn't want to hurt anyone. I even recognised it worked for others. I simply could not do it myself. Their response was always the same: "You know this is how it works in our culture".

Yes. I knew.

My granny was six years old when she was betrothed in marriage. Over the years she shared countless stories about her innocence and the challenges of being a child bride which, while obviously shocking now, was common in her day, and her dramatic retellings were only ever focused on making her grandchildren laugh.

Such early marriages were mainly arranged to ensure the boys were committed from a young age. This didn't always work. Many of my ancestors were also traders who travelled abroad for long periods, in some cases, years. It was quite common for them to take second wives or mistresses in the countries where they were stationed, meaning there could be distant Gidoomal family members – the offspring of those unions – in Japan and the Seychelles. People I've never met or seen.

Many of my siblings were willing to accept the arrangement of their marriages and happily, these have worked well. I, however, was not willing to accept an arranged mariage. So, when it became clear that Sunita and I were like-minded, clicked, and both wanted the same things, I became determined to make it work despite fierce opposition from both families.

To meet a girl I liked, who was not just from an Indian family, but a Sindhi one, seemed like a match made in heaven. However, sharing that heritage was not enough. Sunita's life had been charmed from the moment she was born in St Mary's, Paddington, through her upbringing and then education at the Legat Ballet School in Tunbridge Wells. We were from the same cultural and religious background, but our wealth and castes were miles apart.

In short, she was out of my league.

While I continued to live above the corner shop in Shepherd's Bush, Sunita's family moved from Golders Green to The Bishop's Avenue in Hampstead. While my family ran a slightly haphazard corner shop, hers helped run a slick multi-million-pound business. While I had an accent that gave away my origins, she spoke the Queen's English. And yet, we dared to dream that we might be together.

After the second Diwali function, I knew I had to see her again and came up with the perfect pretext. I was organising a Sitar concert at college for the Indian Society. A good friend of mine, Viram Jasani, was coming to play. We'd made some posters to put up locally to spread the word and sell some tickets. A plan formed in my mind. I managed to wangle her phone number – which I can still recite today – and dialled, a little nervously.

"Yes, who is it?"

The foreboding voice of her mother filled me with terror, but I took a deep breath and plunged in.

"Hello, I'm Ram. I'm at Imperial College. I met Sunita recently and know she goes to the French Institute. I'm looking to put up some concert posters there. Could I possibly speak with her about giving her some?"

Thankfully she didn't query it but passed me straight to Sunita. I repeated my request, saying how grateful I would be if she could help. When she replied with a yes, I jumped in, taking my chances,

"Thank you! This is such a terrific thing you're doing for me. I really think you deserve lunch."

She didn't suspect a thing, and lunch in exchange for the favour of putting up some posters sounded like a business meeting to her family. No questions were asked, nor eyebrows raised. I took her to an Italian restaurant in South Kensington and as we chatted, our common ground grew more and more apparent – mutual friends, mutual ideas and finally, mutual feelings.

But what good are feelings in a culture of castes and arranged marriages? I was not considered a suitable boy, despite my hard work and good prospects. Of course, it could have been a lot worse. If my family's original caste had been the only factor, perhaps it would have been a completely lost cause. We were the lowest of the low and, it was only thanks to my grandfather's great wealth that 'sari weddings' were possible for his sons: dowry-free brides, coming with nothing but the sari they wore and the status of their higher caste, to improve our own. Because of this, my mother and aunt had brought new, 'higher value' blood into the family but, even with this, we were still fairly low in the pecking order.

Between our first 'business' lunch in South Kensington and the later clandestine underground meet ups, Sunita and I got together several times. Enough for the 'putting up posters' excuse to wear thin. Enough for tongues to start wagging. But what really got the Sindhi grapevine going was a slip up of my own doing. Soon after that first lunch, Sunita and her family travelled to Bombay for her cousin's wedding. I had asked for her address, promising to write but, in a moment of extravagance, I sent her a huge bouquet of roses, which arrived the day before the wedding. Her entire extended family assumed they were for the bride, so when they saw the card addressed to Sunita, jaws dropped in shock. On reflection it was this gesture of mine that really triggered the gossip, a gesture which publicised our relationship to her entire family and unwittingly put her reputation at risk. In retrospect, it was a huge social faux pas. In the small world of Sindhi communities, there were of course people there who knew my uncle, Dada Roopa. They wasted no time in dropping it into conversation with him on their return and he took me aside with firm words:

"You risk ruining her reputation. Either declare your intentions to marry her or stop this."

So, if I continued to spend time with Sunita without making my intentions clear, she would be seen as damaged goods – which was ironic because, to me, my intentions were perfectly clear. I would have liked nothing more than to propose to her, if only I were allowed. I had no intention of doing anything except what was right by her. This was not a young man trying to shirk commitment but keen to take it on.

Frantically, our respective families tried to matchmake us with other suitors. Sunita's mother lined up a string of more 'appropriate' boys from her own caste, but one by one Sunita brushed them off, her relationship with her parents becoming a little strained in the process. Similarly, I had no interest in any of the girls being suggested to me. I only wanted Sunita. What we shared simply could not be manufactured in an arrangement. We clicked. We saw eye to eye. For a long time, this stalemate continued. Some years earlier, before we'd met, Sunita had declared she wouldn't marry until she was well into her twenties and her family delighted in reminding her of this. They asked her to promise not to see me anymore, but we couldn't stop.

Maybe the hardest thing was that I totally understood the family point of view. It was normal. We were the ones breaking the rules: rules that were so deeply embedded in our culture it would take a groundbreakingly radical attitude to ignore them. No one was trying to be cruel, it was simply that age old situation of wanting what's best for your children, even if our opinions on what was 'best' did differ dramatically. However unfair it felt, our families were acting from a place of concern, wanting us to be accepted by the community and society. Like all parents, they feared for us. What would happen to us if we broke the norm?

A couple of years prior to this I had embarked on my PhD, although even my admittance to that programme nearly didn't happen. After my degree, having secured a place for doctoral studies in Plasma and Space Physics, again at Imperial, I had applied for the Science Research Council grant, but learned that I wasn't eligible for funding because, once again, I wasn't considered fully British. After all those years living, working, and studying here, apparently, I was still an alien. My university years didn't count towards the minimum three-year residence requirement. Once again, I was considered a newcomer. I was back in Kenya on holiday when the letter came and still remember the crushing disappointment, shock and frustration reducing me to tears.

Hurriedly, my family and I cobbled together a plan. I registered for an MSc in Management Science and Operations Research instead. Fortunately, the fees had been waived following an interview with the Head of Department, Professor Sam Eilon, and my sister Nirmala gave me a £250 loan towards my expenses, including lunches at college – usually chicken and ham pie with chips and baked beans. I stayed at home rent-free and even took a lunchtime job as computer program advisor for students at the college. Every little bit earned or saved helped me towards my goal.

Then I got writing. That summer I wrote letters to over a hundred foundations and companies for internships. And they wrote back. I could have papered the whole lab with the rejection letters I received. But finally, just when I was ready to give up, I was offered an interview for a University of London scholarship. It felt like déjà vu, like I was back applying for my undergraduate grant all over again. I wore my oldest shirt and jeans and still remember the anxious walk from the Senate House reception to the interview room. Over a dozen panellists were seated around a large oval shaped mahogany board room table. I sat on my own at the opposite end facing them, with an anonymous note taker behind me. Within this nerve-racking experience, I made a choice. Feeling I had nothing to lose, I sat upright with quiet confidence and decided I would be prepared to face anything they threw at me. After some very thorough questioning, I breathed an exhausted sigh and waited. To my huge relief and delight, I was awarded the scholarship. Seeing my name listed in the 1973 Imperial College Annual Report gave me a moment of real pride. Receiving the first grant cheque was an even more wonderful feeling!

However, unbeknown to me, my research tutor, Gerry Salkin, had been working behind the scenes, meaning I was also offered a Research Assistant post funded by a grant from the Civil Service. This was worth significantly more financially. So, despite all the effort I had put in, I let the scholarship go to someone else and gratefully accepted the research post.

My attempts to win Sunita's family around coincided with the finishing throes of this postgraduate research, but my elevated education status made no headway with them. I was used to my studious side gaining me traction with adults, but here, although they saw it as a positive thing, they considered it insufficient on its own. They clearly appreciated my academic achievement, but wanted a working son-in-law, someone who could provide for their daughter.

I'm not sure what cracked the tough shell of resistance in our families in the end. Maybe they could just see that we were not going to give up. Maybe they could even see that we worked well together. It helped that my mother and aunt were from a higher caste, a higher stratum of society. It also helped that, although we were just getting going in London, we had a good name among the Indian community in Kenya where we were known and respected as a hard-working, rich, and successful family. We had some mutual friends too, including Aunty Rani Kirpalani, a very wealthy woman from Trinidad, whose family owned the famous Kirpalani department stores there, and who had once stayed with us in Mombasa. She remembered me as the bright, cheeky one who was allowed to stay up late to join in the adults' conversations. Her glowing reports to Sunita's family also edged me a little higher in their estimation.

And then there was prayer. At the time, Sunita was not a Christian, but I was, and had begun to make friends in the Christian Union. A few of them, like our families, warned me away from any connection with her.

"You must be careful," they warned, "She's not a believer."

They were acting out of concern – and, in most situations, I would agree that it is better for a couple to share the same faith. It makes it easier to understand each other at that deep level and support one another through life's challenges. But mine was already such a complicated situation, which very few of my friends at college seemed to understand. When the topic of arranged marriages had first reared its head, rebelliously I threatened that I would just marry a white girl from a completely different background. This was enough to shock my family into a compromise. It was agreed that I could marry whoever I liked, as long as she was Indian. Being a born negotiator, I recognised a deal when I saw one. To marry completely outside of my culture would have hurt my family and broken the agreement. In Sunita I had found a soul mate, way more than I had dared to imagine when my family had first raised the subject of marriage. Also, I could see that Sunita had a strong biblical background from her school days as well as the openness to agree to attend church with me regularly once we were married.

Finally, my good friend, Ranil Perera, came to me and said, "You know Ram, God's grace goes beyond our imagination, beyond our limits. I don't see anything wrong with this and, if this is what you're thinking then who am I to say no?"

His open mind and support meant the world to me. Instead of adding more guilt into an already difficult mix, he offered to bring another friend, Ida Glaser, to pray with me about it. It turned out that this was the very day Sunita was at her lowest, her family's pressure and disapproval weighing heavy on her heart. Later she told me that, without any explanation, her spirits suddenly lifted during the afternoon, exactly when we were praying for wisdom and a way forward.

With this gradual nudging forwards and the clarity that Sunita and I did not plan to give up the fight, our families slowly came around. Sunita's father conceded that he could live with my caste and my background; he could even live with my being a follower of Jesus. But to accept a student as a son-in-law was a step too far. Not that he wanted me to give up my studies, but he wouldn't even consider allowing the marriage until I'd completely finished, and had landed a job. Only then would I be in with a chance. To me, it felt like a delaying tactic, and I was desperate to get around it. I decided to look for work and attempt to finish my studies alongside it.

After the huge struggle to pursue my PhD, it was painful to let it go. I knew I was letting down my tutors and sponsors, and I felt terrible. Optimistically, I told them I'd do my best to write up my research thesis in my spare time, but of course, I had so little. While I did publish a paper on *Stochastic Goal Decomposition* in the Operations Research Journal, also delivering a lecture on it, the full thesis never quite made it to completion.

But eventually it was a choice between a qualification which I could live without, and a woman without whom I couldn't live. Whoever I married would be my partner for life and the thought of being mismatched with someone other than Sunita for the rest of my days, was far worse than losing a few impressive letters after my name. So, reluctantly, I made the decision to look for work, telling myself I would write up my PhD thesis later.

Just to be given this glimmer of hope, the recognition that I might be considered a suitable son-in-law and marry the girl I loved, was cause for huge celebration. Sunita and I rushed out and bought Heart ice creams for her entire family. Later, when the engagement was finally official, we took family and friends to Buboos – a restaurant just across from Charing Cross Station, owned by Sunita's family. Unbeknown to her family however, we had already become privately and unofficially engaged a few months earlier when I blew all my savings on an engagement ring for her – something she kept well-hidden to avoid raising any suspicions. We had planned to mark this with afternoon tea at the Ritz but quickly changed our minds when we saw the prices.

Of course, she did let a few people in on the secret including her sister Celia. She was desperate to share our news with her brother Suneel. We arranged to meet him at Winchester College where he was a boarder. He was 15 and this was the first time I met him. I watched with amusement as she kept trying her best to show off her engagement ring but to no avail. He just wasn't getting it and finally she had to spell it out to him.

There was still deep mistrust between our two families, our two castes. There's a well-known Sindhi saying: "If you see one of them lying dead on the floor, don't even cross over them in case they jump up and get you!" and each family used it about the other caste. Still, despite this wariness and the fact that my father-in-law made me sweat a little before I could even think about asking for Sunita's hand in marriage, I do give her family credit and respect for accepting me, because in our culture and with the differences in wealth and caste, it was an unthinkably huge step for them.

So it was that on 23rd July 1976 Sunita and I were finally joined in marriage. I was 25 and she was 20. Between the ceremonies that day, another celebration took place, this time on my territory – above the shop in Shepherd's Bush. Much as we loved our little shop, it was fairly basic. We kids had chosen the décor and to say it was garish doesn't begin to describe it, so it was rather comical to see a Rolls Royce pulling up outside for the occasion. It was also deeply significant. This was a coming together of differences. A breaking down of barriers, or at least a chipping away at them.

Making it this far felt like a dream come true but organising the wedding itself brought other challenges. How does a born-again Christian marry someone from a traditionally Hindu family?

Where could we get married? I didn't want a Hindu temple, feeling uncomfortable with the declarations I'd be expected to make there. However, to demand a church wedding would be asking too much of both families – I had used all my favours simply to get the engagement approved. Besides, not only was I clueless about how church weddings worked, I wasn't sure I even wanted one. It would have been culturally alien for all of us.

Finally, we decided on a Registry Office wedding. The only challenge here was making sure everyone got there in time for our allocated slot. The Registry Office had stressed and insisted that we must all be prompt, but my sister Babu and her husband had just flown into London from Hong Kong where they were living at that time. Having travelled all that way for our wedding, they were held up in traffic on the day and we had to plead with the registrar to delay the start of the ceremony as I really did not want to get married without their presence and my eldest sister's blessings.

After the Registry Office, in order to fulfil the family wish for a religious ceremony, we had arranged a blessing at the Sikh Gurdwara. My family's history and links with Sikhism made this possible – a gesture of goodwill from the Sikh religious community. I had seen my brother Barry get married to Shalu there the previous year, and I knew that not a word is uttered by the bride or groom. You simply have your blessing – and, at the end of that ceremony, it is recognised that your wedding has received a spiritual endorsement in a South Asian holy place.

Some Christians might struggle with the idea, but this is my character as a negotiator, finding the way that works for everyone, mindful of which values cannot and must not be compromised. We contemplated the symbolism of the many Sindhi marriage traditions before choosing which ones to include. One tradition involves the bride exchanging salt with every single member of both families to represent the washing away of any bitterness or animosity between them so that she has a clean relationship with all and a fresh start in her new home. Hindus do this to cover any negativity from previous incarnations, but I saw it simply as an act of goodwill, forgiveness, and new beginnings: something I was more than happy to include in the celebrations.

There were other traditions too. For three days before the wedding, I had to carry a sheathed knife (historically to protect against any vagabonds who came to disrupt the wedding). To keep another custom, I had to wear my oldest clothes, covered in oil, for the day preceding the ceremony. The men of the family then came in a few at a time and started tearing bits of my clothes off. It's a slightly crazy scene with several men rushing at you at once, looking for all the world as if they're about to attack, when really all they want is to rip off a bit of your shirt. Later, the torn clothes including any loose threads are gathered up and thrown into the sea. Then, yet another tradition involves the groom being covered with turmeric and oil paste, seemingly to give him a good night's sleep and a kind of 'facial', but for the whole body. I laughed when I recently heard this described as the groom being 'marinated for married life'.

Finally, the big day came. It was worth all the waiting, all the persevering, all the sacrifice. My beautiful bride arrived in her sari – because, once again, this was a sari wedding with no dowry expected – and the knot was tied. A bond to hold us together for life. One I have never regretted.

One I have been grateful for every day.

One that I am grateful for every day.

Chapter Seven
Labour of Love

I ripped open the letter, fear and excitement welling up inside me. Could this be the one? The hope was almost unbearable.

I pulled the thin paper from its envelope, my spirits already deflating as my eyes fell on the words 'regret to inform you'… 'high calibre' …. 'application on file'. I scarcely needed to read on. After so many failed applications I'd stopped counting, I could recite the standard rejection letter off by heart. After everything I'd been through in searching for PhD funding this was all feeling depressingly familiar.

They softened the blow with compliments. But the fact was, nobody seemed to want me. I sat down and puffed out a heavy sigh.

Back before the wedding, before the parties and traditions, before the engagement could even happen, I had to prove that I would be able to protect Sunita and provide for her. It is what any father would have asked for his daughter.

"You have to find a job." My future father-in-law's words ricocheted around my head.

"Easier said than done!" I muttered to no one in particular. I had tried everything. I had worked incredibly hard. I had shone academically. I had put my business skills to constant practice, both in the shop and in managing Daddy's Mombasa currency transfers. I had shown I was not afraid of hard work with my holiday jobs. Now, I was completing my PhD with a rather enviable Research Assistant post.

The research was in Program Planning Budgeting Systems (PPBS) for the Treasury, based on a PhD thesis by Timothy Ruefli in the US for the US Treasury, and the experience it was lavishing on me was invaluable. Not only did I have my own office at college and at the prestigious Old Admiralty Building complete with a Civil Service Pass, but I was seeing the finer details of organisational life: learning how minutes are taken and agendas set. Also, very importantly, it taught me the art of report writing, Civil Service style. In the early days, every time I submitted a report, the Permanent Secretary or Senior Official would return it with the words, "I don't like split infinitives!" Of course, first I had to work out what a split infinitive even was, but finally I got into the habit of writing clearly and succinctly as the situation required. On top of all this, I was able to observe senior Civil Servants at work, the recruitment, the promotion systems, and the grades culture. Surely with all this experience, I had something to offer the world of business? Making the decision to put my PhD on hold had felt like the hardest thing I'd done. I never expected the real challenge to be finding work. What more could I do to prove myself?

There comes a point when it's very tempting to give up. There comes a point when you begin to take it personally. There comes a point when you start to wonder if it's you. You carry the constant rejections like a heavy pack on your shoulders. What's wrong with you? There must be some reason why nobody wants you! Because of the situations I had been thrown into, the experience I had amassed in both life and business was well above average for my years. All those lunches listening to my uncles talking about trading; then all through that season when Daddy had returned to Kenya, handing me high level financial responsibilities, complex banking tasks and foreign exchange – not what your average 17-year-old does on a Saturday morning! All of it had been a fertile training ground for a career in business: the skills, instincts, and knowledge soaking into me almost by osmosis. Moreover, my family and I had built up strong working relationships with the wider Sindhi community, both here and overseas. I knew I had a lot to offer.

Daddy had also taught me all about the *hawala* system for transferring currency and I was particularly adept in using *hoondees*, the bills of exchange used for currency transfers and for raising capital. Many years later, concerned about the potential misuse of this system, the Bank of England and the BBC would call me for an interview to find out more, asking me to explain it in simple terms so the public would understand. But that kind of recognition was all in the future. For now, I was left wondering if I would ever find work, doubting myself more and more.

Of course, giving up wasn't really an option. Giving up would not just mean missing out on a good career. No, there was far more at stake. Giving up would mean missing out on any chance of marrying Sunita. Her father had made it clear: "No job, no wedding". I had to keep trying, but with no guarantee of success it was hard to keep my spirits up.

Despondently I flicked through the Sunday Times to take my mind off the latest hit to my pride. It was all beginning to feel rather futile, but I glanced briefly at the employment pages.

Suddenly, however, my eyes were drawn to an unusual advert:

Lloyds Bank International
Open competition for the position of
Operations Research Analyst

I caught my breath. Reading through the advert carefully, excitement began to rush through my veins. My course at Imperial was in Operations Research and Management Science. I could do this. Everything on the job description felt within my reach. Could this be the one? I tried not to get my hopes up too much as I quickly drafted my application, checking every detail to make sure I hadn't missed anything.

Then I waited.

I had been here before too many times. Too many seemingly perfect-for-me jobs that I'd applied for had ended in disappointment, and a job like this was bound to be much in demand.

It was. But out of the 500 who applied, I was one of the ones who was chosen for short-listing tests and interviews. I held my nerve and gave it my all, trying to balance the need for confidence with the fear of disappointment, not wanting to hope too much. I knew I was up against the crème de la crème.

Finally, the call came. They had whittled it down at every round. They had culled some top-quality candidates, gems of intelligence. They had narrowed it down to the final three. I could scarcely believe it when they continued to say that I was one of these.

The final interview came. I was told I'd be meeting the main board finance director, Mr Ferguson. Despite inevitable nerves, I walked in holding his gaze and shaking his hand with rather more confidence than I felt. After the usual discussions he suddenly asked:

"At what time after 1pm will the long and short handles of the clock overlap. Share your thinking on how you have come to your answer. That is the more important issue."

Rather than waste time theorising, I decided the simplest way to answer this question was to make it happen. I removed the watch from my wrist and rolled the dial to just after 1pm. No one had said that wasn't allowed. Very quickly I was able to tell him that it would be between 1.05 and 1.06pm. I shared with him my other observations – that for every 60 minutes the hour hand moved five notches. Mr Ferguson nodded and told me I was on the right track. Finding a simple, practical solution had got me through for now. But I decided to take it a little further and rather boldly asked if I could share a similar problem with him, mentioning that he could even ask the other candidates if he wanted. Despite the rather tight schedule, he seemed happy with my suggestion, so I continued.

"Imagine you are in a desert and have exactly two days of water supply in an irregularly shaped bottle. How would you know when you have drunk exactly half the amount of water from this irregularly shaped bottle with only a bottle cap and a marker in hand?"

He looked a little perplexed, as I drew an irregular shaped bottle to help him visualise the problem. He then attempted to start trying to solve the problem. At this point, I diplomatically helped him by making some obvious suggestions as he was turning around the drawing. Making it appear that the ideas were his, I made some remarks and very quickly he got there. He seemed quite pleased with himself. If I'm honest he really did not have a clue, but it was good to see him satisfied that he had solved the problem by himself! It was perhaps an unorthodox approach, but seemingly my slightly daring cheekiness had put me in good stead because just one day later I got a call to say the job was mine.

The final decision was of course made by my boss, John Porter. I learned as I worked with him that he was a very fair person. His passion for justice, equality and openness meant he was committed to getting the best person appointed, irrespective of race, gender, or ethnicity. I was hugely thankful that people like John existed in the business world.

Sadly, not everyone held such strong principles. Once I'd been appointed, I was eager to knuckle down and work hard, taking any learning opportunities that came my way. I signed up for a correspondence course to take the Institute of Bankers exams, swotting up on my daily commute from Hangar Lane to Bank on the Central Line. I completed four out of the five exams and was even awarded a distinction in accounting. However, I very quickly encountered glass doors and glass ceilings at higher levels. In my mind, a transfer to a commercial banking job made perfect sense, not just for me, but for the organisation. It became clearer than ever when a Senior Executive strolled into our office to chat one day then, looking at me as the only Indian in the group, mentioned, "I'm just off for lunch with Mr Khemchand."

"Oh, I know him!" I said, "He's a very close friend of Sunita's family. They do business with him."

Then another name came up and I said, "Gosh, we're actually related."

For me, such connections were an obvious opportunity for the bank. It was a no-brainer. I could offer them the relationships I had developed with Sindhi businesses Daddy had dealt with. I had plenty of experience and knowledge of these customers and the financing needs of their various businesses, from local corner shops to wholesalers, importers, and exporters.

My family was known and trusted by businesspeople and banks in the Far East, in Hong Kong and Singapore as well as in the UK and USA. I knew these people, had deep relationships of mutual respect with them. I knew I could open doors to new business, new customers for the bank. My family also had vast commercial business and trading connections from our time in East Africa, while other branches of the family lived and worked in Nigeria. Then there was my wife's family and the wider Sindhi community in London. In short, I had at my fingertips a wealth of contacts and opportunities, a vast network of international business relationships and breadth of cross-cultural experience, all of which I offered to the bank along with my thorough understanding and experience in Trade Finance. But when I approached the personnel department with this suggestion it was immediately met with reluctance and refusal. Why? I had worked so diligently. Surely what I was offering deserved at least some consideration?

Perhaps I was a little hasty. I had only been there 18 months and looking back I can see they were thinking "Take your time, there are others ahead of you in this queue." However, as a negotiator I found it incredibly frustrating that they couldn't see the opportunities I was offering them. They stuck with the same old clients, not noticing these new markets right before their eyes. As the Bank of London and South America (BOLSA) they clearly did have some overseas customers. Now they had become Lloyds Bank International (LBI), and I was offering them direct access to a vast international community but there was no interest or take up.

As I continued to work faithfully in my current role despite the disappointment, I then had the additional blow of seeing my boss and another colleague getting exactly the kind of transfer I'd been asking for. It was the final straw, making it crystal clear that opportunities for me were always going to be limited there. Wrong school, wrong tie, wrong accent.

Was it impatience on my part or discrimination on theirs? Probably a mixture of the two. Either way, experiences like this highlighted to me the importance of a level playing field in recruitment and perhaps that's why, later in life, I felt moved to write to *The Times* about British institutions being in danger of cloning themselves and missing out on having minorities join them. Impassioned, I wrote, "Public institutions must reflect the communities they serve." The Commanding Officer of HMS Sultan who recruits for the Royal Navy had taken a lot of flack for discrimination, and was quick to pick up on my letter. He invited me to stay for two days to see the positive changes they had made. As I entered the gleaming premises, every wall seemed to be covered in statements about bringing equality and fighting discrimination. I then sat through the most exhaustive interview process I've ever seen. I was full of admiration for the place, the pursuit of excellence and the rigorous work involved. However, when they asked for feedback, after the obvious compliments I added, "... but the candidates were not even asked one question about their views on discrimination and inclusion. Not only that, but if you look at the interview panel, they are all of the same genre, a certain type of person, for example, headmasters of independent or grammar schools...." I knew how hard it would be for minorities to get past the first couple of rounds with such a panel.

Some years later, I saw another letter in *The Times*. A headmaster was bitterly complaining that naval recruitment panels were removing all the important key people like... headmasters of independent or grammar schools.

I was overjoyed! They had heard me! I immediately wrote another letter to *The Times* commending the Navy for taking on my advice and within 24 hours of its publication, they called to invite me to review the situation again. I was treated like royalty, seated next to the Second Sea Lord at dinner and given an extensive tour of the estate. I was pleased to see there had been dramatic progress, no comparison with the previous experience. Before I left, the Second Sea Lord thanked me.

"Mr Gidoomal, you don't know how grateful I was to read your letter in *The Times*."

He went on to explain that after the headmaster's complaint, Downing Street were demanding an explanation for this outrageous news. However, my letter had softened the situation, relieving them from the pressure. Thinking back to my own early working life, I was only glad to have been able to help others in my position.

Back then, struggling on in my job at the bank, it felt like there was no one standing up for me. No one writing letters to *The Times* about discrimination. I had to just do the best I could.

Finally, with a heavy heart I began to look for other work. By this time of course, Sunita and I were married. I heard of an opening with her uncle's company, Inlaks. They were moving their finance base from London to Geneva because of the draconian taxation regime and strict foreign exchange regulations that were being implemented in the UK to prevent a run on sterling.

Sunita's family had taken a different route to England from mine and were there long before us. At the time of Partition, her parents fled by train from Pakistan to Bombay, where there was already a big enclave of commercial Sindhi families. Her father found work with Bata Shoes in Calcutta, but meanwhile, his brother-in-law, Indoo Shivdasani had started a thriving business in London and Manchester. He needed help to manage the growth and called on Sunita's father. So before Sunita was even born, her parents were living in London, comfortably settled into a successful life. And now there was an opportunity within this company for me too, with her mother's sister Aunty Lakshmi recommending me for the role that had come up.

Although my friends made jokes about the family connection meaning the job was in the bag for me, I knew that business is business. Sunita's Uncle Indoo valued his company and would not give the job to just anyone. I would need to prove my skills and expertise in an interview and inspire enough confidence in him. I also needed to convince Sunita's cousin, Sunder, who had set up the office in Ferney-Voltaire, just across the French border from Geneva.

Of course, the contact helped. This is always the case with relationship, any kind of relationship, not just family. If we make good connections and treat others with respect, we are far more likely to at least be given a chance to prove ourselves. However, at the end of the day we also need to be able to fulfil whatever we promise. In this situation, the family was simply glad to have me on board, working for them, given my training and banking experience. They saw me as fit for the job. There was no pity involved, simply good business sense. Finally, I had a break and felt I was back on the right track.

In complete contrast to LBI, here the value of my contacts and international experience was immediately both recognised and utilised by my boss and mentor, Sunder Advani. In addition, I could use my fluent Sindhi when speaking to the senior executives in Nigeria – they preferred to speak Sindhi when communicating confidential commercial information. Within no time at all I was more than earning my way, helping to swell the company funds with my business acumen and fresh ideas and soon I was promoted to Commercial Director. I was flying high with the freedom to do what I was good at, and to do it to the best of my ability. I gave my all and in return the company rewarded me generously.

Naturally, this new job also involved another life change. Sunita and I moved from our first home in Hangar Lane, Ealing, to the Geneva area, first living in Ferney Voltaire, a small village across the border in France for a few years, and then moving to the city of Geneva itself. Both places were so international that there was never any fear of racism there. Who would you even start with? It made a refreshing change and evolved into a time of freedom and growth.

For us it was also to become a place of beginnings. A place where Sunita came to put her trust in Christ, and also where we set off on the wonderful journey of parenthood.

New life in every way.

Chapter Eight

Fatherhood – Lost and Found

I stared at the tiny bundle of flesh. A son.

My son.

It was 1979 and I held Ravi in my arms for the first time. I was a father, with all the memories and imagined memories of my own two fathers. One fatherhood I had known, one I had not. I had lost both these fathers – my birth father and my Daddy – but now I was experiencing fatherhood myself, like a lost treasure returned to me. The feeling was indescribably wonderful. After Ravi, we went on to have our daughter, Nina in 1981, and another son, Ricki in 1983. All three, with their own unique characters and gifts, brought much joy to Sunita and me.

As with every adventure in life, I was moulded by my past and my family background, but also wanted to be open to all the new things I was learning, applying everything that experience had taught me about the world. Sometimes this would go against the flow of my Indian family.

On the one hand, Indians really know how to do family, so I had vast resources of love and care to fall back on. What had been modelled to me all my life was the importance of prioritising family needs, the mutual support, the security of knowing no one is left behind. But nothing is perfect, and I knew all too well the pressures that Indian families could put on their children, particularly girls. I had seen it with my own sisters. Taking this knowledge, what I had seen and learnt, I adapted the Indian way: keeping the love and loyalty of the extended family while changing the things that I saw as outdated or oppressive.

Unintentionally, the first change we made to tradition came before we had even announced the birth. In Sindhi culture a new baby's name is chosen from a sound given by the priest. When a child is born, the family priest is called and the sound which he gives you – for example, an 's' – inspires how you name your child. It was expected that we would continue with this tradition, but as followers of Christ we did not want to walk this path.

Instead, we wanted to find names that would be easy on them in school yet would fit in with our Indian heritage. Ravi, for example, is an Indian name, but also means 'delighted' in France where we were living at the time of his birth. Nina is a name found in many cultures, but we chose it as we often heard our 23-month-old son repeating the sounds. Then, when Sunita's mother rather surprisingly suggested Ricki as a name for our youngest son, we were thrilled. It was perfect, we loved the name, and it would work wherever we might live, although we spell it with an 'i' as a hint to his Indian roots.

Similarly, we went against the tradition of including the father's name as a middle name, all too aware of the administrative complications it had triggered in our own lives. We chose to simply give each child their own name. Just the one.

Planning for our future family some years earlier, we had bought a three-bedroom detached house in Ealing, with plenty of space for children to grow. However, in the end, all three of them were born in Geneva. When my change of work direction took us to the Geneva area, we sold the Ealing house, and rented a bright and airy two-bedroom apartment in the French village of Ferney Voltaire, just across the Swiss border with France, first staying with Sunita's cousin, Sunder Advani and his wife Kamu in Divonne-les-Bains for six weeks while waiting to move in. Once we moved to Ferney, we found ourselves so close to Switzerland that we always took our passports when we went for a walk as we easily criss-crossed between the two countries, often not even knowing when we had strayed out of France! Geneva airport itself even has a specific exit for the French to go directly into France.

Ferney Voltaire gained the second part of its name in recognition of the French philosopher and all he did for the community while he lived there. There is also a Voltaire museum. Other than this, it is a pretty and fairly typical French village, complete with several boulangeries for our daily baguettes, and a fishmonger who came every Tuesday. This was particularly important whenever my mother was visiting, as we would want to buy cod for her to make her amazing fish curry.

Although Ferney is a small village, it was in no way insular. Being close to Geneva, it was full of different nationalities, and all were welcome. My office was also in Ferney, and was close enough for me to walk home for lunch. The company I worked for was part of the Inlaks group named after the founders (Sunita's Uncle Indoo and Aunty Lakshmi). Being family, and living just a stone's throw from the office, we often entertained them and other business contacts over lunch.

We spent four happy years living in Ferney, although we did move from the flat to a farmhouse, six weeks before Nina was born.

With the births came a crash course in French/Swiss administration. Registering Ravi's birth, for example, brought an unexpected challenge. Being a relatively new Christian, I was understandably clueless when it came to different branches of the church. So, when I first went to fill in the birth registration forms and the registrar asked me whether I was "protestant ou catholique" I looked at her blankly. Of course, I had heard of the different kinds of churches but had no idea which one I belonged to. I replied the only way I knew how:

"Chrétien". I was a Christian.

"Mais ça n'existe pas!" the Registrar cried. That doesn't exist. There was no option on the computer for 'Christian'. I needed to work out which camp I fell into. Confused, I went to find my pastor, who gave me a whistle-stop tour through the history of the church, explaining about Henry VIII and the forming of the Protestant movement. Finally I understood some of the history, but I still couldn't reconcile it to anything I had read in the Bible.

After three days of arguing with the registrar, on the day of the deadline, she looked up at me and smiled:

"Ah, Monsieur Gidoomal, look at this," she said pointing at the screen, "I've created a new box here for 'Chrétien' and we've even changed the computer programme!"

And so, we were able to both name and register our children in the way that felt right to us. Choosing our own way of naming them seemed like a statement to the family. However, we were not doing it to stand out or to be difficult, we simply felt it was the right thing for our family, for their future. A few days later, when my mother called to tell us she had sounded out a Hindu priest, it was too late – our new-born son had already been named and registered as Ravi. Both our mothers were a little shocked at this deviation from tradition, but eventually it was accepted as our choice. Later, when our children became parents, they found their own ways to name our grandchildren, reflecting the richness of all their various cultural influences – Indian, English, Jewish, Hungarian, Swedish...

It is just one example of how things change down the generations. While we, who had sometimes felt like outsiders, wanted to help our children fit in with local culture, our children, who are more confident and at ease in their British skin, are prioritising their root cultures again, wanting their children's names to carry this uniqueness and identity.

As time went on, we continued to do things our own way but always tuning in to the wisdom of our Indian roots too. It was the Indian community that had provided me with role models throughout my life, and with the arrival of fatherhood, I looked to those role models again. I had lost my first father when I was only seven weeks old but always knew what a father was, because my Daddy was more than enough. Losing him when I was 18 devastated me, but again, other father figures stepped in to support me and advise me. I will always be grateful for this.

When I first met my father-in-law, despite the initial challenges to being accepted as husband material for his daughter, I was immediately impressed by his values, his commitment to equality and justice, and how he lived these out in everything he did. He quickly became another strong role model for me. Of course, he still maintained his position as head of an Indian family – the patriarch – with all the rules and respect that entailed. However, he did this with an underlying wisdom and a recognition that he was living between two cultures: the one he brought with him from India, and the one all around him in England. Of course, when it came to me going out with Sunita, his Indian influences were very strong and the western ones less so; but in comparison with my own biological family, he was notably more liberal and open.

Shivi, or Dad as I called him, was an educated man, and understood the customs of the people among whom he had chosen to live. He was also astute and experienced in business, having worked for Bata Shoes in India before coming to London to join the Inlaks Group. However, it was his attitude to his family that struck me the most. His love for his children was obvious, but what stood out was the way he treated Sunita, Celia, and his son Suneel completely equally. In a culture that hails the male offspring as higher and more valuable than his sisters, this made me sit up and take note. My own community had always treated their sons as kings while considering the daughters - with their need for a dowry - a bit of a liability. Seeing the genuine and equal care Sunita's father had for all his children made me respect him and want to do the same for my own.

This striving for equality and justice was a vein that ran through the family. Sunita's great uncle, H.B. Shivdasani, for example, was a senior member of the Indian Civil Service, held in high regard at the time of Gandhi's Salt March. Recognising the injustice of the salt tax, he found himself siding with those marching and defied the orders of his British superiors, refusing to arrest Gandhi. Later, when independence came and tables were turned, he was generously rewarded for his decision to do the right thing.

Such shining examples of integrity among our predecessors shaped our own attitudes and decisions. We came from these people, Sunita and I. We came from families with strong characters and strong principles and now it was our turn to hand these on to the next generation. We wanted our children to grow up with the same kinds of strength, the same kinds of values.

However, while lofty ideals are wonderful, in the day-to-day experience of being a father, I realised just how much I had to learn. As well as my original Indian roots, there were new influences I wanted to incorporate in my parenting. My relatively recent decision to follow Christ meant that I wanted to bring my children up in His way, but I didn't always know how. Things that were obvious to other people had simply never been modelled to me, and I had to learn by asking friends for advice and reading books, in particular *The Effective Father* by Gordon MacDonald.

The church also became a lifeline for such learning. After four years living across the border in France, we made the move to Geneva. As with our time in France, we found ourselves part of a vibrant and diverse international community where everyone was welcome. There was no place for discrimination because everyone was different. The church reflected this community of inclusiveness, and we quickly found our place there with like-minded supportive friends. We became close to

Philippe and Wendy Berthoud, who were also to introduce us to Prabhu Guptara – someone who would later become a dear friend and colleague. Equally, Douglas and Rosemary Marr showed us great kindness, taking us under their wing, with Rosemary being instrumental in Sunita coming to Christ. We also met regularly with three other mature Christian couples who were able to give us wise advice on the areas we found new and confusing. With this small trustworthy group, we studied the Bible using another book, *Strike the Original Match* by Charles Swindoll, which ran alongside a study programme the church was hosting to help couples improve their marriage relationships. In a city where many people worked in global UN agencies or banking, stress levels could run very high, often to the detriment of the family unit. I still remember the Bible teacher sharing how he balanced his work commitments with his family's needs as best he could. One example was how he would assess his work situation at 5.30pm every day, checking his in-tray for any outstanding tasks and, if nothing was life or death urgent, he would leave it for the next day so that he could go home and support his wife with his children's bedtime routine. He knew that for his wife, after a day at home with the children, this was the most difficult time of day. His point was, where are all the fathers at this time of day when they are most needed by their families?

I thought this over and decided to follow his idea, the one difference being that my urgent shipping and cargo tasks actually couldn't be 'left until tomorrow'. Any delays would be heavily penalised by the hour. Therefore, I came up with a plan. At 5.30pm every day I would walk out of the office – waving off the jokey shouts of "Oh, another half day Ram?" from my colleagues knowing that I would be with my children for dinner, baths, bedtime stories and prayers. I then went back into the office at 8 or 9pm and put in another few hours, much to the surprise of those who had teased me on my earlier departure. Many of them didn't appreciate or understand why I did it, but it was one of the best moves I ever made to reassure Sunita of my priorities and to invest in the children at such a key time in their lives.

The children's bedtime thus became a precious ritual for me. I even learnt to play the guitar so that we could sing together before they went to sleep. As well as these songs and stories, we went through a routine of 'Sad, Bad and Glad' every evening. Each child would tell me one thing they were sad about, one thing they felt bad about having done and one thing that had made them glad, teaching them the principles of prayer for help, repentance to get any feelings of guilt off their chests and thankfulness. It gave them a framework of security and is an exercise we still continue today whenever we look after any of our seven grandchildren (although of course, as had happened earlier with their parents, they sometimes struggle to think of anything bad they have done!).

So, an early fear of holding tiny babies the wrong way quickly gave way to a practical hands-on love, a desire to know them, protect them, and be with them. Becoming a father was such a special thing for me and I wanted to give it my all. When they began to take piano lessons, I learnt alongside them to encourage them and show them we weren't asking of them something that we wouldn't try ourselves. When Sunita was expecting Ricki, I loved looking after the older two, giving her an opportunity to rest. I have wonderful memories of walking in the woods together before returning home to bake cakes (although admittedly, normally with ingredients and instructions all pre-prepared by Sunita).

Back in the UK some years later, when I had left my executive business career behind me, I had the privilege of doing the children's school run, something I would never have experienced had I remained in the executive corporate world. I loved watching them greet their teacher at the start of each day with a tip of their caps and a "Good morning, Miss" – I always hung around until this little ritual had taken place. The playground itself was rather an unusual environment for an

Indian man in the 1980s, or perhaps I should say, I was a bit of an anomaly there. Today the school run is done by mums, dads and grandparents of every colour and nationality but back then it was often a mums-only zone, and pretty much all of them were white. It's fair to say I stood out a little, but what I gained from that time with my children far outweighed any awkwardness about being different. It didn't matter that sometimes not much was said on the car journey to and from school. My presence was what counted, I prayed with the children and often there would be one little gem of conversation shared that would make it all worthwhile. It is lovely to see this tradition being taken forward by the children themselves.

It is often in these ordinary, unspectacular daily moments that bonds are strengthened and children see what is truly important. I am reminded of William Martin's poem, *Do not ask your children to strive*, which celebrates such moments.

Do not ask your children
to strive for extraordinary lives.
Such striving may seem admirable,
but it is the way of foolishness.
Help them instead to find the wonder
and the marvel of an ordinary life.
Show them the joy of tasting
tomatoes, apples, and pears.
Show them how to cry
when pets and people die.
Show them the infinite pleasure
in the touch of a hand.
And make the ordinary come alive for them.
The extraordinary will take care of itself.

Another wonderful thing about the community in Geneva was the mutual understanding about the pressures and demanding schedules of our careers. When needing to prepare materials for the teenagers' Sunday school class, church friends would often arrange early morning meetings at the airport where we could pray and chat over good coffee and croissants before hopping onto our flights to New York, Paris, Rome or wherever else we were heading to fulfil work commitments. This is something I really missed on returning to London where, at the time, nobody at church seemed to recognise that anything might take priority over the sacred rota! As one Sikh follower of Christ put it succinctly, "When I became a follower of Jesus, I lost my family, and all I got in return was meetings!" Thankfully this wasn't the case in Geneva. With such a transient international population, the church there completely understood the need for welcome, community and belonging. Every Sunday the older, more permanent members of the church would spontaneously invite another family or perhaps a few single people for lunch. Everyone felt included and welcomed into the church community. Often people were on short term contracts, spending only six months or a year in Geneva, and without this tradition of hospitality they would have come and gone without any relationships forming. For us, the welcome we received was warm and deep, and we tried to replicate it for others.

Our children also understand such feelings of transience. Their early years were spent moving around wherever my job took me. During the first four years of my working life in the Geneva area, when we lived just across the border in France, we benefitted greatly from the combination of Swiss income and French expenses, making us very comfortable financially. However, when Mitterrand came to power in the early 80s, we knew those days were numbered. He changed the fiscal rules so dramatically that we applied for Swiss residence permits and moved to Geneva itself for a further four years. There we rented a newly built four-bedroom chalet style house. We especially loved its light and spacious living-cum-dining room with double doors opening onto a small garden facing Mont Salève, also known as 'the Balcony of Geneva'. On warm Sundays we would eat lunch in the garden, watching colourful gliders take off from Le Salève, and fly right over our house. Meanwhile, on Saturday mornings during ski season, we could get up early and cross the border to the French resort of Les Gets, still managing to be home for lunch and the weekend's household chores.

When those four years drew to a close, I was called back to London for what I thought would be a temporary stint of three months. However, fairly quickly I was told my presence was needed back in the UK permanently. Sadly, I closed up the house in Geneva and our Swiss days came to an end. Then around six months later, just as we began to put down new roots in London, I found I was required to travel up to Scotland on a regular basis to keep tabs on business interests there.

Having understood that the move to London was a permanent one, we had bought a home in Sutton and set in motion some building work there. We might not have rushed to do this had we realised I would be commuting to Scotland most weeks with poor Sunita ending up home alone, with three young builders staying in the dining room! And we almost certainly wouldn't have begun the renovation work if we'd known what was coming next. The chairman suddenly sprung on me that I needed to move to Scotland to take charge of a seafood processing plant we had acquired there. His plan was for us to build a global speciality seafood business, and he allocated me a multi-million pound budget to achieve this. It turned out to be no hardship to move to Perth. We were always made welcome. I have often told the story of my first visit to the seafood processing plant there.

I had flown from Geneva to Aberdeen to see the processing plant which Inlaks Group had taken over. The acquisitions had made me Managing Director of Highland Seafoods, and this was the first time I would be meeting the staff there. I landed on a clear Scottish afternoon and immediately noticed a tall dour-looking man holding up a sign bearing the company name. As I went over to make myself known, I was surprised to see his face light up with a genuine smile. He shook my hand enthusiastically, introducing himself as Foster Gault, the Production Manager. As we drove through the lush Aberdeenshire countryside, he pointed out various landmarks until finally we saw the seafood plant, tucked away next to a beautiful estuary, a wisp of smoke curling up into the blue sky from the salmon smoking plant. We pulled into the car park, and I saw that the staff had gathered together as a welcoming committee. None of them looked exactly delighted at the prospect of meeting their new Director. In fact, they looked decidedly tense, knowing that a change of ownership might mean the end of their jobs, unaware that we planned to re-employ them and even take on more staff.

As I approached the gathering, just as with the encounter at the airport, I saw their faces transform. One by one, their downcast expressions became beaming smiles. This happened again and again throughout my visit. It was a complete mystery to me, but a few months later when I had got to know people better, I felt able to ask Foster why. He paused a moment, then smiled and said, "Well, to be absolutely frank Ram, we all thought we were getting an Englishman!"

It was both ironic and amusing that my foreignness, which had caused me so many problems when I first arrived in London all those years ago, was here seen as something positive, something that made me more acceptable. And while I don't condone any kind of prejudice, it was a refreshing change to have it working in my favour.

The decision to move to Scotland was therefore not a difficult one for us. We settled quickly in Perth, the community there embracing us as their own. We joined North Church, Perth, having been introduced to Ann and Richard Mazur who became great friends of ours there, along with Atholl and Caroline Laing. We formed a homegroup together and these two couples gave us invaluable support, quickly making it feel like home.

Of course, I was still travelling around like a maniac, but Scotland was my base. That is where we were living when I made the trip that would change my life. It was the Scottish church community that gave me a solid foundation providing strength, challenging teaching, and thinking space as I mulled over my future direction. However, as it turned out, we would not be able to stay there for long. Out of the blue we received the news that my boss was seriously ill. We found ourselves relocating to London once more, this time for good.

Every place brought us something different and hopefully we gave something too. Through all the changes, the different countries and homes, our family life was the constant, the strength of our bond seeing us through and overcoming any other uncertainties. Our children learned resilience and confidence from the moves, influenced by the diversity of cultures they encountered. As for me, my adventure with fatherhood continued – surprising and blessing me even to this day.

By my early twenties, I had lost two fathers but gained a heavenly one in God. I had lost two fathers but found the love of my extended family was there, waiting to catch me, to guide me with strong role models and supportive care.

And it was this love and guidance, both from my Heavenly Father and my family, which built the foundation stones of fatherhood in me, teaching me how to be a father myself.

Chapter Nine
India, My Beloved Country

"Caviar Monsieur? Champagne?"

I stared blankly at the Air France hostess in front of me. I heard her words, but they made no sense. Nothing made any sense.

She began to repeat her offer, but I shook my head, holding up my hand to refuse. Normally I welcomed the perks of First Class travel but how could I think about eating caviar now? I didn't even know if the sickness I felt was physical. All I knew was I needed to be alone with my mess of thoughts and feelings.

Finally, the lights dimmed, and I exhaled, all the tension and emotion I'd been holding back flooding out as I broke down in tears. I was too traumatised to even begin to piece together what I had seen that day. Stopping at the office on the way to Bombay airport, I had been numb, unable to even pick up a pen from the desk. What on earth had just happened to me? As I wiped my eyes, more tears came, along with questions: What was I doing here on this planet? How could I live like this after what I had seen?

It was April 1988 and I had travelled to India to study the potential and feasibility of buying and shipping prawns for the seafood plant in Scotland. It was meant to be a business trip like any other, ten days, there and back. Simple. The kind of trip I made all the time. I could never have imagined the impact it would have on me, how it would be a springboard to a complete overhaul of everything I knew.

It's true that for some time prior to my trip I'd been wondering how I could put the teaching of the Bible more into action. I kept hearing people at church talking about 'calling' but, without a Christian background, I never quite understood. I knew it meant that you changed direction and did good things, but how exactly did you get this 'call'? Time and time again, I would hear people announce they'd had a call to go to, say, Morocco, and I would genuinely wonder whether someone had been in touch with them by phone.

Of course, I did my bit at church and tried to support those in difficulty. Even as foreigners ourselves, during our time in Geneva, we had always looked out for anyone who needed a helping hand. In particular, we had taken an Ethiopian Christian refugee under our wing, remembering only too well my own battle to find my feet when I first went to London. He was struggling to find work and support his family. I asked our HR director if we could help him. Our office had no openings but through a contact with another HR director, he was able to find work in his field as an electrician, with opportunities to train further and get his Ethiopian qualifications accredited in Switzerland.

So, I was trying. Trying to serve others in the church. Trying to do my best, and with genuine motives. But I couldn't help noticing that when other people talked about 'calling' it seemed like more than that. It sounded somehow deeper and more compelling.

Testing the water a little, I had made contact with the Association of Biblical Counselling who had advertised for a

CEO. I wanted to see if my skills could find a place with them, but it seemed I was far too young for the role they had on offer. However, seeing my desire to make a difference in the world, they introduced me to their Chair – Dr. Raju Abraham – who was also a consultant neurologist. Instinctively, they sensed he would guide my efforts in the right direction and indeed, he was to have a profound influence on my life through his wisdom and example. Between him and my good friend Prabhu Guptara, I was reintroduced to my Indian roots. There were things happening in India I'd had no idea about. They told me about the poverty, the persecution, and the struggles of missionaries trying to help. They talked about the privilege I had as a Non-Resident Indian (NRI). The Indian government knew there was enormous wealth, ability, and genius in the diaspora, with Indians generating huge amounts of disposable income – billions in the UK alone. People like us, Raju told me, were in a unique position. Considered gold dust by the Indian government, we had the power, skills, and resources to change things in our mother country for the better. This was a gift – and it was, he said, my responsibility to use it.

Although my love for India was something that was rooted deep into my soul, nestled at my very core, I had simply never thought of it from this angle before. Not having ever lived there, it still felt somehow removed and I had never taken the time to find out more or to develop an interest in Indian missions or charities. Inspired by my friends' words however, I agreed to meet up with Raju's brother Viju during the trip to Mumbai. Viju worked with the International Fellowship of Evangelical Students there, serving the poorest of the poor in the city's ghettos.

The business trip itself had all gone to plan. I travelled around India's colourful ports, lapping up the vibrant atmosphere, beauty and cuisine between visiting factories and meeting fishermen. We organised deals, shook hands and signed on the dotted line. The job was done, I was free to go home. However, whenever I visited companies in countries where poverty endures, I like to find out what they are doing in the community. What are they doing with their profits? How are they using their power to help the disadvantaged? On this occasion, of course, I had Raju's brother Viju to show me. As planned, on the final day I met him, along with a group of Christian pastors.

"You want to see what we're doing?" he said, "Come with me. This is where the need is. This is where we work."

I followed him, my eyes wide with fearful fascination as he led me into the shanty towns and ghettos, into Dharavi, where *Slumdog Millionaire* is set. I had heard of the slums of course. I had seen pictures. I was sure it would be shocking, and I believed I was in some way prepared. Steeled with the armour of knowledge, perhaps I would nod sadly and thank them for their good work?

I had no idea.

I had imagined the worst, and that still fell an enormous way short. I had no clue, no inkling what was coming, and how it would shake me upside down, the loose change of confidence and 'belief in the system' falling out of my pockets. Because nothing could have prepared me for what I saw, heard, and smelled that day.

In shock, I walked with Viju through alleyways lined with makeshift homes and rubbish, past the ragpickers and the prostitutes. My ears rang with the din of shouts and cries: the noise of too many people. The noise of need. Feeling nauseous, I stared at a small boy in front of me, ragged, dirty, and thin. He must have been about five. Just like my own son. My mind automatically sprang to my children, safe, well fed, healthy and educated back home. Although we tried not to live too extravagantly, they had never wanted for anything.

"Where does he live?" I managed to ask, my voice muted by the crushing devastation I felt. "In one of these boxes?" It seemed unbelievable that a child should live in such conditions. But worse was to come.

"No, not in a box. The slumlord won't let him. He has to sleep in a water pipe instead."

The words registered with me slowly. A haphazard box was apparently too good for this child?

"Show me" I demanded.

He looked me in the eye, frowning.

"I'm sorry. You wouldn't cope with the stench. It's too much, even from a distance"

Desperately I tried to maintain some kind of composure and gather more information. I kept thinking of my own children, imagining them in this horrendous place. The mere thought was unbearable.

"But . . . his parents. Where are his parents? Surely they can do something?"

"Parents?" my friend gave a sad laugh. "Dad? Forget it. And his mum can't do anything. She works over there."

He nodded towards some cages where girls, some only on the cusp of puberty, were locked up, their expressions blank and hopeless. It took very little imagination to realise what was going on. I swallowed hard, my stomach turning. I was overwhelmed with a grief I couldn't express. As I tried to compute what I was seeing, I understood both too much and too little all at once.

I held myself together for the rest of the visit, but the vision of that little boy and his caged mother would not shift from my mind's eye. I would never unsee them. Slaves of a system that they were powerless to change or escape, their life was a recurring nightmare, while just a few blocks away people like me wined and dined on the finest food. I had enjoyed the colourful sights of India but had closed my eyes to the reality of her poverty. Now, condensed in one place, I could ignore it no longer.

On the plane, I watched the cabin crew move away from me, continuing to serve delicacies to my fellow passengers as I wept quietly, asking myself, "How can I be a Christian in such conspicuous luxury, doing nothing about what I've seen? What am I doing on this planet? I call myself a follower of Jesus, but what am I doing?"

What I was doing was helping make millions for the family business. Many of the deals I was involved with resulted in significant profits sometimes doubling and even trebling our margins. I thought back to a recent business trip made by private jet, complete with my own G&T chiller. Suddenly none of it seemed quite so impressive because, while I was making all that money, who was doing anything for these people?

The ideals I had built my life upon – ambition and hard work – were crumbling to dust before me. There is of course nothing wrong with working hard and having a successful career, but my recent focus on amassing more and more profits for the coffers suddenly felt meaningless in the face of such raw human need and inequality. Finally, I understood what a calling feels like: an overwhelming need to respond to what I had experienced there in Mumbai, the sheer horror and devastation that screamed at me for a reaction and a response.

The rest of the journey passed in a blur. Finally, I arrived back in Perth and walked back into my home, back into my life. On the surface, everything was exactly as it had been ten days earlier but, in reality, nothing could ever be the same again. I crashed down into a chair.

"Sunita, something's happened to me. We have to talk."

Breaking down again I shared every detail of my experience with my wife, the one person I knew I could talk to about anything, my best friend and confidante. I knew she would understand. We talked for hours, praying together, and taking an honest inventory of our lives and future. From the outside, I had made it. I was rising steadily to the highest ranks of the company with the promise that seven figure bonuses were just around the corner, but already I was bringing home far more money than we would ever need. The truth was, we had no desire for yachts and flash lifestyles, and struggled to even spend the interest on the money I earned.

Even the very home we were sitting in told the same story. When looking for somewhere to live in Scotland our rental budget would have stretched to a castle, but that would have been far too showy. When my secretary spotted an advert for a bungalow, I felt far happier with the idea. We were even more encouraged when we learnt it was the home of David and Marjorie Souter who needed to let their home in order to go to Zimbabwe as missionaries. We simply didn't need or want anything more.

Funnily enough, we had had similar conversations previously, but Sunita and I had never quite been on the same page as each other. At one point she had suggested change, but I wasn't ready, too entrenched in the success I'd worked so hard to achieve. Another time I had wondered about stepping down to do something different, but she had worried about whether the timing was right. This time however, everything converged. We were in the same place at the same time, both convinced that this change needed to happen.

How would we survive though, without the income and luxuries we had grown accustomed to? Making careful calculations, we realised there were numerous places we could make savings. We could manage without private medical insurance. We could put the children into State schools. We didn't need a five-bedroom detached house in Greater London. Certainly we could manage with one car rather than two. Slowly, as it dawned on us that we really could do it, we made the mental leap. This wasn't impossible. It would be hard and would involve sacrifices, but it wasn't impossible. And so, over the coming weeks, Sunita and I planned for a different kind of future. One that would bring hope and life to others, rather than just to ourselves.

As the months passed, we thought about it more. Possibly it was no coincidence that our church there, North Church Perth, happened to be running a series of talks on careers at the time. The minister there was Rev. Bob Sloane, who subsequently became the Queen's chaplain at Balmoral Castle. When he came to the talk on 'Money', it was so powerful. I will always remember his words, "Enough is always a little more." It struck me deeply because every time I had thought about leaving work, I would remember the next bonus and think, "Just one more and then we'll be fine." But such thinking can go on forever because 'enough' never comes.

Not wanting to make the decision hastily though, I took time to talk with the pastors of the three churches I'd been involved in during the years leading to this point: the one in Geneva, the one in Perth and the one in Sutton. My soul was searching for something beyond my own understanding, and I knew I needed wise counsel.

Around the same time, I had been reading a book by Tom Sine called *The Mustard Seed Conspiracy*. In it, he makes the very simple point that if one person makes £1 of difference, then a million people can make a million pounds of difference. No one's contribution is too small. No one's contribution is insignificant. I also read his thoughts on those who climb the corporate ladder only to find there's nothing at the top. The more I read, and the more Sunita heard me talking about it, the more she said, "You know Ram, I think maybe the time is right now."

As an aside, having made the decision to live with comparatively less, we were overwhelmingly grateful to learn we had a pension fund large enough to cover the cost of our house. Alongside this, another unexpected financial gift came in. We had taken the plunge, prepared to give up everything, and God had given this back. We could keep our home and the children could remain in their schools.

The next steps would be hard, however. There were challenges ahead. But armed with the knowledge that we could manage financially, I felt confident to talk to Azad Shivdasani, who was both the chairman and Sunita's cousin. Once we had moved back down to London, I arranged to meet him for dinner at The Antelope pub, just around the corner from our Belgravia office.

It is always difficult to hand in your notice when you like your colleagues. How much harder when they are family! How do you explain to this family who has given you such a lucrative work opportunity, that you no longer want to be a part of it? In their eyes I had come good. Being part of and leading a commercial team that helped make millions for the company, I had become a highly valuable asset. They were not going to let me go in a hurry. Nor did I want to jump ship and let them down. I knew they had plans to take my career even further, but none of this could convince me. It wasn't even that they disagreed with what I wanted to do. The chairman was all in favour of my ideas to help combat poverty but suggested I do it alongside my work. Couldn't I just donate some of my huge earnings? That in itself would make a big difference to others. For me, however, this wasn't enough. I needed to be involved at the heart of the work of changing lives, not just a slightly removed donor.

"Look," said Azad, "There will potentially be a lot of people working here for whom you will be responsible. You have a market and an audience for your cause. Why can't you work out your calling within the business?"

"True," I admitted, "But my calling is to do it in the name of Jesus. To go out in the name of Christ to serve the poor, to serve the community I've seen."

At this point he conceded and said he would honour my calling. I went on to explain my plan.

"We can do this slowly. To begin with, I can still work four days a week for you, but I'd like to be released one day a week. I have to be honest though - my long-term plan is to leave completely."

Even though, in those days, with the Inlaks Group you were either in or out, Azad blessed this plan for me to transition gradually out of the group. We agreed to our new 4:1 working week and my salary was adjusted accordingly.

Of course, it wasn't just my boss who wanted me to stay. Sunita's aunt was the matriarch of the family, so when I had a call from Aunty Lakshmi I knew it was serious.

"So, what is this I hear you're leaving. Are you crazy?" she began, "Let's have lunch."

Knowing she was a force to be reckoned with, I agreed to go only if her daughter Bina came too. I knew she would listen impartially and understand. We met in an upmarket Japanese restaurant in Mayfair where I was given a very thorough grilling.

"This is a terrible idea! How will you pay the school fees?"

"Aunty, it's all taken care of."

"But the house? How will you pay the mortgage?"

"It's all sorted Aunty, really it's fine."

The tirade of questions continued until finally Bina, an alumnus of Cheltenham Ladies College, exclaimed in her own inimitable way, "Mummy! Stop bullying Ram!"

"Ram has made up his mind. He is not joining the competition, and he has understood your concern about caring for Sunita and the children. He does have enough to take care of them in the manner they have been used to."

In fairness, her mother hadn't intended to pressurise me as such, but she was a strong character with a passion for her family's wellbeing. She couldn't bear to think of any one of them struggling financially or not being taken care of.

So, finally, I had, if not the family's blessing, at least their acceptance. They could see my mind was made up but also that I remained loyal to them. Sadly, my immediate boss had become seriously ill, and I knew they needed me more than ever while he recovered. I could not have just walked away. As agreed with the chairman, I made the break gradually, first giving them four days a week, using my day off to study at Spurgeon's College, then slowly shifting the balance until, within four years, I was only giving one day a week to Inlaks, and the rest of my time to Christian philanthropic work. Even when I made my final break, I made it clear that I was always available by phone to give them help and advice with company matters. They are my family and the last thing I wanted to do was cause them any trouble.

And gradually, as they saw what I was doing, perhaps they understood a little more. As for me, I finally realised what my purpose was, what it meant to be called to something. I had always tried to live by the strong values of equality and care for others that had been modelled to me since birth. I had always had that sense of duty to mankind. But what happened to me that day in Dharavi overturned everything I'd known earlier.

In a moment, in a flash, my desire to help others had been catapulted from something born of duty and kindness, to something propelled by a powerfully unleashed compassion. Suddenly, it was not a matter of 'trying to do my bit'. It was life or death. It was no longer a little extra to tag onto the end of a business trip but an all-encompassing urge that demanded my full attention. It was my reason for being here on this planet.

Calling was no longer an abstract concept. Now it was crystal clear. I had a job to do, and I would have no peace until I made the choice to do it. Looking back, it makes perfect sense that this life-changing call should have happened in my motherland. Every time I visited India, I had felt that same powerful feeling of being home, that connection to my people and my history, but my experience in Dharavi was on an entirely different level. It was beyond powerful. The strength of emotion it inspired was a turning point, a call to new things. The calling was clearly from God, but India was the backdrop, the place that has always had such a sure place in my heart, once again stepping in to powerfully change the course of my life.

Chapter Ten
Pulling the Cracker

Something a little unusual was happening in our plush Belgravia office. There, in the waiting room, sat a man who didn't fit our normal demographic. His scuffed boots sank into the deep pile carpet and, unlike most of our regular visitors, there wasn't a designer suit in sight. However, the fact that he looked completely out of place didn't seem to faze him at all. As I walked in, he gave me a broad smile.

"Steve Chalke" he said, shaking my hand.

I invited him into the board room and the youth worker confidently pulled up a chair at the gleaming marble table. I smiled at the incongruity of it all. We were more used to hosting the movers and shakers of the business world, leaders of successful money-making companies. But this was a meeting with a difference. Here was a leader with a difference.

Because it turned out I was not the only one who had visited Dharavi. I was not the only one who had wept in shock and had my life and complacency shaken into action. A few months before my own trip, Dr Raju Abraham had also arranged for Steve to visit the Mumbai slum. Steve was Anglo-Indian and his father's nostalgic idealism about the motherland had made him eager to see it for himself. Aware how deeply we had both been affected, Raju arranged for us to meet, confident that our combined gifts and skills would be far greater than the sum of their parts. And while on face value, our backgrounds, careers, and life experience seemed worlds apart, as soon as we started talking about Dharavi, everything overlapped. This experience could only truly be understood by those who had lived it too. There was a relieved recognition as we listened to each other's stories: someone else gets it.

However, we had not arranged to meet simply for mutual understanding. Both of us had been inspired to do something. But what? Between us, surely, we could do something big? Prior to the meeting Dr Raju had briefed me, "Look Ram, you're a businessman. You take ideas and translate them into action. Steve has ideas but needs help managing them and fundraising for them. Can you work together?"

He told me about a small but exciting project Steve had been running with his youth group in Tonbridge, Kent. It worked as an 'Eat Less – Pay More' initiative, where teenagers cooked and served meals made with cheap or donated food but charged first world restaurant prices, with all the proceeds going to famine relief projects. It was a brilliant scheme and Steve had been wondering how to extend it to other churches, wanting to see if it could even work nationwide.

With my business background, it only took a matter of seconds for the word 'franchise' to pop into my mind. If it could work in one place, why not replicate it nationwide? Charity restaurants could be set up in temporarily vacant high street shops. Instructions could be sent to churches wishing to follow the model Steve Chalke and his youth group had used. Funding

Gagandas Dayaram Gidoomal and Vasanti Gagandas Gidoomal

Naraindas Dayaram Gidoomal (Daddy) and Janki Naraindas Gidoomal

OUR MOST RESPECTED (LATE) PRESIDENT.

KATHIAWAR SPORTS CLUB.

MR G. D. GIDOOMAL.

Mr. Gagandas D. Gidomal, our late President, who by his untiring, selfless and devoted efforts made the existence of our institution a reality. In appreciation of his work and revered memory we humbly dedicate this souvenir to his lasting memory and as a monument to his work.

OUR SHORT HISTORY

Nor can we forget the late Mr. Gangandas D. Gidoomal, who was our President. A man of considerable foresight, he also looked into the future — never backwards. He brought, during his tenure of office, new life to the club's activities and by his personal example prompted others to strain their very nerve in achieving all-round progress. The club owes him a great deal for bringing it to a position of eminence among sporting institutions, enabling it to sponsor the current tour of the Indian cricketing stars.

Kathiawar Sports Club 1957 Programme featuring a tribute to
Ram's father, Gagandas Dayaram Gidoomal

A generation who pioneered the silk trade from Japan to the ports of
East and South Africa – Ram's father, who was the eldest son of Dayaram Gidoomal,
with his uncles – from right to left: Dada Jethanand Gidoomal,
his wife Aunty Sita Jethanand Gidoomal, and Dada Hiranand Gidoomal

BIOGRAPHIES

The Late Mr. Dayaram Gidoomal

THE very sad and sudden death of Mr Dayaram Gidoomal, which took place at Capetown on Friday, Oct. 23, after a very short illness, removes from the life of the Indian community of the Union a patriotic and a generous hearted fellow-countryman. The late Mr. Gidoomal came to this country in 1907 at the age of fifteen with his uncle, the late Mr. C. P. Luchhiram, who was also a prominent Indian merchant and had won the esteem of his countrymen through his public-spiritedness. He opened a silk merchandise business in Johannesburg in 1918 which has developed into the now well-known firm of Japan Bazaar, of which he was the senior partner. Japan Bazaar has its branches in Mombasa and Nairobi in East Africa, in Kobe and Yokohama in Japan and in Hong Kong in China. The late Mr. Gidoomal was one of the prominent leaders of the Transvaal Hindu Seva Samaj to which institution he donated liberal sums. He took keen interest in public affairs in South Africa as well as in the struggle for freedom in India and never hesitated to open his purse liberally in any deserving cause. Unlike many men of fortune the late Mr. Gidoomal did not wear an air of arrogance which usually comes in its trail. He was humble and a lover of the poor. By his business acumen and his general knowledge of the world he had come into contact with many Europeans as well as Indians by whom he was liked and respected. He leaves behind his sorrowing widow, three sons and four daughters and two brothers to mourn their irreparable loss. The death of Mr. Gidoomal is a loss first to his family, then to his firm, the Japan Bazaar, then to the Hindu community and last but not least to the Indian community of the Union for we have but few such noble hearted and public-spirited men in our community who alone are fit to guide the destiny of their people. We extend to the bereaved family and to the members of the Japan Bazaar our deepest sympathy.

GIDOOMAL, Dayaram ; *b.* Hyderabad, Sind, 1892 ; *educ.* Hyderabad, Sind. Came to South Africa in 1907, settled in Johannesburg. Here joined the firm of his uncle, D. P. Gidoomal, silk merchants. In 1918 with partners, started the Japan Bazaar, which has been developed into one of the leading Indian establishments in the city of Johannesburg. While retaining interests in the firm, has made a long stay in India. Has been a generous giver to all deserving funds. *Address :* (In India) Khiatotando, Hyderabad, Sind. (In South Africa) The Japan Bazaar, 63, Eloff St., Johannesburg, Transvaal.

Ram's grandfather – his entry in the *South Africa Who's Who 1937*

His obituary as featured in a South African Indian magazine, *Indian Opinion*

Rukhmani Dayaram Gidoomal (Ama)

Roopchand Dayaram Gidoomal
(Dada Roopa) and
Kamla Roopchand Gidoomal

Ram's inspiration and role model, Aunty Hari (Dr. Hari Sen, the founder
of the Tagore International Schools), with her husband, J. K. Sen

The three flats in which the family lived, on Kilindini Road, Mombasa –
photographed in 2017, 50 years after they left in 1967

J H Gidoomal Shop on the corner of Salim Road and Kilindini Road, Mombasa

Entrance to the H H Aga Khan High School (AKHS), Mombasa

AKHS Class of 1967, School Reunion in Toronto in 2005

Ram and Sunita with her parents, Tirath Tekchand Shivdasani
and Vishni Tirath Shivdasani at their wedding reception

Signing the Wedding Register at Hammersmith Registry Office

Ram and Sunita at Buckingham Palace following the Investiture

Her Majesty Queen Elizabeth II congratulating Ram Gidoomal at Buckingham Palace after investing him as a CBE (Commander of the most Excellent Order of the British Empire) for services to the Asian business community and to race relations

HRH The Queen at St George's, University of London.
Ram was Vice Chair and the Chairperson was Baroness Julia Cumberlege, CBE, DSG, DL

With Nelson Mandela in Brixton Market at an event organised by
Business in the Community and Race for Opportunity

Coming to Britain
an immigrant's story...
with Ram Gidoomal

"...an unusual blend of ethics and enterprise..."
Management Today

"From buying smoked salmon to selling charity"
Financial Times

"Great guy, great story, great video"
Cliff Richard

Meeting Amitabh Bachchan and Jaya Bhaduri at a charity event.
On the left, Ajitabh Bachchan

Visiting a well in Mirzapur, UP, funded by the Rotary Club
of Puerto de la Cruz, Tenerife, Spain

Opening the New Hospital Wing of Kachwa Christian Hospital, India,
built with funds donated by the Mitchell Family

In Turkey, speaking on Cotton Connect

At Queen Mary University of London with students;
in the Refectory, during the London Mayoral campaign 2004

Keynote speaker at AKHS Class of '67 Reunion in Toronto in 2005

Being interviewed for the Today programme on BBC Radio 4
during the 2004 London Mayoral Campaign

Imperial College
London

Receiving the Fellowship of Imperial College in 2010

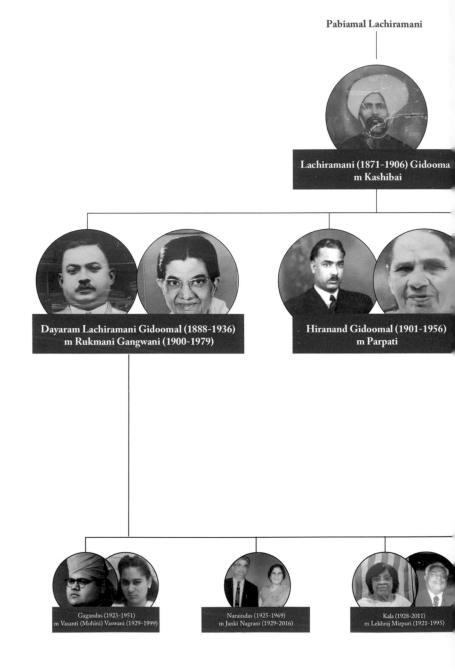

Pabiamal Lachiramani

Lachiramani (1871-1906) Gidooma
m Kashibai

Dayaram Lachiramani Gidoomal (1888-1936)
m Rukmani Gangwani (1900-1979)

Hiranand Gidoomal (1901-1956)
m Parpati

Gagandas (1923-1951)
m Vasanti (Mohini) Vaswani (1929-1999)

Naraindas (1925-1969)
m Janki Nagrani (1929-2016)

Kala (1928-2011)
m Lekhraj Mirpuri (1921-1995)

Gidoomal Family Tree

**Jethanand Gidoomal (1903-1960)
m Sita (1916-1973)**

Kaushaliya (1929-2006)
m Tahilram Nagrani (1925-2010)

Daya (Mohini) (1931-1996)
m Nariandas Vaswani (1920-1980)

Roopchand (1933-2014)
m Kamla Daryanani (1931-2002)

Ishwari (1935)
m Sunder Mirpuri (1937-2011)

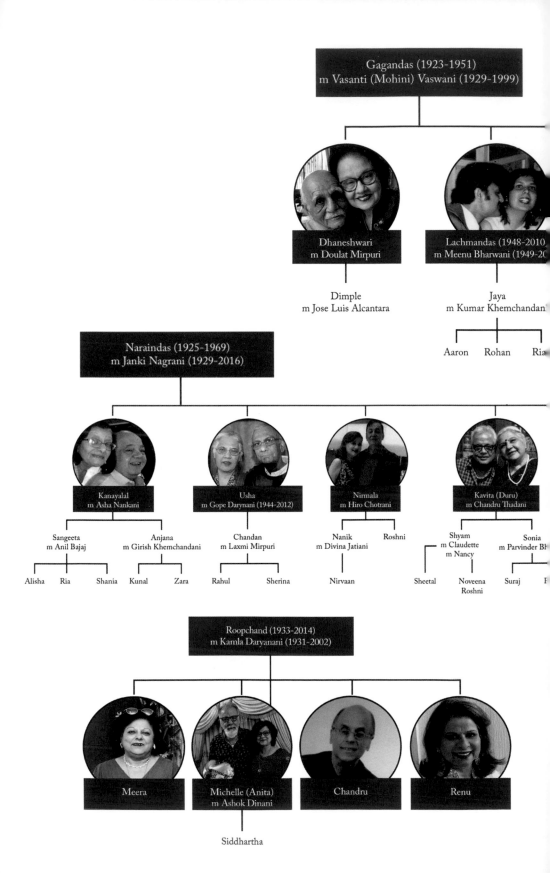

Gagandas (1923–1951)
m Vasanti (Mohini) Vaswani (1929–1999)

Dhaneshwari
m Doulat Mirpuri

Lachmandas (1948–2010
m Meenu Bharwani (1949–2(

Dimple
m Jose Luis Alcantara

Jaya
m Kumar Khemchandan

Aaron   Rohan   Ria

Naraindas (1925–1969)
m Janki Nagrani (1929–2016)

Kanayalal
m Asha Nankani

Usha
m Gope Darynani (1944–2012)

Nirmala
m Hiro Chotrani

Kavita (Duru)
m Chandru Thadani

Sangeeta
m Anil Bajaj

Anjana
m Girish Khemchandani

Chandan
m Laxmi Mirpuri

Nanik
m Divina Jatiani

Roshni

Shyam
m Claudette
m Nancy

Sonia
m Parvinder Bh

Alisha   Ria   Shania

Kunal   Zara

Rahul   Sherina

Nirvaan

Sheetal

Noveena
Roshni

Suraj

Roopchand (1933–2014)
m Kamla Daryanani (1931–2002)

Meera

Michelle (Anita)
m Ashok Dinani

Chandru

Renu

Siddhartha

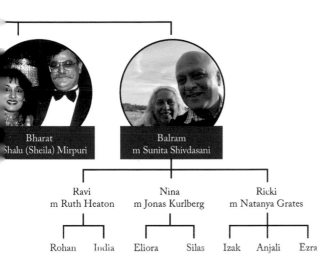

Bharat
m Shalu (Sheila) Mirpuri

Balram
m Sunita Shivdasani

Ravi
m Ruth Heaton

Nina
m Jonas Kurlberg

Ricki
m Natanya Grates

Rohan   India

Eliora   Silas

Izak   Anjali   Ezra

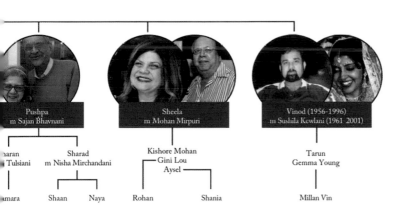

Pushpa
m Sajan Bhavnani

Sheela
m Mohan Mirpuri

Vinod (1956-1996)
m Sushila Kewlani (1961-2001)

Sharan
m Tulsiani

Sharad
m Nisha Mirchandani

Kishore Mohan
Gini Lou
Aysel

Tarun
Gemma Young

Tamara   Shaan   Naya

Rohan   Shania

Millan Vin

The family attending the wedding of Ram's nephew in 2016

was needed of course, but my business skills would come into play there.

Something was worrying me though. I wondered if it would affect the whole project. I needed to voice my concerns before we got in too deep.

"The problem with teenagers," I sighed, "is that they're so apathetic."

"Teenagers? Apathetic?" Steve stared at me in disbelief. "Can I make a suggestion?"

He proposed I go to a nearby secondary school just as classes were finishing for the day and stand near the bus stop.

"Listen to the sheer noise, energy and vibrancy there, and then come back and tell me if you think they're apathetic."

It was enough to convince me. If we could harness that energy and put it towards fundraising with good works which, at the same time would build much needed confidence in the young people of our country, how wonderful would that be?

Admittedly, Steve didn't have much of a business plan, but he was dynamic and full of inspiration. He also had a natural connection with young people. We began to move things forward. The original project had been called 'Beggars' Banquet' but neither Raju nor I were happy with the idea of calling those in need 'beggars'. We put our heads together to come up with a new name for the restaurants that were to run during the festive season. The name 'Christmas Cracker' was chosen as it seemed appropriate to name them after something with a gift at the centre.

Of course, pretty quickly we ran into the question of funding. We had been looking at ways to raise awareness of the project throughout the country. Raju introduced us to Paul Clowney, a graphic designer who went to his church. We asked Paul to create all the branding and graphics and he came up with an innovative neo-Zulu design which we used across the board. Steve then suggested he should go to India to make a short film which could be shown to tens of thousands of people at Spring Harvest, a large Christian convention held every Easter. He had access to the youth there, our target audience.

"How much do you need for that?" I asked.

"Well, I'll need to take a cameraman with me…" he began.

I decided that one way of simultaneously cutting costs and supporting the local economy would be to use an Indian cameraman. This would mean we only needed to pay one airfare rather than two. But starting from scratch, even that was a big ask. As we discussed money, I sensed all eyes at the table resting on me: Steve, Dr Raju, and Hilary Saunders, editor of 21CC, a youth magazine which was already a partner in the venture and would become a great support, regularly promoting the project. I suddenly realised they were expecting me to pay.

Of course, on that one occasion I probably could have, but my mind was ticking. I knew I was entering a new phase, a new world. My income had already dropped and if I was expected to open my chequebook for every financial need, I would be bankrupt in no time. Thinking carefully, I said, "Leave it with me."

Really, I had no idea how I was going to sort it out, but I recalled having met the manager of Air India at a cocktail reception and, despite not being confident that he would even remember me, I decided to give him a call. Dropping Inlaks into the conversation was a good start – we had been very loyal clients, sending huge amounts of air travel custom his way. So, when I gave a brief overview of our project he immediately responded with enthusiasm.

"That's a great cause. How many tickets do you need?"

How many? Of course, I just asked for the one as planned, but I knew then that, with my business connections, this kind of help was available. Of course, it was on the understanding that their support would be mentioned in any publicity material we produced, but it made all the difference in those early days. The following time when we really needed more people there, I asked for three and the airline generously agreed.

With the publicity out there, more and more youth groups had caught the vision, signed up and were making plans. The franchise idea meant that all the individual projects' start-up costs had to be raised locally by the volunteers in each area.

There was also some wider fundraising, including an auction at Spring Harvest during which Steve Chalke donated his leather jacket. One young Christmas Cracker helper named Vicky was so taken by the idea, she decided she would stop at nothing to get it, eventually using her entire week's budget to pay for it. Later, when her local Christmas Cracker project decided to run a similar auction, Vicky sacrificially put the now legendary jacket up for auction... only to buy it back a second time!

Of course, other charities had tried the 'Eat Less, Pay More' approach with schemes like World Vision's 'Fast for the Poor' but harnessing the creativity of our young supporters led Christmas Cracker to develop snappier slogans like 'Bite for Right' and 'India's baking – she needs dough!' Once the young people and their leaders were on board, there was no end to what we could achieve – they brought all the extra vibrancy and enthusiasm we needed. Of course, we wanted to channel their energy and prepare them properly for what was ahead, with each local project team having to attend a one-week training course on mission, and on Jesus' response to poverty – and a second week learning basic business and accounting skills.

Meanwhile, when it came to cost cutting, we learnt a thing or two from the slums themselves. As Viju had shown me around Dharavi, I was struck by the number of different NGOs working together there, around ten in all. Instead of each having an office with all the overheads that incurs, they pooled their resources resulting in more being left over for those in need.

This impressed me so much that, when we set up Christmas Cracker, we followed this idea: a lesson from the slum to eventually benefit the slum. Instead of setting up a new office I said we would have agreements with those whose assistance we needed and pay for services rendered. Christmas Cracker owned nothing:

no building, no staff, no photocopier, nothing. Everything was outsourced or subcontracted. When we needed people to travel around the country, I asked the staff at Oasis Trust where Steve Chalke was the director to do so, and to charge us for their time. Through the seven years of its official existence, we never had a single direct employee or an office. South Asian Concern (SAC) which Raju and I had by then established, provided the administrative services managing the finances, book-keeping, accounts, and overseeing the disbursements of funds raised. Meanwhile, Oasis had contact with 200 youth groups. They were the ideal people to man that side of the job. The principle was to avoid wasting money setting up something new - and it all came from that one simple example in the slums when I saw ten NGOs managing to share a photocopier.

Finally, with the start-up costs covered, and the preparations made, the restaurants – also known as Crackerterias - could open. I took my family to New Malden to see one in action. It was housed in an old British Gas showroom which had been given a bright festive makeover. Although it was mostly run by the youth, there was a huge amount of support from parents and other church members. I was delighted to learn that all ages and denominations were getting involved, and that nobody was excluded for any reason. The lady who took our order was a Roman Catholic in her seventies. She was deaf, and was thrilled to be able to join in the project.

I chatted to the young staff there and they explained how, every evening, they would do the rounds of the local shops, asking what food was being thrown out. Then they would take anything that was still legally edible, for free.

Knowing this was a charity venture and that the café wasn't competing with them, all the shops were more than happy to comply. So, any cakes or doughnuts that hadn't been sold were usually up for grabs. They would also go to the butchers and pick up all the end trimmings that nobody else wanted and a local Chinese family would transform these into the most amazing sweet and sour chicken. The creativity it unleashed was amazing. It was phenomenal to see what the young people could do.

As the years went by, the project developed. Food related health and safety regulations made the Crackerterias a little harder to maintain and, although some groups kept these going, others moved on to different projects. Steve, in particular, was aware of the need for new ideas to keep the young people energised.

This is where first Radio Cracker and then Cracker newspapers stepped in. We realised there was a window of opportunity in local radio. Legislation was about to change, but we had a couple of years before it did. Back then, as is the case now, the younger generation were brilliant with new technology. I met with an engineer from Imperial who said he would be able to develop and provide all the necessary equipment, but at a cost of around £2000 per station. My heart sank. Our target was to have 100 stations, but where would I find £200,000? Without even checking, I knew we had nothing in reserves. The whole principle of Christmas Cracker was: whatever we raised, we gave away. Every year, the bank account was cleared out, the balance going back to zero. It's a good discipline - not hanging onto money when it's desperately needed by others, but of course in business terms it's considered bad practice. Honestly speaking, one reason for this was because I had only ever intended to be involved for a year, but once Christmas Cracker got going, it became a self-perpetuating force.

Without any central reserves, the radio start-up costs fell to each individual group. £2000 is a large but achievable amount to raise between a group of enthusiastic young people. Starting in the summer holidays, they did everything from car washing to cake sales until the full amount was raised. This meant that once each radio station was up and running, they could offer advertising that would go collectively to millions of people, and every penny of income from this could be sent to those in need.

The advertising was sold at different levels: Bronze, Silver, and Gold, with your publicity aired more frequently the higher up the scale you went. In Sutton & Cheam, the young entrepreneurs realised they had a contact with the Chief Executive of Direct Line in Croydon and managed to persuade him to buy a Gold package for £10,000.

In areas where they had both Crackerterias and radio stations, the two worked in perfect harmony – the radio advertising the restaurant and the restaurant playing the radio as background music, as well as collecting any paid requests. Some would put a big basket in the corner of other local cafés and businesses too, for people to add music and other ideas. For example, a grandmother brought in a cassette recording of her granddaughter playing violin to be played on air for a small donation.

From here, the idea of newspapers came up – such as The Newbury Cracker. The young people would compile the information, find a printer, sell the papers and have additional income from the advertising space they sold. They worked with the local community and churches to gather relevant stories and announcements. Around Christmas everyone needed to know what was going on, so they had a captive audience. With the restaurants and radio, this became a triple media blast into the community. Again, in addition to raising money, working on the newspaper taught young people valuable editorial skills. It's not been unusual over the years for me to be interviewed and then hear the journalist saying to me, "Oh yes, I cut my editorial teeth on the Cracker newspaper!"

Working together we achieved a huge amount. All through the various years and different permutations of Christmas Cracker, we worked as a team. Steve was dynamic, the perfect front man. I was happy to mill around in the background, making sure the business side of things worked. One aspect of this was making sure all the monies raised were sent to the correct projects. Overall, we raised nearly £5 million, but even in the first year, it was nearly half a million pounds. How do you transfer this kind of money to those you want to help? Do you set up a development agency with all the associated costs or donate to an existing one? Many development agencies in the

West charge even to transfer money to charities in the Majority World. Notably, one was asking for 33% which would have been soul destroying for our young people after all their hard work. We arranged a deal: the agencies would just hand over the money on our behalf without deducting a penny. Some agencies did still have fees and we asked to be informed of these upfront, but others said they would transfer the money for nothing.

Unfortunately, one aid agency, despite this agreement, deducted 20% of the money we were sending to Fortaleza, Brazil. We had become involved in a project there helping a group of slum kids with a bakery business. We resolved this simply by asking for all the money back and sending it directly. With a £20,000 donation that meant £4000 at stake. We were firm on this because, without lifting a finger, these agencies were receiving our money. They gave us a portfolio of potential projects which the team would evaluate before allocating the income generated, with the young people also having their say in the geographical area and the main focus for the year. As people ate in these pop-up restaurants, there would be videos to watch and pamphlets to read, explaining that their money was going perhaps to build water wells in India or hospitals in Belize. Each year the videos would feature a theme song such as 'Harvest for the World' by The Christians, or 'Another Day in Paradise' by Phil Collins, often donated without any royalties needing to be paid.

The young people had the satisfaction of knowing their hard work was paying off. They learnt new skills in the process, and had a lot of fun, especially when it came to PR events. With the younger generation on board everything felt possible. They were living proof of my motto "Don't let what you can't do stop you from doing what you can" and a prime example of not fearing the battle, nor being put off by obstacles. They were an inspiration to me, always looking for possible solutions, always asking "What *can* I do?"

For example, I *can* go to my local lawyer to hassle them to give us the site on the high street despite being told No. I *can* go to the then Foreign Secretary, Douglas Hurd and say, "Will you come and ride on an elephant to open our restaurant". He said No, but it was worth asking and, undeterred, the young people instead borrowed a bear from the local zoo for the day and had 'The Bare Necessities' blaring out in the street.

This can-do attitude extended even beyond their own expectations. I remember the very first meeting, discussing plans and asking the youth for ideas. There was this drawing of a Christmas cracker and I asked,

"What are you going to do with that?"

"Well sir, we were thinking of pulling the longest cracker in the world to get into the Guinness Book of Records and raise awareness of the project, but it's going to cost money and there's none spare."

Very quickly I jumped in. "We'll get money for that! You get the cracker built."

I had connections with a company who agreed to pay all the costs in return for having an ad in the middle of the 120-foot cracker. Meanwhile, the renowned cultural analyst and journalist, Jenny Taylor, had been seconded by the mission agency Interserve as Christmas Cracker's National Launch Press Officer. Her work with Christmas Cracker won nationwide media coverage for our new concept in fund-raising, including airtime on BBC Radio 4's *Today* programme. It was Jenny who took the young people's cracker idea and ran the launch event, *The World's Biggest Christmas Cracker*, on London's South Bank. In the end it was featured on the BBC's *Newsround* programme, on Sky TV, and in *The Daily Telegraph*, among other places. The publicity more than paid off for the company, and our project also got the coverage it needed.

As for the cracker itself, it took several classes of schoolchildren from the Faraday School on the South Bank to actually pull it. An independent inspector came to measure it and sure enough we made it into the Guinness Book of Records.

The media loved it, but even better was the exhilaration and reactions of all those involved.

Spurred on, the young people then produced the largest cheque in the world, which also got into the Guinness Book of Records. We found a company in Scotland capable of producing paper big enough, because this couldn't be something held together with sticky tape – we wanted it to qualify as a cheque that could be banked. In the end they succeeded in making one complete continuous cheque which was accepted and cleared by one of the banks.

One year, we also decided to do an alternative Christmas Cracker – in the summer. This was to raise money for the Disaster Emergency Fund. It was around the time of the famines in Africa and Bob Geldof's work there. We called our new project 'The Alternative Christmas: 48 hours to change the world'. It started and finished in a single weekend, 24th and 25th June, exactly six months before Christmas. I knew the director of Midland Bank and he organised the donation of 500 shiny new £1 coins, one going to every group to get them started. Following the Parable of the Talents, we told the young people to see how much they could multiply their £1 in 48 hours. They had from when school closed on Friday night until a special youth service on the Sunday evening to make as much as they could from that pound.

Of course, we offered some ideas to get them going. For example, they could buy paper and generate dummy share certificates or loan documents to sell to church members in order to have enough money to do something bigger (the idea being that they could pay them back at the end of the project, still having a lot left over). Some groups bought bread on Friday evening and made sandwiches to sell to shoppers on Saturday morning. Another group decided to buy washing up liquid and sponges to clean cars with the motto "Wash for Dosh" and another bought shoe cleaning materials and polished shoes in the high street. In the space of two days, this project raised £125,000, which is really not a bad return on the initial £500 investment.

The main Christmas Cracker project ran for seven years, raised just under £5 million overall, and mobilised some 50,000 teens. Even after the official organisation of it ended, many places kept going. The last I heard, there was still a radio station on air in Rugby. There was also one Crackerteria restaurant in Ballymena, Northern Ireland which just kept going, run by a man called Jack. The funds they raised continued to help the same project in India: Emmanuel Hospital. Having built strong links, they often sent the young people over there to be inspired further.

This was in line with the Christmas Cracker philosophy. Right from the start we had sent our young people out to visit the projects. Jokingly we offered rewards for those who made the most money. Third prize would be one week in a slum. Second prize, two weeks in a slum. And, first prize, you've guessed it... three weeks in a slum. While such terminology did not raise eyebrows at that time it is clearly not acceptable practice today.

Of course, the young people lapped this up and all wanted the three-week prize. As for us, we had two reasons for sending them. Mostly to give them an unforgettable and life changing experiences – inspiring their future choices. However, it also served as a form of audit. Here we were, sending money abroad in trust. Was it being used effectively? Was it going to the people we intended it for? The mandate we gave the kids was to go, do your bit, but also come back with your stories, your experiences, tales of how you've been impacted, and tell us how the money is being used. It is a huge scandal when charity funds are misused, and this was one mechanism to insure against that. Thankfully, although we did pick up on a few challenges, these were quickly resolved and, on the whole, there were hardly any problems.

Another thing we had to bear in mind was the mental health of the young people travelling. Despite the joke about prizes for the highest fundraisers, in actual fact the young people self-selected, and we had strict conditions and screening to ensure that those planning to travel could cope with what they would see. I knew from my own experience just what an impact the sights of the slum could have.

We did offer to cover the flight costs for the top three, but none of them claimed it, all having raised their own airfares. On arrival they were looked after by local churches, creating wonderful partnerships for the future.

The visits stirred up even more ideas. One group of girls who were learning fashion design here in the UK had noticed that young women trying to escape prostitution had no idea how to make money to live. The girls requested to use the funds raised to send sewing machines and said they were prepared to go out to train the women themselves. They came up with designs that could be made there, and then sent back to the UK to be sold here. Suddenly these former prostitutes had a new business.

As for me, the whole project was a hugely exciting way of starting this new phase of life. News of the project spread, and the Financial Times ran a story, quoting me as saying, "The creative use of business skills and links makes things happen. It gives me all the excitement of deal-making, not for making money for myself now, but for getting others excited, getting them to go beyond themselves – which is, after all, the reason that Jesus came."

It was true. My motives had completely changed. What good is it to amass wealth here? Life is transient - my past experiences had already taught me that. My family worked hard to be prosperous and lost everything, twice. Twice they had been plunged into the inevitable feelings of terror that brings. Twice, their lives had been turned upside down through circumstances beyond their control.

Now, my life was once again being turned upside down, but this time it was my choice, my doing, my own decision. I wasn't losing anything, rather I was choosing to give it up, choosing to live on less rather than piling up wealth for no reason.

Twice my family lost everything and had to struggle to survive, but now, having chosen to let go of my excess riches, I found that we always had enough.

Chapter Eleven
South Asian Adventures

"Ram! How much space do you have in your dining room? You see I've got these invoices…"

I glanced around my home. Already we had turned one small room behind the garage into an office where I worked on our charity ventures. Already the line between work and family life was at risk of getting blurred as paperwork spread first into the laundry room, and then the kitchen. So, when Chatru, our accountant and good friend, described the bagful of 200 invoices he needed to spread out and sort through, I had visions of our finite family space being swamped beyond recognition.

"Hold on for now," I pleaded, realising we urgently needed to find a proper office.

I couldn't deny it was a good sign. We had more than enough work to keep us busy and were clearly meeting a need. We just needed more space. We needed to expand.

The seeds of this new venture had all begun in 1987, before Christmas Cracker, even before I had been on my life changing journey to India. Already back then there had been a niggling thought in my mind, a question about my true purpose and a desire to make a bigger difference in the world than just 'doing my bit' at church.

Having met Dr. Raju Abraham earlier in the summer, Sunita and I invited him and his wife, Catherine, along with our mutual friends, Prabhu & Philippa Guptara, to our London home. We were amazed at how well our children got on, even at their first meeting – they were all very close in age.

In the garden, we chatted over a leisurely lunch of barbecued Nigerian King Prawns. Raju talked about the challenges faced in the Indian subcontinent. It was then that he and Prabhu encouraged me to recognise my value as a Non-Resident Indian. However, at that time I just couldn't see my role. I had always loved India and of course Inlaks had business interests there – they owned tea estates in Coimbatore and had an office in Mumbai. On top of this, both Sunita and I had close relatives spread across the country, but still, I felt I had lost my deeper connection with my motherland.

As the summer breeze rustled through the leaves, I confessed I'd been thinking of leaving the world of commerce altogether to go to Bible College. However, Prabhu jumped in, imploring me to keep up my business links, pointing out various key factors in my life. Firstly, I was a Sindhi. The Sindh province straddles India and Pakistan, and our people are renowned for being industrious, pioneering and savvy in business. Secondly, I had a proven personal track record in business myself, with clear expertise and skills in this area. Thirdly I had contacts. There were so many Asians with whom I could share my spiritual journey and meanwhile, I could also raise awareness of the practical and spiritual needs of other South Asians, whether in the UK, the diaspora or in India. Similarly, these extensive connections would allow me to be a bridge between South Asian Christians and my

Christian business or church contacts. The combination of these different strands, he said, made me quite unique.

His words were a revelation to me. It was a lesson in the importance of being who you are rather than just jumping into what you think is expected. Be who you are and use your God-given skills. My God-given skills were in business – a world that can sometimes seem a little greedy, self-absorbed, and focussed only on profit. Could I really use these skills for the common good?

With any new idea or decision, I always ask ten questions, and this was no different. What do you want to do? Why? Why this? Why now? With what? By whom? By when? How much? What are the consequences of doing it? What are the consequences of not doing it?

I mulled it over and, after my visit to Dharavi, when I made my decision to gradually leave Inlaks, I realised that God did not call me to become something that I wasn't, but instead to use what I was and what I had been given in new ways.

That's when I agreed to take steps into this venture with the others. Everything was pointing towards a holistic project based on the principles Jesus taught, with a business edge that could serve the Indian subcontinent through fundraising, while also serving UK-based South Asians through friendships and partnerships. The more we talked, the clearer the vision and purpose became. And very quickly, I saw that with the right motivation, business could provide an incomparable source of funds and goodness to change lives for the better.

So, with the invaluable support of Sunita, I joined Raju, Prabhu and another friend, Robin Thomson, who had just returned from India with his wife Shoko, in setting up South Asian Concern (SAC). Having been born in India, Robin was more Indian than Sunita and me! I have learned so much from him about India and missions generally over the years.

Later others joined too – in particular, Paul & Su East helped strengthen our links to the Emmanuel Hospital Association, also my brothers-in-law Deepak and Suneel became trustees and travelled on various missions with me – but in the beginning there were just the four of us, building something completely from scratch. We were all very different, but our deep friendship and common goal meant that we always worked well as a team. Any group of people will occasionally have disagreements, but we had a strong foundation and the willingness to discuss issues with mutual respect. I recall Sunita commenting on the friendships at the time, saying how we always pulled together to find solutions.

Apart from anything else, the way we operated was indicative of our very 'Indian' approach to running an organisation – bringing in friends and family, using everyone's skills, recognising that spouses are as much part of the organisation as the individual. It was, in fact, our spouses who at our first Trustees meeting challenged our initial plans to organise a conference of those interested in South Asia and suggested that, in the first instance, we simply listen in humility, by inviting participants to a prayer consultation and together seeking the Lord's will.

By the time of the charity's launch in 1989, Sunita and I were members of Chiltern Church, who also became very involved in supporting SAC, even organising a service of commendation for us as we began this new path. Their friendship and prayers have sustained us ever since. One of our guests at this service was our friend, Chatru, who would eventually become our accountant. We had met Chatru and his wife, Jyoti, in Tenerife some years earlier. Interestingly Jyoti is the granddaughter of one of my grandfather's best friends, Rai Bahadur Watanmal Boolchand, whom I met during my very first hours in India at the age of 14. Chatru and Jyoti invited us for dinner and chess and, in time, we had got talking about the Bible.

"I think I'll try and get hold of a copy of this Bible you're talking about," he said.

"Well here, have ours." I handed him the well-thumbed book.

He was speechless, touched that we would give him our own copy of what is our most holy book. It set him on a path of reading the Gospels and eventually deciding to accept the friendship that Jesus the Lord offers in our walk through life. We were so grateful when he and Jyoti moved to England and became involved in SAC.

The charity's purposes were multiple, but the common thread was supporting South Asians, both in their homeland and here in the UK. One notable achievement was organising the very first gathering of South Asian Christian leaders living and working in South Asia. The only place it was possible to do this was Kathmandu. This location meant we were confidently able to invite representatives of all seven of the countries that made up South Asia at that time: Bangladesh, Bhutan, India, the Maldives, Nepal, Pakistan, and Sri Lanka. During that meeting, we were invited to have tea with the Nepali Prime Minister who had been educated at a Christian school and was very much in favour of our work, even confiding that he mistrusted his own people when it came to attacks on Christians. Unable to make the opening ceremony himself, he sent along his Tourism and Aviation minister who began his inauguration speech with the words:

"I hate Christianity..."

We shot each other panicked looks. What was coming next?

"But I love Jesus," he continued. "The 80 plus of you in this room have the power to change South Asia, because I have seen what is done by your faith."

Besides the spiritual element, there was a big emphasis on fundraising for practical aid in emergency situations and, in fact, in 1991 we also set up the South Asian Development Partnership (SADP) to focus specifically on such needs. I had a passion for this, and ran SADP pretty much single-handedly until 1995, when my brother-in-law, Deepak Mahtani, came to join me.

Thus, in 1993, when a devastating earthquake hit Latur, Maharastra, in the west of India, we were ready to spring into action. Working with Christmas Cracker of course meant huge amounts could be achieved. By this time, Steve Chalke was the GMTV (Good Morning Television) vicar! Coincidentally, in order to renew their licence, GMTV needed to demonstrate that they were doing something positive for the community and the wider world, so Steve mentioned to me that they were looking to support an overseas project. Although six months had passed since the earthquake and the media hype had died down, I immediately thought of Latur.

"You know what happens? There's an earthquake and everyone rushes to help, but after the initial surge of overseas aid, it just gets forgotten!" The fact was, they were still suffering, struggling to get back on their feet. There was no hospital in the area and people needed medical care. I suggested we support the building of a local hospital to serve the area. Emmanuel Hospitals Association (EHA) had also seen the need and wanted to set one up. I made the pitch via Steve, and GMTV agreed that for one week, their fitness guru, Mr Motivator, would run a nationwide 'Lose Pounds, Give Pounds' campaign. People wanting to shed a bit of weight could be sponsored or make donations, with all the money going to our hospital fund.

Since we were a small and relatively new charity, we were completely unprepared for how huge the response would be. We didn't really have the infrastructure. This was well before online payments, so cheques and cash came flooding to SAC's P.O. Box, sacks of them, full to bursting, every day – all of which Sunita & Jyoti had to manage, along with a tireless team of volunteers. It was essential that there was a group of people present, to ensure integrity and to witness correct procedures; but it was also essential for the sheer scale of work. On the first day, the sack was opened and the money counted. The volunteers worked solidly until 3pm and then headed to the bank. Time for the next shock. The small local branch had never seen anything quite like it and, after one very late night, processing hundreds, possibly even thousands of cheques, they pleaded with Jyoti and her team to bring the donations in at regular intervals during the day.

Opening the envelopes, you never knew quite what you would find. Some of the letters that came with the donations were incredibly touching. One elderly lady had just had a £2 increase on her pension and sent two £1 coins in an envelope, wanting to give her 'little extra' to the hospital. Interestingly, there were also a lot of cheques for odd amounts, like £101. We knew immediately that these were from Asians, as some traditions believe that round numbers are unlucky. Sunita also noticed that there was not much of a system to begin with, meaning that huge cheques were being left on the desk, while tiny amounts were being paid in. With her gift for administration, she was able to organise her team to prioritise banking the bigger cheques first.

While Sunita and her helpers were wading through paperwork, other members of the team went to the BT Tower every day to answer phones and receive donations that way.

However, back before any of this could even begin, I had had to secure seed funding of £10,000 to pay for the project to be overseen. Without that, I couldn't authorise this to take place under the Christmas Cracker name. I happened to be going to Switzerland to meet my former employers and finally persuaded them to donate the required sum, explaining that, from that £10,000 we were expecting to raise £100,000. What kind of business deal does that? But as it turned out I had my projection all wrong. We didn't raise £100,000. We raised £400,000!

With that huge sum, we were able to help EHA build the much-needed hospital, which opened in 1996. One heart-warming story amidst all the tragedy in Latur, was of an 18-month-old baby girl who was pulled out of the wreckage, unconscious but breathing, after nearly six days buried in rubble. Her metal cot had fallen over her in such a way that she had been protected from harm while dripping water had kept her alive. Her name was Priya, meaning 'beloved', and she became a symbol of hope. Therefore, it was decided to name the hospital after her. The Priya GMTV Hospital opened in 1996 under the Emmanuel Hospitals Association and is still faithfully serving its local people to this day.

A wonderful by-product of this campaign was that I developed a great friendship with the then Indian High Commissioner, His Excellency Dr L M Singhvi. GMTV was keen to have him on air on the Friday of that week's campaign. As I already knew him a little, Dr Raju and I went to meet him at 5 o'clock that morning and we all then travelled together in his car, IND1, to the studios where, on behalf of the Indian government, he was able to thank the public for their generosity. After the show, and a photo opportunity with Mr Motivator, the High Commissioner, Steve, Raju and myself, Dr Singhvi, invited Raju and me to his home for the most sumptuous Indian breakfast imaginable. After sharing this experience, throughout the time he held office South Asian Concern was always given the privilege of organising and leading the annual Christmas service at the High Commission.

SADP was also involved with relief work following the devastating 2004 Indian Ocean earthquake and tsunami, and many other terrible disasters. However, we also wanted it to be a catalyst for change. So, in addition to the practical support, we put a lot of effort into education – raising awareness of human rights infringements across the world. We often ran conferences, one highlighting human rights violations in Gujarat, for example, and another aimed at reconciliation in the aftermath of the 7/7 bombings to name just a couple.

One of the patrons of SADP, Dr Prem Sharma, was so inspired by the Gujarat Conference and its outcomes that he decided to take on the task of organising SADP's peace conferences and engaging young children and teenagers to attend. With his influence he was able to invite senior Government Ministers and MPs to participate, and to be committed to act on the outcomes.

Meanwhile, we continued working with Christmas Cracker. One thing that always made us smile was the fact that the trading company – a wholly owned subsidiary – operated as "Cracking Up Ltd". Answering the phone with "Hello, Cracking up here" always gave us some kind of reaction at the other end, whether laughter or momentary confused silence!

To cover its up-front costs, Christmas Cracker partnered with a number of big charities, agreeing deals whereby they invested a proportion of the funds towards our annual running costs, and we then distributed the funds we'd raised pro rata between all those charities who had invested. They were more than happy with this – we had a great track record with young people who they could access for their projects, and they always received back a significant multiple on their original investment, which could then be used for those in need.

One charity we worked with was The Leprosy Mission in England and Wales. In the early nineties, they had organised a fundraising lunch at the prestigious Carlton Towers Hotel in Knightsbridge and their patron, Princess Diana, always a keen ambassador for them, had agreed to speak there. They were eager to have a diverse audience, but their contacts with the Asian community were limited. Therefore, they got in touch and asked if I would be able to fill a table, with Asian businesspeople. With such an offer coming free of charge, it didn't take much persuading, although of course all my guests did send generous donations following the lunch.

Princess Diana made sure she spoke with every guest, and I had a lovely chat with her about Christmas Cracker and was able to share how well we had been doing. Sadly, however, she told me her own charities had been struggling somewhat with fundraising at the time.

Meanwhile, all the big charities that Christmas Cracker worked with were delighted because not only were they receiving the fruits of the restaurants, radios, and newspapers, but they also had access to a database of around 50,000 young people who had a heart for the poor. Every year the project took on a different focus - the first year the money went to help those in the slums of Mumbai, the place which had set everything in motion. Other years it homed in on Fair Trade, helped Aids victims, or those trapped in the sex trade.

Of course, at that time, Christmas Cracker was practically a household name – especially in church circles but elsewhere too. However, very few people knew much about the small but influential charity backing it up. SAC however was busy and thriving, and – bearing in mind Chatru's huge bag of invoices – in need of stretching space. This came, almost miraculously, in the form of a phone call with a solicitor friend, Alistair Watson. It turned out that a local law firm had some offices near Sutton station that SAC could use rent-free. This also benefitted the firm as charities were exempt from paying rates.

Later, when we needed to move again, we were stunned to find we were receiving an inheritance from a lady I had once met who supported our work. She had willed a substantial sum of money to the founders of Christmas Cracker, including SAC. This allowed us to buy our office building, at just the right time, enabling us to continue the work more effectively.

Perhaps some of the only people who felt a little disappointed when SAC moved its office out of our house were my children. They loved to come home from school to find Steve Chalke's car in the drive and click that a Christmas Cracker meeting was in progress.

"Great!" they shouted, "Leftover pizza for tea!"

However, we were happy to settle into our new office and continue the work. On occasion, we did extend our remit beyond South Asia, the most notable example being the Kosovo refugee crisis. Around that time, Sunita's cousin Bina was hosting a dinner party in her Mayfair home and had invited a Sindhi businessman who ran a UK and US hedge fund. He had been watching the television reports with horror. The streams of innocent refugees fleeing their homes brought to mind harrowing reflections of the Partition. It felt a little too close to the bone and he was keen to help. That evening, impassioned, he offered £50,000 to any charity who would make a direct impact on the situation. He didn't want his donation getting lost in a government agency or eaten up with charity administration costs.

"Well," said Bina, "I think I know someone who can help with that."

She called me and I jumped at the opportunity, explaining that we could ask doctors and nurses from EHA in India to travel to Kosovo and provide medical assistance for injured victims. The donor was delighted with the idea and his enthusiasm sparked the generosity of other business contacts, one of whom matched his donation. In the end, over £100,000 was raised and Indian medics were mobilised, crossing dangerous territory to serve in the refugee camps of Northern Albania, just along the border with Kosovo. EHA has over 2000 staff. They sent teams of doctors, nurses, lab technicians and pharmacists to help with both practical and reconciliation work. As Deepak commented at the time, "The message of Hindus giving to Muslims through Christians was powerful and was affirmed by the Regional Director of UNHCR as well as receiving a lot of positive press." Indeed, the Evening Standard was quick to run a story with the headline: "Indian Aid for the Balkans".

Another notable achievement through SADP came when we undertook some critical research based on the 1991 census. When the reports started coming out from the census, we could see that for the first time they had identified Indians, Pakistanis, and Bangladeshis in the demographics. We decided we should grab the opportunity to analyse every single constituency.

The resulting report was published in 1992 and identified that the 1.5 million South Asians in the UK presented a £5 billion opportunity for Britain's businesses. It also made it apparent that 90% of South Asians had settled in the M6-M40 corridor which runs between London and Birmingham, passing through southern Buckinghamshire, eastern Oxfordshire, and central-southern Warwickshire.

We invested a good deal of time into analysing the data with the help of talented social researcher and recent university graduate, Stephen Morris, who was temping with us at the time. He waded through the huge volume of data, studying it and pulling out anything that would provide useful information about British Asians. He was with us for a year and produced a hugely significant piece of work that proved very valuable to both SAC and SADP, as well as their clients and partners. Even today, many years later, organisations are still asking the same questions about how to get minority communities to engage with the public sector.

"We just don't have enough information!" is the common cry.

I always reply, "Yes, but the census has it all. Why don't you target them according to that?" And with that, I am once again able to point them towards our report.

Although SADP still exists and, with the help of Dr Sharma and our colleague Robin Thomson, has continued to help run peace initiatives in the UK, the level of activity is significantly less now. However, SAC continues to send support to emergency situations overseas. Notably, we stood with the Indian people through their recent Covid crisis, when we raised £230,000 for oxygen generating machines and ventilators to be sent to several different hospitals there. For me, it feels like a testimony to our original goals that we are able to keep serving in this way. SAC and SADP were never big, well-known charities, and yet we have made a difference, often quite a significant one. Similarly, I never felt the need to be upfront in any of the campaigns. As long as the work got done and the money was sent to those in need, I was content. During the big appeals, particularly Christmas Cracker, my one principle was that you would find me in the back room. It was partly that I felt very aware of my Asian roots, aware that we were running campaigns for white majority churches in a white majority country, but it was partly also because I just didn't feel the need to be seen. That was not my place in the process. Steve Chalke, with his thriving youth charity, Oasis, was perfectly positioned for this. It suited his gifts, personality, and resources. It just worked. That was his calling, and I was following mine.

Following a call is a challenging but rewarding experience. It does not always mean giving up your job. In my case it did, but even then, the thing that surprised me at first was that I needed to stay in business and use my skills rather than stumbling into completely new territory. As a result, I always advise the younger generation of South Asians to recognise whatever resources they have at their fingertips and to keep asking "What can I do with what I already have?"

Perhaps not everyone will agree with the need for SAC's spiritual element, but the practical work we have achieved speaks for itself. Our aims were to help and support others, to build bridges and open doors. Although my personal choice is to follow Jesus, I am still part of Hindu, Sikh and Muslim communities and I have great respect and love for people of those, and indeed any other faiths. When I share my own values, I try to be sensitive to this, entering into dialogue rather than argument, and always apologising if my words ever unintentionally cause offence.

I have learnt so much from my colleagues at SAC. I have learnt so much from the projects, the successes, and the challenges. But perhaps one of the biggest things SAC taught me, was the value of tenacity. When we started the work of SAC all those years ago, there were plenty of raised eyebrows from people wondering what on earth we were trying to achieve, given that there were already many other agencies working in South Asia. What I learnt was not to be put off by mockers. When you're taking a step of faith, doing something different or out of the ordinary, there will always be sceptics. Let them say what they will. Your calling is your calling.

And I knew mine.

Chapter Twelve
Telling the Story

"What happens to them? I've always wondered. What happens to all those brilliant girls?"

The teacher who said this to me was looking at me intently.

"I would teach them for years," she continued. "Their giftedness was so exciting. I was sure these girls would do it all. They'd be the doctors, professionals, and leaders of the future. But after their O-levels they'd simply vanish. Finally, a few years later, I would see them at the bus stop, married and pushing buggies. And I never really understood before now. I never knew the magnitude of the pressures and expectations they were dealing with."

I had just given a talk at my sons' school, King's College Wimbledon, about my book, *Sari 'n' Chips*. The Head had had a similar reaction after reading it saying, "We have so many excellent South Asian boys here, but I had no idea what went on behind closed doors." Wanting his staff to gain a deeper understanding, he had called me in to speak to the teachers.

While I was sad to hear the teacher's experiences at her previous school, it completely affirmed my reasons for writing the book. I had grown up with six sisters and four brothers and, even in a loving supportive family like mine, the expectations were crystal clear. I could see the pressures on the girls especially, but also on the boys, not just to get married, but to marry the right person, in the right way. And when I say the 'right' person, of course, it was not necessarily the young person's definition of 'right' (though I'm relieved to say all my siblings did end up in happy marriages). Family honour or *izzat* took precedence over everything else. Making the right connections, the right impression, paying the right dowry, doing the right thing. For us, it was about safeguarding the money Daddy had left for his daughters' dowries after he died. None of us boys were allowed to touch it. It was set aside for the weddings, for saris, jewellery, airfares, and receptions.

Family honour is of course not a bad thing, and in most families – my own included – it was simply a form of maintaining our social standing in the community. This in itself is something which has brought tremendous angst for Asian young people in the past, often causing huge stress and the feeling that their own choices and individuality are being repressed.

However, all this pales into insignificance in the face of what happens when such honour is taken to an extreme. Because across all Asian communities there have been incidents where the pursuit of honour is taken to a far more dangerous degree. Tragically, there are some individuals who regard honour as so important that any non-compliance with it demands vengeance at any cost.

So, while *Sari 'n' Chips* is partly autobiographical, its main purpose was to explore some of the issues faced by the Asian community here in the UK. I covered everything from culture shock and identity, to work and religion, but throughout the book there is a huge focus on family, especially on women. Because it was really the experience of Asian women that inspired me to write it. Hearing one too many horrific stories on the news about domestic violence, or teenage girls beaten or stabbed to death by their own relatives for not behaving quite as their families required, I felt physically sick and knew I could keep quiet no longer. Why was no one doing anything about this?

Originally, it wasn't even a book, but a dissertation idea. The weekly studies I had begun at Spurgeon's College after my visit to Dharavi continued to inspire me. I felt hungry for more, wanting to have a deep-rooted understanding of the Bible, so I signed up for a correspondence course, also with Spurgeon's College, to complete a Cambridge diploma in Theology. Part of the course requirement was to set up a prayer support group. I asked Professor Donald Wiseman if he would chair the group and he graciously accepted. The group also included the pastor of Chiltern Church, Peter Morris, and a couple of the elders, Brian Adams, and Roy Coad, as well as Chris Lee, the pastor of North Cheam Baptist Church, where I went when I first arrived in London. The group met monthly to pray for me and was a huge encouragement as I studied.

When the dissertation requirement arose, I decided to write about my ethnic background and culture. But soon it became clear both that there was too much to say, and that this was too important to just file away with my other coursework. Along with Mike Fearon, I developed the ideas into a full-length book which was published by Monarch in 1993. Then I waited for the reactions.

I wanted to speak up, but I had no idea quite how much I would be in demand once I did so, with requests for radio and TV interviews suddenly flowing in. I was called by *The Telegraph* and *The Times* and, for a while, I also became a regular interviewee on Radio 4's *Today* programme whenever they needed a comment on such issues. I spoke with emotion about a young girl and her unborn child who had been stabbed relentlessly by her mother and brother. Then there was the Turkish girl who had begged the police for help, petrified by the pressure her father was putting on her. Later she was found dead in her bath with 31 knife wounds. Live on the *Today* programme and in the company of a senior police official from her area, I questioned what on earth had gone wrong. Why had no one listened to her? Where were the police? Where were her teachers? How can this have happened without anyone really noticing or taking her fears seriously? My comments caused quite a stir and I found myself invited by Hammersmith Council's education chief to discuss ideas that might bring change.

In the book itself, I also told the controversial story of an Asian woman who had suffered such an extreme level of domestic violence that she eventually killed her husband out of self-defence. Of course, I would never condone murder, but in this case her action was the only way out of a daily living hell. She was imprisoned for manslaughter but eventually released on grounds of clemency, something I applauded as just and proper in this particular case.

Of course, not everyone was going to love me for these views.

"Stop hanging out our dirty laundry in public!" one elderly Asian man shouted at me on a radio phone in. Another accused me of milking the situation, of criticising my own culture publicly to line my pockets. Fortunately, the programme's presenter was Ramola Bachchan, director of TV Asia and a force to be reckoned with. She stepped in very quickly to remind the caller and all her listeners that this really wasn't the case.

"Actually, Mr Gidoomal isn't making a penny out of this. All the profits from book sales are going straight to charity."

Despite these negative reactions, there were others – many, many others – who thanked me for speaking up. People who had seen the problems unfolding. People who had listened to the news with the same horror as I had. People who wanted these young Asian women to be able to live free from fear. Gradually the calls started changing, the comments supported me rather than attacking me, saying, "Yes, we need more discussion. We need to be able to talk about this without fear or shame."

And it wasn't just public comments and media reactions. There were individuals too. I had decided to go out on a limb and put my phone number and a contact address at the back of the book. I wanted to be available to help any readers who might have further questions or need support. I received letters from every viewpoint imaginable. Many were grateful I had spoken up, but of course, inevitably there were some who did not want their boat rocked, and others who complained because I had not included their specific ethnic group in my studies.

Overall, however, I felt I had achieved my goal in fighting for justice. Back then, only a few people were talking about domestic violence within South Asian communities, unintentionally giving the impression that everyone within their community was willingly compliant. As far as I know, I may have been one of the first men to speak out about it on national media, but once the debate was open, more and more people added their voices. Gradually, more women began to speak up for themselves, starting their own campaigns and charities, taking their petitions to the Foreign Office. I willingly took a step back, happy that they felt able to take on the mantle. It was what I'd always hoped would happen. I was delighted to see groups such as the long-established Southall Black Sisters attract more funding and gain momentum. If my voice had anything at all to do with these new manifestations of courage, then I had fulfilled what I set out to do.

While my primary purpose in writing *Sari 'n' Chips* was to stand up for women and speak out against domestic violence and honour killings, it also told my own story and seemed to reach people on other levels too. One day, while I was out, Sunita took a call from a young Asian girl in Doncaster who had found our number in the back of the book.

"I've just read Ram's book and I want to follow Jesus too," she began. Sunita told her she would get me to call her but, before I did, I wanted to make sure I could put her in touch with a local woman in her community - it had to be a woman, this was our culture. I called the Christian bookshop in Doncaster, and they confirmed that someone had bought a copy of my book. I was just wondering how to proceed in finding someone who might tick the boxes of being first a woman, then a Christian and preferably also Asian - to fully understand this girl's background – when the person at the other end of the phone said,

"Hang on, someone's left a note behind the till."

A Christian Indian woman who was new to the area had specifically come into the shop to leave her name and contact details, just in case anyone wanted to talk to her about any of the issues in the book. Even more remarkably, when I called the young girl back with this information, it turned out they shared a postcode. I was able to connect them. Remarkably, when this same girl moved to Wales sometime later, exactly the same thing happened again. We had kept in touch, and she wrote to ask for help in finding a local church. In the same pile of letters was one from a woman in Cardiff offering help and support to anyone in her area. Putting the two letters together, I saw that not only were the postcodes the same, but they lived on exactly the same street. Through such connections, we have seen this young woman grow in strength and character, becoming a leader in her church.

Other people contacted us about different cultural issues. The parents of a young English girl called me. Their daughter, a student, had fallen in love with an Indian boy, but his parents were panicked by this and threatened to take him out of university. Through reading the book and discussions with me, they all managed to negotiate a path ahead. The young couple stayed together and are now serving as missionaries overseas.

Meanwhile, the book was also reaching an international audience. In the States, Indian immigrants have their own characteristics. The stringent immigration policy there only welcomes in the absolute crème de la crème, the highest-achieving Asians. This conjures a certain respect, but problems arise when these high-flying Indians have children. The pressures on their offspring to go to the next level is immense and has led to major mental health issues. After writing *Sari 'n' Chips*, I found myself invited by the North American Council of South Asian Christians to go and talk openly to families there, sharing my experiences and advising them on managing expectations.

The book seemed to have taken on a life of its own, sparking both debate and hope for change. For me, I simply wanted to help. I didn't do it for the kudos. When my input was sought, my question was always, "Will it help society, the church, and beyond?"

It seemed to be reaching people. When the National Library for the Blind wrote to me in 2003 to ask permission to produce a braille copy, I was delighted and immediately gave my consent.

Meanwhile, having turned my original dissertation idea into a book, I now needed to find something else to write about for my course at Spurgeon's College. With my complex religious background, it seemed obvious to focus on Pluralism. Again, this idea grew legs of its own when the Cambridge Exam Board awarded it a Distinction and offered me a job as a Cambridge examiner in A-level Hinduism. Any egoism I might have developed about this, however, was quickly crushed when they admitted they were desperate! Still, it was a fascinating experience and something completely new for me with my business background.

Several other books followed, all written with the desire to promote cross-cultural understanding in different ways. Then a slightly different book opportunity came up when I later ran for Mayor of London, and was asked to record my experiences and political standpoint. The result was the book *How Would Jesus Vote?* All the books I wrote were in collaboration, with others working alongside me, and sharing their wisdom.

My studies continued and, in addition to my Cambridge diploma in Theology, I was awarded Spurgeon's Oasis Diploma in Church Planting and Evangelism with Distinction. For one of my assignments, along with SAC, I set up an evening class to provide training in East-West differences and relations. Unaware of the importance of such matters, the college had set up a small room with a handful of chairs. I'm happy to say they had hopelessly underestimated the interest. More chairs and tables were brought in and eventually we had to move to a larger room to accommodate the 'sell-out' numbers.

In everything I did I was working towards an atmosphere of cultural sharing and awareness, but my original aim of supporting women was still strong. Many readers of *Sari 'n' Chips* comment that there is a very feminine trait to the book and that is true, because with six sisters I have seen first-hand the pressures these girls are under, the things they go through, and the unfairness of the family system where all the privileges and rights are automatically handed to the boys. I wanted people to get under my skin and feel this injustice along with the young women who suffered it. Young Asian women face genuine challenges when they marry and move in with their husband's families. It's easy to imagine how they might feel. Often, they had no voice, no say in anything.

Although my desire was simply to tell the truth and raise awareness, my book had a couple of unexpected by-products. Most notably, I was invited to become a Fellow of the RSA (the Royal Society for Arts, Manufactures and Commerce, a network of nearly 20,000 professionals). After some consideration I made the wise decision to accept, becoming a lifetime member. This was something I would never regret.

It was the RSA that later gave me the platform to deliver my lecture, "Building on Success – The South Asian Contribution to UK Competitiveness" which was later featured on the *Today* programme and in several top newspapers including *The Evening Standard*, *The Times*, *The Scotsman* and even *The Hong Kong and Shanghai Post*! This was at a meeting in 1997 chaired by Bob Ayling, then Chief Executive of British Airways, with audience members including Prue Leith (chair of the RSA at the time), Barbara Roche (the Shadow Business Secretary), and the former High Commissioner to Pakistan, as well as many other high-profile guests from politics, business, and financial institutions.

In fact, it was this lecture that formed the basis for two more books because, having listened intently to my talk, my audience started asking questions like, "Who are these South Asians?" and "We've never heard of these people," so I said, "Ok, let me explain." And six months later I produced *The UK Maharajahs* describing some of the most prominent and successful British Asians. It was a quick project because all the research had already been done for the lecture. It simply needed adapting into book form. It was a similar story for my subsequent book, *The British and how to deal with them*, which was the fruit of that same lecture, but also benefitted from significant input from my brother-in-law Deepak Mahtani, an award-winning cross-cultural trainer and consultant. In it, we gave more practical advice about doing business with ethnic minorities in Britain, the twist being that, when mentioning 'The British' in the title, I was referring to people from Minority Ethnic communities who have made their home here and are as British as the next person. The book was written to help Britain's businesses successfully deal with the diverse ethnic communities, also making the point that Asians, as a migrant group, have made significant economic contributions to the UK.

When I think of these two books, I am reminded of an interaction I had at the Appledoorn conference in Holland a few years later. The conference was focusing on themes such as diversity, inclusion, and citizenship. Mayor Cohen of Amsterdam made a dramatic statement in his opening speech, saying, "This is an important issue because, by the year 2020, Amsterdam is going to be majority non-Dutch."

I waited my turn to speak then said, "Mayor Cohen, I appreciate you saying Amsterdam will be majority non-Dutch, but can you not see that Amsterdam will be 100% Dutch, just that the definition of 'Dutch' will have evolved?"

My remark was met with huge applause, and I have used a similar statement here about the British. Sometimes we need to be prepared for our definitions to change.

Thinking back to that season of book writing, I am reminded of the enormous help David Porter gave me. Not only did he help with the writing of *How Would Jesus Vote?* but he was also the one who helped me with the research for that pivotal RSA lecture on the South Asian Contribution, followed by *The UK Maharajahs*, and more. In addition, he assisted me with drafting my message and prayers for the Radio 4 *Daily Service* which I did live every few weeks from Didsbury, Manchester (it was always strange to see my name listed in *The Radio Times* when I was scheduled to lead the service). David sadly died of a stroke some years ago, but I will always remember him as a mentor, whose advice I valued hugely.

With so many challenges, I am very grateful for all the help I received at that time. And as I reflect, I am also reminded of the other surprising and happy by-product of *Sari 'n' Chips* which was that I found myself with a number of kindred spirits looking out for me: women who could see I was fighting for greater equality. Unlike the women I had been speaking up for, these were the ones who had defied the odds – women in high places who did have a voice. While I had never had ulterior motives in standing up for women's issues and championing their causes, a time would soon come when I would be very grateful that I'd done so.

Chapter Thirteen
Unlocking the Door

"PULL HIM!"

"No, no! This way! You pull his head. I've got his shoulders."

Panic was rising in me as I tried to shout at my brothers to stop, let go! Not for the first time, I wondered what had possessed me? How had I got myself into this mess, stuck here? Literally stuck. I needed to tell them, but no words would come out, only indiscernible grunts.

It was 1961 and blisteringly hot. Just another day in Mombasa. The sun had been beating down on me all afternoon as I played with my brothers and sisters in the courtyard. Torn between the joy of the game and longing for water, we kept going despite sweating profusely and getting thirstier and thirstier.

Finally, I could stand it no longer. I needed water. Ice cold water from the fridge across the courtyard. And once I started to think about that ice cold water, I could think of nothing else. But I would need to be quick. If I waited much longer, or even gave a hint that I was going, my older brothers and sisters would race to the fridge first and then there would be none left for me.

That's when I had my 'brilliant idea'. I would run to the fridge before them, open the top compartment and lick the ice directly from the freezer. I was already imagining how exquisitely refreshing that would be on my parched tongue! What bliss!

So while the others were distracted by the game, I made the ten yard dash across the courtyard. Of course, they immediately twigged and, within seconds everyone else was running too, desperately trying to overtake me. I had three older brothers, all bigger and faster than me. I didn't have time to think. I just had to make the most of the few seconds' head start I'd grabbed for myself.

Panting, I arrived at the fridge just before them! I'd made it! Quickly, I opened the freezer compartment and started trying to give the ice in the freezer frantic licks. The cold air was heavenly but within seconds – disaster – my tongue had completely glued itself to the ice. I couldn't even lick it. I was well and truly stuck. I tried to scream but, rather like in a nightmare, no noise came out.

Together, my older brothers tried to pull me free but only succeeded in pulling my body one way while my tongue stuck to the freezer. The pain was excruciating. It felt like my tongue would be ripped away if they pulled any more. Of course, I tried to tell them to stop but without a working tongue, what chance did I have?

Hearing the commotion, the servants and cook came running to help. To my horror, some bright spark suggested pouring boiling water onto the ice where my tongue was intimately joined with the freezer. Thankfully, at that point, my mother and eldest sister arrived on the scene and calmly suggested switching off the fridge and allowing the freezer to thaw naturally. It took time, but eventually I was released. My aching tongue moved around my mouth, delighted with its newly regained freedom, grateful for the possibility to form words again. I knew I would never make that mistake again.

Sixty years on, I can still remember every detail. You could say it's been frozen into my memory!

Forever more in my family, this sorry tale would be known as the 'freezer lick story', usually mentioned with a chuckle. The fact is, not every 'brilliant idea' that pops into an 11-year-old's mind works out quite so well in reality. When you run ahead to beat the others, and then everyone catches up with you to see you stuck to the freezer by your tongue, it's a little humiliating. Painful too.

Things don't always go the way we plan. Growing up, I had many ideas for my life, but of course deportation set me on a different path – and, with no other choice, I followed it. Later, even with multiple achievements under my belt as an accomplished businessman and successful charity founder, I became stuck once more, hitting the wall of rejection time and again. I knew I had more to offer. I dreamed of contributing to society in new ways, offering my hard-earned expertise on boards and in the public square.

In a way, I still had the same drive and determination of that thirsty 11-year-old desperate to get to the freezer. In the face of prejudice, I needed such resolve more than ever. Yet even with that, every idea and application was met with obstacles – this time, not from my own naivety, but from the way doors can slam shut in the faces of those who don't fit.

Numerous times I was encouraged to apply for governorships or positions on boards for companies, charities, or health trusts. Each time, I was told it was a sure thing, "Ram, you're exactly what we're looking for!" Spurred on by their confidence and assurances, I went out of my way, often giving up precious family time to put my requested application forward, or attend an interview, but time and again I would end up rejected while the usual suspects were awarded the coveted positions. Gradually, it became clear that these decisions were *faits accomplis*, with me just a pawn in the application process, ticking a box for them and making it seem that procedures were being followed. They were giving ethnic minorities a chance, they would say – they had interviewed an Asian candidate! But the reality was, the colour in the boardroom was monotone white.

One time, applying for a governorship, I was rejected as overqualified for the position. They then proceeded to appoint someone equally educated and experienced. I tried not to take it personally, but every 'no' was crushing. What would it take to open this door?

When following a dream or a deep vocation, the secret is to keep pushing. Sometimes however, it feels like doors are not just closed, but completely locked. Sometimes you need to find the key. After the success of *Sari 'n' Chips* the people who held such keys were women in positions of power. Women became my allies and encouraged me, wherever possible acting on my behalf to open up opportunities. To some, this may sound like nepotism, but that's not really the case when you consider I had only made these contacts through my own hard work, striving for justice for others.

Networking can sound like a dirty word, utilitarian and exploitative. It conjures up visions of talking to one person while already looking elsewhere, wondering "What's in it for me?" I refuse to partake in such things. Instead, I use the term 'relational networking': developing and nurturing deep and genuine relationships. Rather than using people and contacts, we must value them as individuals. The result is real human connection, and this pays dividends beyond the imagination.

Between my own persistence, the encouragement of these women, and the contacts formed in the RSA, I finally began to get some breaks. I received a letter from the Ministry of Agriculture, Forestry and Fisheries (MAFF) inviting me to join the Apples and Pears Research Council as an Independent member. They had picked up my name from the public appointments database, but the person sifting through the potential candidates happened to have been involved in Christmas Cracker. It was a huge thing to be offered my first public appointment at last, but the actual position seemed rather insignificant. When I heard that my fee would be £40 per meeting, I called a number of South Asian friends.

"Is this even worth taking? It looks like a tiny thing, and I know nothing about apples and pears research! Will I be able to contribute anything?"

I wasn't worried about the money itself, more that this was an indication of the role's importance. Would I be able to contribute anything? After some deliberation I did decide to go ahead. After all, I had not been invited as an apples and pears expert but as an independent member. And it truly was a valuable experience. It's where I cut my teeth, learning about governance under Professor Sir Colin Spedding. He had invited me onto the committee set up to examine the APRC's governance because they were due a review by the Ministry of Agriculture. And, usually, a review means bad news.

However, Labour had just come into power, and I was in tune with their thinking. Their buzzword seemed to be 'stakeholders' and picking up on this I decided that's where our focus had to be too.

"Who are our stakeholders?" I asked, "Can we do some analysis, consultation, and research?"

Somehow, speaking the right language was another key, opening up lines of communication. The rest of the committee – white conservative orchard owners and farmers - sat up and listened, and I realised I'd begun to make my mark. Before that, I was an outsider. It was clear they couldn't quite work out how an Indian independent had ended up sitting in their midst. However, although I had not been invited for my fruit expertise, we did happen to have around 25 apple trees in our garden, meaning I was able to hold my own in their discussions. Meanwhile, my scientific background gave me confidence in analysing the research documents. Surprised at how the different strands of my life had come together in this most unlikely place, I suddenly realised I had been prepared for this after all.

It is easy to look down on opportunities that seem smaller than we hoped for, but often we can grow and flourish from these. Quite apart from everything I learnt there, I suddenly found I had a foot in the door. The door that had been shut in my face so often and for so long had opened a crack and I was not going to let it swing closed again.

Not long after this, I found myself appointed to a public board under the oversight of a Government Ministry. My public sector experience played a part here, but mostly it was through a woman's good word. Anne Page wrote to the Minister about me, who in turn told the Permanent Secretary. I had seen the advert for this role and applied, but without any reply. Suddenly I got a call from the Permanent Secretary, asking me to send my CV directly by fax both to him and to the Chairman of the Board. Before I knew it, I was being invited to a breakfast meeting with the chairman the very next morning.

"But... what about the Nolan rules?"

Lord Nolan had chaired the committee responsible for establishing the regulations for public appointments, all of which we seemed to be bypassing.

He cut me off with a quick, "We'll do Nolan afterwards!"

I had a moment to choose. Perhaps I should have challenged it, but I knew this was on the strength of a recommendation. I decided to go to the breakfast interview and, although the chairman was angry, he had clearly checked me out, and I found myself appointed to the committee. Another breakthrough.

Around the same time, I had been contacted by a prominent family in India, whose young daughter was suffering from leukaemia. They had raised a significant sum of money to pay the deposit for treatment at Great Ormond Street Hospital (GOSH), but with no possibility of acceptance until they could raise the full amount required for the two-year treatment.

Someone suggested I call Lord McColl, the then Parliamentary Private Secretary, serving as a special advisor to Prime Minister John Major. It was the first time I had dialled a Downing Street number and I admit to feeling a little in awe. In fact, I couldn't believe it when Lord McColl not only returned my call, but was also quick to listen and intervene. I gave my personal assurance to him that the balance of funds would definitely come in as several appeals were ongoing in the Asian media. GOSH admitted the child following Lord McColl's intervention and, sure enough, in the end, several times the amount required was raised.

Ironically, once the breakthroughs begin, once the door opens, and you finally get a chance to move forward, opportunities tend to snowball. That initial contact with Lord McColl developed into a personal friendship that led to my appointment as a governor at James Allen's Girls School (JAGS) in Dulwich. At the time, Ravi and Ricki were pupils at King's College School Wimbledon and, when the Head there heard about my JAGS appointment, he nominated me for governorship at KCS – I had gone from no governorships to two. Suddenly I was in demand, being requested to give speeches, invited onto all sorts of government quangos and agencies, even becoming a government advisor, working on policy. I was invited to join Blair's Better Regulation Task Force which opened up a range of new relationships. I was then stunned to hear that, one after the other, I was to receive honorary doctorates from Middlesex, Bristol and Southampton universities. In addition, I was invited to be a Visiting Professor in Entrepreneurship and Inner-City Regeneration at Middlesex University, and that Archbishop Runcie had chosen to appoint me as an honorary member of the Faculty of Divinity at Cambridge. I shook my head in disbelief at the turn life was taking.

Sadly, even within these success stories, occasionally the sting of discrimination would still strike. I had written my book, *The UK Maharajahs* about how much my community was contributing to the UK economy, but there were still some who refused to see this. One of my responsibilities on the Better Regulation Task Force was to chair the Small Business Regulations Subcommittee and this, in turn, led to the Federation of Small Businesses inviting me to be a keynote speaker at their annual conference, a highly prestigious event.

Optimistically packing up the car with copies to the book to sell, and all ready with my speech on opportunities and regulatory challenges for small businesses within South Asian communities, I made the long journey to Kenilworth with my brother-in-law Deepak. The hotel conference room was packed with several hundred guests. They listened to the first and second speakers – two very high-profile names – but when it was my turn to take to the podium, the entire room cleared. Everyone walked out. It is hard to describe just how crushing that moment felt. Of course, the organisers themselves were mortified and tried to lure people back in with promises of champagne. One took me aside and, with huge embarrassment, confessed that it was a very tough crowd who, until just a few years previously, had allegedly passed motions to 'Send them home' – meaning: to send all immigrants back to wherever they came from. Eventually the planners managed to rustle up enough of an audience from within their own staff and, determined not to be overcome, I gave my speech. Then Deepak and I faced the journey home, still numb with the shock of this humiliation, and yet somehow not entirely surprised.

Experiences like this, and the memory of all my past rejections spurred me on to fight such ongoing discrimination. From the mid to late nineties, I also served as a trustee on a Business in the Community initiative – Race for Opportunity – pushing for more diversity in business and especially for ethnic minorities to have greater opportunities. One interesting by-product of this came when Prince Charles was visiting The Neasden Hindu Temple and the Palace was keen that he should have people around him, walking alongside him during the tour, particularly as that was the day his separation from Princess Diana was announced. They made contact with Business in the Community who, given that this was a visit to a Hindu temple, suggested I would be the most suitable person to meet, greet, and accompany the Prince around the temple.

Then, in the summer of 1997, I was surprised to find in my post one morning a letter on House of Lords headed paper asking me to speak at the National Prayer Breakfast. It was simply signed 'Crispin'. It seemed unbelievable and, at first, I wondered if it was a joke. I called the number given and was quickly put straight. This was a letter from Viscount Brentford himself and yes, of course it was genuine. Viscount Brentford and his wife Gill have given me invaluable support for which I have always been grateful.

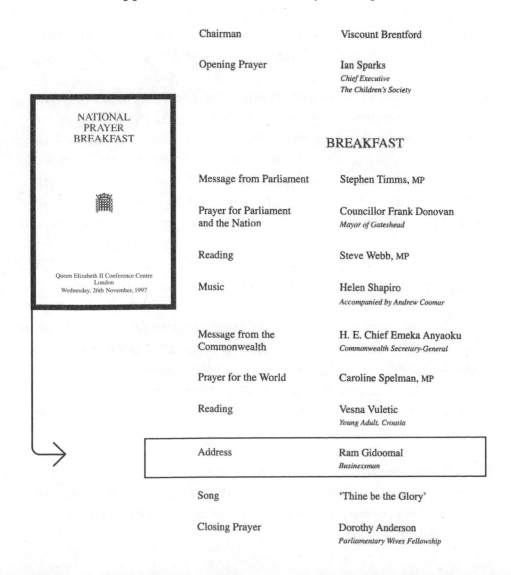

Chairman	Viscount Brentford
Opening Prayer	Ian Sparks *Chief Executive* *The Children's Society*

NATIONAL PRAYER BREAKFAST

Queen Elizabeth II Conference Centre
London
Wednesday, 26th November, 1997

BREAKFAST

Message from Parliament	Stephen Timms, MP
Prayer for Parliament and the Nation	Councillor Frank Donovan *Mayor of Gateshead*
Reading	Steve Webb, MP
Music	Helen Shapiro *Accompanied by Andrew Coomar*
Message from the Commonwealth	H. E. Chief Emeka Anyaoku *Commonwealth Secretary-General*
Prayer for the World	Caroline Spelman, MP
Reading	Vesna Vuletic *Young Adult, Croatia*
Address	Ram Gidoomal *Businessman*
Song	'Thine be the Glory'
Closing Prayer	Dorothy Anderson *Parliamentary Wives Fellowship*

I spent months working on my speech. The National Prayer Breakfast attracts the highest flyers: parliamentarians, ambassadors and business and church leaders, so this was both a huge honour and an opportunity not to be taken lightly. I wrote my speech, rewrote it, tested it, rehearsed it. Then, by chance, I met Harvey Thomas. Harvey had written speeches for all sorts of famous people and organisations; household names. He was Billy Graham's communications chief and had been head-hunted by Margaret Thatcher for the same role in Downing Street, not to mention delivering training at the Foreign Office. As I chatted with him, I mentioned I was doing this speech.

"That's great Ram! Well look, I'm a professional speech writer but I've really enjoyed talking with you so I'll happily have a look at it for free."

His generous time and input were the icing on the cake. Although he didn't change the text much, his advice on intonation, when to pause for laughter, and when to raise my voice was invaluable, a godsend – just days before the Breakfast. Later we would use his consultancy services as part of our wider work with Winning Communications Partnership, raising income to support our projects.

Finally, that autumn, the time for the National Prayer Breakfast came around. I looked out at the sea of faces in the QEII Conference Centre, took a deep breath reminding myself of all Harvey's counsel, and went for it.

I'd chosen the title "The worldwide nature of the family of Jesus Christ" and, as well as relating it to current global issues and news, I told my own story of meeting Jesus at the pub, my struggles to understand church, then my experience in Dharavi and how it raised my awareness of the shocking rich-poor divide and our responsibility to make a difference, to love our neighbour as ourselves.

There was a brief silence after my final words before the place erupted in applause and I breathed in relief. Afterwards, people queued up to speak with me and I was surprised to find Jeffrey Archer among their number. As he shook my hand enthusiastically, he said, "You know, I've spoken at these kinds of things, Ram, and what you did today was outstanding."

Later on, someone else mentioned that the American Ambassador had been weeping during the speech. He sent a message saying he wanted to meet me, and I found myself invited to the Embassy and also to his Regents Park home twice for the 4th July celebrations – a much coveted social engagement. Similarly, there was a Labour Minister who had been suffering from depression. No one had seen him smile in a long time, but that morning he couldn't stop laughing. As a result, he invited me to dinner at the House of Commons. "No reason," he said when I enquired, "I just want to chat. I really loved what you said and want to get to know you." We talked and ate T-bone steak together, the night before it was banned due to BSE.

The Indian High Commissioner was also at the Prayer Breakfast. He had initially thrown his invite away but dug it out again when he realised I was the speaker. He often repeated bits of my speech saying, "This man Gidoomal, he met Jesus at the pub!"

Things were definitely on the up, but nothing could have prepared me for what came next. A few weeks had passed when, in late November, my phone rang as I was driving home.

"Ram, there's an unusual looking letter for you here", Sunita's voice came over the car's speakers. "Marked strictly private & confidential."

"Oh, interesting…"

I arrived home, intrigued and tore the letter open, giving a gasp as I saw the Buckingham Palace logo and the opening words "Her Majesty the Queen would like to confer the honour…"

My eyes quickly scanned the page…a CBE. Ok, nice, but what exactly was that? I'd heard of an OBE. An OBE was really good, wasn't it? We threw suggestions around, perhaps CBE was a 'Chaplain of the British Empire'? Maybe it was for my religious work? Despite my obvious excitement at the award, I secretly felt a little crestfallen not to get an OBE. Eventually, realising speculation was getting us nowhere, we pulled the Webster's Dictionary from the bookshelf and thumbed through the pages.

"It's not Chaplain…it's Commander!"

There it was in black and white. A CBE is 'Commander of the Order of the British Empire' as opposed to an OBE which is an 'Officer of the Order of the British Empire', and MBE, a 'Member'. And what really took my breath away was the listing made it very clear that a CBE was the highest of the three.

I genuinely hadn't seen it coming, but now that I had the letter in my hand, it rang a bell. I was on the board of Business Link (having tried and failed three times to get a licence for Business Link London South, I had finally succeeded – meaning tax payers' money would now come to this public board). Some weeks earlier, I'd been flicking through their magazine and seen that, around this time of year, people start receiving mysterious confidential letters informing them of Honours being awarded to them.

Now, having received such a letter, in my excitement, I folded the letter, put it in an envelope, and sealed it, ready to post off. Thankfully Sunita was there.

"Ram, wait, stop! You haven't actually accepted! You need to sign it!"

"Oh my goodness, you're right!"

Sunita ran into the kitchen to steam it back open. This time I made sure I ticked the box to accept, and signed the letter, before resealing it and rushing to the Post Office to send it recorded delivery.

On the day the 1998 New Year's Honours List was announced, I called the whole family home to be with Sunita and me. Someone organised a huge cake and we celebrated into the night. It was a wonderful evening of good food, conversation, laughter, and occasional cheers, only interrupted by the constant ringing of the phone with loud congratulatory calls from family and friends. The news was being broadcast on Indian radio, with half-hourly announcements of any Asians being honoured. Every time my name came up, someone new would hear and feel compelled to get in touch.

Once I'd got over the initial exhilaration, I was itching to find out how it had come about. Who had nominated me? And how had they gone about it? So, after I had received the award from Her Majesty the Queen in a magnificent and unforgettable ceremony, I called up a civil servant I knew from the Better Regulation Task Force.

"Listen, this whole thing came like a bolt from the blue. Have you any idea who nominated me?"

He explained a little about the process and how nominations and citations are requested from different arms of government to show how you have served the country. In my case it turned out to have been for services to the Asian business community and race relations.

"I must say, Ram," he added, "The file that came around with your notice was double the size of almost all the others."

"Ah, so it took me twice as much work to get it?" I joked.

On this occasion, I didn't mind. The truth is, I was serving on so many different boards by then that my file was bound to be huge. Gradually I began to see pieces of the puzzle, things that had happened over the previous months. Firstly, we'd been invited to a Buckingham Palace garden party, an honour given to people working in public service. Then there were the requests for my naturalisation certificate, with people casually asking "Oh, by the way Ram, when were you made a citizen?"

Despite having begun my life in the UK as a British Protected Person, I had eventually gone through the process to become fully British. Naturalisation was an official tick by my name, but the acceptance I was now finding in the public square felt like the real thing. Perhaps not surprisingly given my CBE, 1998 was also the year my name appeared in Debrett's *Who's Who*.

My CBE wasn't the only time I had the honour of meeting the Queen. In addition to the earlier garden party, Sunita and I found ourselves invited to Buckingham Palace thanks to my role as Fellow and Trustee of the RSA, on its 250-year anniversary. On this occasion, I perhaps became a little over confident. It was towards the end of the afternoon and many people had left already, but due to a sudden downpour, we decided to take cover for a while. The Queen's equerry had gone to fetch an umbrella and we invited her back into the marquee to keep dry. Some contacts I'd made were very keen to meet the Queen and hadn't had the chance, so I approached Her Majesty and asked if it would be acceptable to introduce these people to her. Happily, she agreed. Perhaps that is what gave me the confidence to make the very bold offer to escort her back to the Palace.

Of course, she politely declined, explaining that her equerry was returning. When he did, we all walked behind her, and our afternoon ended on a high, especially when I was able to find a connection with one of the Queen's footmen! I had recently spoken at a business lunch at the Dorchester Hotel and the host had mentioned in conversation that his nephew was a footman to Her Majesty. I remembered his name and made a point of looking out for him at the Palace.

My slightly cheeky offer to the Queen reminds me of another time when I decided to seize the moment, resulting in an impromptu interview with Edward Heath. I had been invited to attend an event at Kensington Palace in the mid-nineties, celebrating the contribution of the East African Asian community in the UK – as you can imagine, a very special occasion for me.

As I arrived, I saw the former Prime Minister, entering just in front of me, followed by a TV crew from a well-known Asian network.

I recognized the journalist leading the crew, and quickly asked him if I could use his mike to take the opportunity to thank Mr Heath for what he had done for the many Asians who had been expelled from Uganda. Years earlier, as Prime Minister, he had taken the bold decision to honour the British Passports of East African Asians, and allow us the right to enter and settle in the UK.

The journalist agreed to my spontaneous request, and passing me his mike, simultaneously gave his TV crew clear instructions – LIGHT, CAMERA, ACTION! Mr. Heath assumed I was one of the journalists, and responded to a couple of my questions saying how much he appreciated me thanking him on behalf of the Ugandan and East African Asian communities.

But Kensington Palace officials were watching this unfolding scene with great consternation. Concerned that the strong lights could damage the precious ancient paintings in the room, they came running through the crowd of arriving guests as quickly as they could to stop the filming. "This interview is not listed as part of the official program!"

I apologized to the palace officials, and they immediately relaxed as the director had by then instantly reacted and switched off the filming lights.

Edward Heath himself was quite relaxed about my having "ambushed" him – for him, it probably brought back memories of that sort of thing happening all the time when he was Prime Minister!

A year or so later, the interview clip was included in a video which TV producer Crawford Telfer made about me. Crawford had spotted me on a BBC programme, *Kilroy* – which, at that time, was usually broadcast live, late morning once a week, covering controversial issues. Crawford contacted me for "a short interview" which developed into *Coming To Britain,* a 30-minute documentary!

However, even with all the success, I would never forget how hard I needed to push, nor the injustice of some of my rejections. In fact, I'd had such a run of disappointments applying for NHS board positions that I'd decided to waste no more time on them.

Once I'd had a letter from an NHS regional office encouraging me to apply for a role. The letter's tone was highly positive. When the interview came up, we were literally en route to our holiday. I had a car full of luggage and excited children. We took a detour and I asked them to wait for me while I went to discuss the position

– it would probably take an hour. The fact that I'd been invited to apply made it seem worth the sacrifice, but that just meant it was all the harder when the inevitable letter of rejection came.

"Fine," I said glumly, "Then who did get appointed?"

"Oh, the deputy chair got it."

Why, I wondered, did they hassle me so persistently to apply? Still, I accepted that the best man got the job. When it happened a second time: the same organisation, the same sugar-coated letter, and yes, the same outcome, it became clear that I was being used as political correctness fodder. What they didn't understand was that while they ticked their diversity boxes, they were playing with my time and feelings.

Finally, I gave up. This was never going to work. When the next letter came I said, "Sorry, I'm just not interested."

Around that time, I attended a lecture at the RSA. Milling about in the foyer beforehand, the buzz of chatter all around me, I got talking to Elizabeth Vallance. Married to Sir Iain Vallance (then chairman of British Telecom) Elizabeth was an accomplished academic, magistrate and activist in her own right. She could easily have insisted on being addressed as 'Lady' but was far too down to earth and personable for such things.

While we were waiting for the lecture, she mentioned she was the chair of St George's Hospital, and I shared with her the frustrations I'd had with NHS public appointments.

"Really?" she said, "Well I'd love to have you on board. You should apply."

"No, it's fine," I said, shaking my head, "I've had it with them."

She was insistent however, assuring me that this time my application would be taken seriously. So, I gave it one more shot. And this time, with her backing and another good word from Anne Page to Frank Dobson, who was the Secretary of State for Health, things were rather different. It shouldn't be about who you know, but their support certainly helped, and I found myself deciding between two offers: the Royal Marsden in Chelsea, and the Epsom & St Helier. In the end, I chose the latter, being keen to support my local hospital. Later, I was also approved as a member of St George's Medical School board, which had a special relationship with Epsom & St Helier hospital.

Afterwards, I sent her a copy of *Sari 'n' Chips* and received a lovely note back saying, "If only for this book, Ram, you deserve your CBE!"

Finally, I was getting somewhere. As with my freezer lick experience, there had been moments of pain and humiliation, this time however, imposed by the forbidding structures of society. And, as with the freezer lick, I was once again finding I needed the help and wisdom of others.

The struggle was real, but the lessons learned were invaluable. There is power in patience, in taking small steps, and trusting that you will get there at the right time. Those bolted doors were finally unlocked by others who had seen my work, but I still had to push them open. And in return, I have always tried to open doors for others. Particularly, having learnt so much from the wisdom of my elders, I have tried to do the same for the next generation. This is relational networking. This is community.

Chapter Fourteen
Who Is This Man?

What on earth was I doing here?

Winter sun streamed in through the windows of Toynbee Hall's meeting room. I stole a glance along the platform at my competitors. We had been seated in order of our party's importance. On my left sat people like Frank Dobson, Stephen Norris, Glenda Jackson and Ken Livingstone, all big heavyweight names with their heads held high. And then there was me. The fifteenth candidate. The last in line.

In front of us, the oak panelled room was packed with interested spectators, journalists ready with their questions, and photographers homing in on the other, more famous, candidates.

How did I end up at these hustings? It certainly wasn't my idea. Politics was one game I had never intended to play. Yes, my public appointments had begun to bring me into contact with politicians - something I always found interesting – but it wasn't a sphere in which I saw myself working.

My contribution to the Better Regulation Task Force involved advising on policy making and was an amazing experience – like being a minister without being a minister. You had all the influence without being elected. This was how I liked it. I was happy to provide business input, but to be a politician? No thank you. I simply didn't need it.

Being at the heart of government for the Task Force already brought me the kind of opportunities I'd only dreamt of previously: newspaper articles, Radio 4 interviews, television. There were meetings at number 11 Downing Street, the Old Admiralty Building, and the Cabinet Office at 70 Whitehall, not to mention dinner at the banqueting hall.

Then, when Peter Mandelson asked me to serve on the Department of Trade and Industry's National Competitiveness Advisory Committee, I even found myself invited to a breakfast meeting at number 10 Downing Street.

When the day came around, however, it coincided with the start of the Iraq war. Tony Blair had been up most of the night talking with the Americans, so we all wondered if the breakfast would be cancelled. I turned up anyway, which was just as well, because it did go ahead. Walking into a magnificent dining room with about 20 others, I found my place at the table, nodding to my companions – all well-known business leaders. I held back a gasp as I studied my personalised seating plan and realised I would be sipping tea and munching bacon and eggs just a couple of seats away from Tony Blair. It meant that I was able to speak up for small businesses, complaining about how they were treated by the larger companies, many of whom were represented at the breakfast. Later that day, two Permanent Secretaries I knew called me to say they'd seen my name in Dispatches. I'd managed to make my voice heard.

While I placed deep value on all this experience, none of it had ever increased my desire for actual involvement in politics.

However, I was always happy to speak up for what was right. One of the most memorable opportunities to do so was on BBC2's

Newsnight programme with Jeremy Paxman in 1996. A researcher had called me that morning to discuss some new research by an Oxford professor stating that Asians were the new money-makers, taking the Jewish path, while Caribbeans were finding it harder to get ahead. They were heavily pressuring me to comment on both cultures and I realised over the course of discussions that they would have happily put me in a difficult spot, something that became even clearer when the other guest turned out to be a professional West Indian woman. However, when Jeremy asked me to comment on Indians and Pakistanis being the 'new Jews' a thought popped into my mind. I warned him very politely that using such shorthand descriptions, albeit based on research by an Oxford don, risked offending the Pakistani communities in the UK, given that the majority of them are Muslim and may not wish to be referred to as 'the new Jews'.

I have never seen Jeremy Paxman do such a quick U-turn, suddenly becoming very polite and non-aggressive, enabling me to sail through the rest of the interview unchallenged and free from controversy. A senior BBC executive who was involved in the programme happened to have children at my son's school and, a few days later, told me how the control room burst into laughter when they saw Jeremy thrown off track, commenting "Very few people have done this to him!"

But it was after another television interview that I met someone who would set me on a new course. I had been interviewed for a BBC South Asia report and was just leaving White City TV studios when I felt a hand on my shoulder.

"Ram, great interview! I've just seen it." David Campanale caught up with me. "By the way, have you heard about this mayoral race? They're looking for candidates."

"Oh interesting," I smiled at him. "I'll mull it over and send you some ideas."

Later, true to my word, I sent him a list of half a dozen names, a mixture of people who were speaking up against violence and injustice, plus some business leaders. Blair had made it clear he was interested in people like these. Having sent David the list, I felt I had done my bit and thought no more of it, until a couple of weeks later when he called me up.

"Thanks for the suggestions, Ram. Good to have a list of names, but, er… we've been discussing this as a committee and we think you would be an ideal candidate."

I was momentarily speechless. It was flattering to be suggested of course – especially as I knew this was a group of young people, millennials who were concerned about their city, and needed a spokesperson. I shouldn't have been surprised: it was youth-led. Thinking back to Christmas Cracker, I knew how inspiring young people could be. It was always their enthusiasm and optimism that moved me to make changes. It was always young people, with their fresh take on issues, their keen eyes seeing right through inequality and discrimination. Young people who had not yet been ground down by the 'cannots' of this world, instead able to see the genuine needs and the possibility to act on them. Once again, they were showing me my own mandate: Don't let what you cannot do stop you from doing what you can.

But a mayoral race? That was the last thing on my mind. All the careers advice I had ever had back during my Kenyan teens guided me towards worthy professions such as Medicine or Law, possibly business. But not politics. Never politics.

Partly to buy some time and partly to avoid being immediately negative, I told him I would go home and talk to Sunita about it. I was pretty convinced she would agree with me and then I could just go back to David and say, "So sorry, the wife says no."

But she didn't say no. What she said was, "Well, don't we usually pray about these things?"

I sighed. "Okay then." What I was actually thinking was, "You pray your way and I'll pray God says no". So we prayed and we waited. There was no lightning bolt, no immediate certainty either way, but over the following weeks, the more I looked around London, the more I saw injustice. Around the same time, I was at a business board meeting for the Training

Enterprise Council and a consultant we had engaged showed a map of London from 100 years ago, comparing it with a current one. Both maps were colour-coded to show areas of wealth and poverty. There were a hundred years between the two maps, and those colour-coded areas had not changed. To satisfy my disbelief, I delved into the statistics. It was true. Even then, in the year 1999, a baby born in Hackney had six years less life expectancy than a baby born in Westminster.

London is my city. I came here as a refugee and, despite some hard times initially, it has been amazing to me. But this map, these statistics, I couldn't believe this was the same city. What could I do to help change this?

Of course, I hoped I was already making a difference through my many public appointments. I was speaking up for the underprivileged and the disadvantaged. The Better Regulation Task Force, where I served as a small business representative, was chaired by Lord Haskins and was overseen by the Cabinet Office, and through this I was made chairman of the Anti-Discrimination Legislation subgroup, a UK-wide initiative. Labour had just come to power, and I found myself regularly called upon by Downing Street advisors, such as David Milliband, his brother Ed Milliband, Andrew Adonis, and others. Many of the ministers were just cutting their teeth in their new roles. However, because of the number of ministers in charge of different kinds of discrimination, my work was becoming a challenge. Lord Haskins stepped in and said, "Don't worry, we'll talk to Jack Cunningham."

Rumour had it that Jack Cunningham was the one who wore size 12 boots. He was Tony Blair's cabinet enforcer. With him on our side, the task became much more straightforward. He gathered every minister who had anything to do with discrimination under one roof for me, giving me the opportunity to share ideas and consult with them and their advisors all at once on this crucial topic.

I certainly didn't feel compelled to take on another challenge just yet. But, as time went on, it occurred to me that maybe there was something more I could do. Maybe I could make more of a difference to the inequality in my city. The Biblical values upon which the country had been founded were being side-lined and while I, more than anyone, understood we lived in a multi-cultural society, the core principles themselves had served us well and were being undermined for no good reason. Could I stand for such values? To me it was blindingly obvious they were exactly what the city needed.

Perhaps what really qualified me was that my burning desire for truth has always been stronger than my need to stay safely quiet on issues. On seeing discrimination or injustice, I have to speak up. For example, during a meeting at the Old Admiralty Building for the Competitiveness Advisory Panel, I was shocked when the chairman of a successful company commented, "We've got to watch these shady Asian countries and shady Asian businessmen. They behave in ways that are not quite ethical and then we have problems competing."

I looked around the room at the press, political leaders, well known chief executives, waiting for someone to condemn this statement. A large majority of those present had recently signed a public document confirming they would speak up against racism but now there was silence. Eventually, I put my hand up.

"May I please remind the gentleman on my right that he's forgetting what took place in our very own Parliament where we had cash in brown paper bags exchanging hands between MPs so that questions would be asked in Parliament. Is that ethical or unethical? Please let us be careful before we point fingers at these countries and communities."

Again, deadly silence. I moved on, knowing at least that I had spoken up, but a few weeks later I happened to meet a Downing Street transcriber at a Bank of England lunch. Recognising my voice from the meeting's recording he praised me for speaking up, having felt horrified at the racism he'd heard. A couple of weeks after that, I received a call from Robert Peston, wanting to include this story in the Financial

Times. Sadly, it was blocked. It was impossible to get the transcript from Downing Street, which would have served as the necessary evidence. Even though the story never came out, I was always grateful to Robert Peston for the huge effort he made to promote the truth.

I still had no interest in becoming Mayor of London, but I began to feel convinced I could contribute positively to the London Assembly. However, in order to gain one of the 25 seats there, a goal I had assessed as achievable, you had to have profile. You had to have some traction. You had to run for Mayor.

So I joined the Christian Peoples Alliance and was elected leader. We created a manifesto around their six principles of Social Justice, Respect for life, Reconciliation, Active Compassion, Stewardship of Resources and Empowerment. The point was that although these are indeed Christian principles, the genuine life-enhancing goodness they aim to achieve is universally recognised. They are based on giving fair opportunities to all, and on narrowing the rich-poor divide. Although these six principles are solidly biblical, they are also honoured by men and women of goodwill everywhere. In short, you don't have to be a Christian to support Christian principles. For me, having 'Christian' in the party name was not a sign that we were against other faiths, but a guarantee that we ourselves would respect them. In fact, much of my support did not come from Christians at all but from other minority groups.

Even while I was still deciding whether to proceed, we were totting up the costs: £10,000 to register, another £10,000 for your name to appear in the booklet, then money for a team, office, and staff. That's a tall order. It was looking like £100,000 just to wash your face and say, "I'm running."

However, I knew that, with the contest for an Assembly seat calculated on proportional representation, if I even got 4% of the vote, I would have a seat. I looked at the Christian population of London and I looked at all the other contacts backing me and thought, "Why not try?"

The support I received from the Asian community was a huge encouragement. One of Sunita's cousins was quick to get out his chequebook and pay the £10,000 registration fee, then funds began arriving from others to meet the remaining costs. Hindus, Sikhs, Muslims, Jews, and agnostics put their hands in their pockets to support me financially, as well as rallying all their friends and staff to vote for me.

With such incredible backing from people from minority groups, the Christian support looked rather flimsy in comparison. However, there were some who helped me significantly. In particular I met Brian Souter at a Downing Street reception. He was the brother of David Souter, whose bungalow we had rented in Perth. Brian was a great encouragement to me during the mayoral race as well as being a supporter of SAC. Similarly, Sandy Millar at Holy Trinity Brompton gave me invaluable support throughout.

Most churches held back however, perhaps out of concern for reputation. There was a risk that the whole church would be tarnished if things went wrong. Of course, they were right to worry on one level. The media were immediately out to get me, looking for skeletons in the closet. My response was, "Well, do let me know if you find any. I'd be really interested." They called the house and hassled my son who has the same initials as me, but all to no avail. For them, I was disappointingly scandal-free, hopelessly squeaky clean.

Sadly, it wasn't just the church which held back its support. The BBC refused to give us a political broadcast. I went to plead with the director herself asking "Where's democracy? We've paid our £10,000 but we're not getting an equal say". It's impossible to visit every home in London, but these other parties would appear in everyone's living room on TV. However, she would not budge. I left the meeting in tears. What chance did I have?

The Times however, found me a little more appealing. Breaking the embargo on the press release, they jumped in with the headline "Former refugee throws his hat in the ring."

That did the job! Refugees began to believe this was their city too, and when it came to that first hustings at Toynbee Hall, it seemed that half the immigrant population of London had turned out for it.

I looked down the row of accomplished political faces once more, reminding myself exactly why I was among them. As the meeting got under way, the speaker turned to the line of candidates and asked us,

"What would you do for London?"

Three minutes. That's how long each of us had to put forward our case. As I listened to the slick long-timers talking suavely about transport, housing, and crime I began to panic. At the end of each three minutes spiel, the house filled with applause. If there had been a clapometer, they'd have been up there with six, seven or eight out of ten. I breathed deeply. What should I say? I thought about what Jesus would do. Why are you running? I asked myself. You came as a refugee, you know the refugee world well. You've got to speak up for the disadvantaged.

So I did. I spoke for three minutes and said, "If I'm elected, I will work for the homeless, the jobless, and the carless."

The place erupted in cheers and applause, the Richter scale going up to 12, 13, 14 out of ten. The other candidates stared in astonishment as if seeing me for the first time and wondering, "Who is this man? Who is this upstart who's just made the place explode?"

I went home, feeling a lot better. Just as we were about to go to bed, BBC Radio London news came on.

"Let's have a quick listen," I said to Sunita.

The interviewer was talking to the favourite candidate about his manifesto.

"What do you see as the three biggest issues for London?"

"Well," he began confidently, "I would say the homeless, the jobless, and the carless."

We looked at each other and burst into surprised laughter. "How wonderful," I thought. "If, in one meeting, I have switched the agenda of the London election so that everyone's focussing on the homeless, jobless, and carless, then my work here is done. I don't have to be Mayor of London. They can do it for me."

Another electoral event was held at the Royal Geographical Society, chaired by the journalist Simon Jenkins. A number of people had tipped him off about me, and he was confident he could call on me to comment.

A question came up about English Heritage. What would we candidates do about it as an institution? I raised my hand and said, "Look, I love English Heritage, but now I speak as a former refugee, and when I visit a place like the Ismaili Cultural Centre in South Kensington – an outstanding site of architectural beauty - I wonder, can that mosque genuinely be classified under 'English' Heritage? If I were mayor of London, I would create an institution called 'London Heritage' and I would suggest similar formulae for other cities where there are places that we can all share as our heritage with a common identity."

At the time, Dame Rennie Fritchie (now Baroness Fritchie) was the Chief of the Independent Public Appointments Office. She made a point of commenting to me, "Ram, I loved your intervention at the debate, I thought it was very good." Simon Jenkins also quoted it in his piece in *The Evening Standard*, adding "The Conservatives should beg Gidoomal to join them!"

So, although I struggled to get backing from some people, others exceeded all my expectations. For example, Lady Susie Sainsbury and Viscountess Gill Brentford wrote a joint letter to *The Telegraph* publicly affirming and recommending me. This was in addition to one that Prue Leith had written to *The Evening Standard*. Once again, I felt the tremendous power of female support and was moved that they would make such efforts for me.

Meanwhile, another tremendous boost was coming. *The New Statesman* ran a blind web-poll called Fantasymayor.com. They put up six manifestos: Labour, Conservative, Liberal

Democrats, Greens, Ken Livingstone (running independently), and mine. When people were initially asked to vote by their party preference, I didn't do very well. Around 56% said Ken Livingstone. A mere 3.5% went for me.

Next however, voters had to answer 15 policy questions asking what they wanted from their mayor on a range of issues. This time they voted 'blind', purely on the policies, without knowing whose they were. The website then matched their aspirations with the policies of the candidates. The results were incredible. I came out top and beat Ken Livingstone by a substantial majority,

The voters were no doubt surprised to see who they had voted for. Many would not have wanted to be associated with the word 'Christian'. But these were not 'Christian values' in some impersonal, abstract sense. These were 'people values' because Jesus came to live among people and to help them. As the art historian Hans Rookmaaker said, "Christ did not come to make us truly Christian but to make us truly human."

Unsurprisingly, the Fantasy Mayor story caused quite a stir and was even picked up by Time magazine in the States. Every national paper here also admitted, "If this election were on policies alone, Gidoomal would win by a landslide."

But alas, elections are not won simply on policies but on personalities and profile. I knew that. Still, it was a huge affirmation to find I was so in tune with the people of London. The fact that my policies were the most closely matched to the aspiration of Londoners was a profound statement. More importantly, it spoke volumes about what people really wanted. Everything in my manifesto had Biblical values at its roots. For me, the only obvious conclusion to draw was that people wanted and needed such Biblical values, but just didn't know it.

When the actual election came around on 4th May, of course I didn't win. It had never been my main goal or expectation. Unsurprisingly, Ken Livingstone stole that particular show. I did, however, save my deposit, because even with no track record and very little media coverage, we managed to gain nearly 100,000 first and second preference votes, coming fourth out of the political parties. Much as I love the Green party, I was incredulous and rather proud to learn that I had come out higher than them, despite their 25-year-headstart in history.

Although I thought that my 4% of the vote was fairly meagre, I was surprised by the number of people who got in touch to congratulate me, assuring me that in politics, that was quite an achievement. Suddenly I realised everyone was talking about me, in the House of Commons, the House of Lords… everywhere was the murmur of "Who is this man?"

Even if my result was no landslide, I had theoretically secured enough votes to win the 25th seat, under the D'Hondt Rule. However, there was a further twist. Just before the vote, the Minister for London had come to see a group of London leaders and pointed out that the BNP might also win a seat under the current rules. He suggested that the threshold for any seat qualification should be 5% and we all agreed. The day after the election we held a service to celebrate the result and that was when our election expert called me to say "You do realise, that 25th seat was technically yours?". *The Evening Standard* also picked up on this, with the headline "Seatless Victory", recognising the huge ground we had covered. It did indeed feel like a win. Besides this, I was repeatedly told by a number of people, including politicians from the main parties, that the fact that I ran and gained that share of the votes had been a significant factor in preventing the BNP from gaining an assembly seat during that first election.

Four years later, I ran again. If I'm entirely honest, it was less my own desire and more out of a sense of duty to my donors and supporters. Sunita's cousin once again promised to pay the registration fee, urging me not to back down. There was a general sense that I was on a roll and would be letting the side down if I didn't try again.

As a businessman I knew that once you've had your first drive you're a known commodity. Therefore, whereas I was completely ignored by the mainstream the first time around, this time they took me seriously. I even had the party political broadcast I'd so badly wanted. On paper, things should have been much easier. The problem was that by then, groups like the BNP had begun to target me, trashing my photos and posters, and adding the slogan 'Don't trust this refugee!'

In one hustings in Bromley, Kent, I had the privilege of taking the main platform but unfortunately a BNP fundamentalist in the crowd became aggressive and started shouting that it wasn't a free election, that he needed his chance to speak. I held up some BNP materials featuring someone like me in a hangman's noose.

"Well," I said, "If this is what you plan to do with people like me, it's only right that you're denied the platform. Remove such inciteful content from your publicity and I'm sure you will be given a voice."

Although most people refuse to engage with such venomous propaganda, there will always be a proportion who are swayed. But it wasn't only that. I just never quite got the momentum up the second time around. So, while I kept my support in the constituencies where I'd been strong previously and did manage to save my deposit, other parties overtook me elsewhere. I did my best but, right from the start, the competition was tougher. I knew I'd hit my limit and it was time to step down.

Meanwhile, I was gradually losing my enthusiasm for the CPA. Certain policies didn't sit well with me. Their negative stance on same-sex marriage bothered me both on a policy and a personal level. Firstly, I felt we needed to comply with the law of the land; I didn't want to make statements or take actions that were inconsistent with the country's legislative framework. Also on a personal level, I had no peace about their anti-LGBTQ+ views, because of the many people I knew and respected from that community.

Taking a wider view, a new group of people had joined the party and were beginning to theologise the policies. They seemed to be forgetting this was a political party and not a church. This was a political party which, while based on Biblical values, was open to everyone. Furthermore, the main funding base was not actually from Christian sources, it was simply from people who valued our principles of care for others.

When I wrote my book *How Would Jesus Vote?* with David Porter in 2001, I made the following point: "If in your local constituency, a Muslim has the policies that fit your aspirations the best then I would say vote for the Muslim." Christians are sometimes shocked by this, but we cannot just vote for a Christian candidate simply because the label is right. The policy and content must be genuinely in line with what we believe to be best for our community. In the political sphere we can work together with others for the common good, respecting other people's freedom either to practice their own religion or to be atheist.

The same point was made in a rather more comical way during the book's launch, when Nicky Campbell interviewed me on BBC Radio 5 Live. Someone called in and said,

"So Mr Gidoomal, this book is about how Jesus would vote?"

"Yes…"

"Well, didn't Jesus walk on the water? So that makes him a 'floating voter' doesn't it?"

"Exactly!" I laughed.

That was the point of the book. Be floating voters. Don't let your vote be taken for granted by any party. Check them out, scrutinise them. See what difference they will make on a national level. Then cast your precious vote.

Another caller commented that my six principles would not come cheap.

"True." I replied. "But what is the cost of not doing them?"

To take one example, I wanted to improve access to work for those with disabilities. The cost of those people not being able to work was much greater, both for them personally and for the wider community, than the cost of enabling them.

I appreciated this chance to have a voice. Of course, there would always be some people who wanted to look for the negatives. The day after the first election, the media were quick to contact me.

"So Mr Gidoomal, you didn't win."

"Yes," I agreed, "And 11 others didn't either."

I didn't win, yet I knew that I had managed to get my points and ideas across. I didn't win, but I knew I had pushed some worthy issues higher up the political agenda. I didn't win, but the idea in my manifesto for creating a Boost Bond for East London (inspired by Michael Schluter who first set up such a bond in Sheffield) became a reality and has now issued £1 billion of bonds for social impact across the UK. I didn't win, but I didn't need to. Good things still came out of the time, energy and money that had been invested.

As before, when I had had the impact of a minister without actually being a minister, I realised that sometimes the secret of changing the world is to have influence without power. It's the art of letting other people have your way.

Ram Gidoomal CBE
Chairman of the City and East London Employment Bond

requests the pleasure of the company of

....

for breakfast hosted by
the Rt Hon Paul Boateng, MP, Financial Secretary to the Treasury

*at 11 Downing Street at 7.30 for 8.00 am to finish 9.30 am
on Thursday 6th December 2001*

to preview the City and East London Employment Bond

RSVP
Citylife Ltd
Jubilee House
3 Hooper Street
Cambridge CB1 2NZ

*No admittance without this invitation card
and appropriate identification.
This card is non transferable.*

Tel: 01223 566333
Fax: 01223 566359
Email: citylife@r.f.clara.net

Was I the first person of Asian origin to organise
a breakfast meeting at 11 Downing Street?

Chapter Fifteen
All in a Day's Work

"Ram, I've had a very strange question from my boss in Michigan."

Ricky Shankar had come into our charity offices the previous day to follow up on some of my business contacts for Syntel, where he was the UK CEO. I'd met him about a week earlier at a Sunday service where South Asian Concern was presenting its work.

As we got talking that first day, he'd explained how his company needed to make local connections in order to recruit staff here, specifically software engineers. Contacts was something I never lacked, so I'd invited him over to discuss it. Between business, we got chatting about our families, leading to this rather unusual phone call the following day:

"So, my boss says, how are Bharat and Lachman?"

"Oh yes, very funny." I laughed. It wasn't the first time I'd heard my family likened to the Diwali story of three brothers: Ram, Bharat and Lachman. In our family of course the birth order is different, with Lachman the eldest, Bharat second and I last, but the names themselves are the same.

"No, no seriously. He said you'd think it was a joke, but it's not. He's genuinely asking after your family. He used to play with your cousin at school."

"Hold on. What did you say his name was again?"

"Bharat Desai."

"Bharat Desai?" My mind whizzed back over 30 years and I pictured my younger cousin's friend, who I'd lost track of, since his family uprooted from Mombasa to India. "Yes, of course I remember!"

It was unbelievable to learn that this boy I used to hang out with in the playground had become a giant of the business world, running Syntel, a software company that his wife and he bootstrapped from a standing start into a multi-million dollar NASDAQ listed company. I was delighted that this chance encounter had put us back in touch and, sometime later, I was finally able to meet up with Bharat himself. It was 2nd May 1997, the day after Tony Blair's historic landslide election victory. Bharat had flown down to interview some software engineers for Syntel and we met at the Royal Lancaster Hotel. It was the first time we'd seen each other since he had left the junior Aga Khan School in Mombasa, so we had a lot to catch up on.

In addition to a fair amount of reminiscing, we talked business, and he appointed me to his European board – where, for eight years, I would support him in setting up UK operations and helping develop the business here.

To be on a NASDAQ board was very prestigious and looked wonderful on my CV. However, it was when his wife Neerja came to London with him the following year that I gained a deeper understanding as to why he had done it. As we mingled at a fundraising dinner at the Grosvenor Hotel, she turned to me with a huge smile.

"Ram, you have no idea how excited my husband was to meet you again. He told me all about how generous you were, always splitting your tuck money!"

"Tuck money?" I frowned, delving into my memories, "Oh my goodness! I had completely forgotten that!"

Suddenly I was back in that school quadrangle in Mombasa, the classrooms on one side, the toilets and tuck shop on the other. In the queue, my cousin Dogo Lachu, Bharat and I would ponder the all-important decision of what to buy with our pooled resources – rose syrup milkshakes, jammy dodger style biscuits, chewy fruit sweets, or maybe a bag of crisps to share. Democracy ruled with everyone having their say, then finally we would wander around the playground, looking for a suitable palm tree to shade us while we enjoyed our treats.

I chuckled at the happy memories of those school days. I might have forgotten, but Bharat never had. He had never forgotten, and he'd told his family. For me, it was simply a good deed from childhood, a logical action. In my mind, it was unfair that he had less than me. I had the power to redress the balance, so I did. It seemed so insignificant I would never have guessed it could come back to bless me all these years later. Sharing that little bit of tuck money, a few shillings here and there, really felt like nothing. Now I had been repaid a hundredfold with a high-status position on his board.

This was not a favour for a friend, however, but a business decision based on his memory of me as a person of integrity. He remembered my instinct for fairness and generosity, and therefore knew he could trust me. It is impossible to guess the impact of our actions, what they mean to others and how they might return to us later. I had no idea how much Bharat had appreciated that small kindness of our school days.

Of course, this was all back in the mid to late Nineties, when I was enjoying a kind of snowball effect with appointments, constantly gathering momentum as one contact led to another. Admittedly, things became a little harder again after the two mayoral races.

One time, I applied for a role with a major national public board, was shortlisted and, after the final interview, received a call from the then Permanent Secretary. He informed me I was the independent interview panel's choice and all that was needed was to run it by Downing Street and the Minister.

"I can't foresee any problem Ram, but I'll let you know in a couple of days."

He finally called me that Friday with the news that No 10 had okayed my appointment but the Minister had blocked it, saying, "Ram is politically dangerous!". The fact that I had run for London Mayor and Assembly on behalf of an independent party, which at the time had less than 100 fully paid-up members apparently made me a threat. Of course, I was disappointed about the position but took his comment as a great compliment. To have scared a senior Cabinet minister into thinking I was politically dangerous was quite an achievement.

However, as time went on, the influence of such ministers became clear. A number of times I was appointed for new boards and committees, going through all the correct channels, only to be blocked at the eleventh hour by a government minister. It seemed not just unfair but wrong that my 'dangerous' reputation and the whims of ministers could undo an officially appointed position. It was quite sad to think that ministers behaved in this autocratic manner, overriding independently appointed interview panels. Unfortunately, it reinforced my view that the Independent Public Appointments Commission was really a farce and lacked any teeth.

I began to realise it would not be easy for me to get any more public appointments or even to be reappointed for the ones I had. For three years I had served on the board of English Partnerships (now known as Homes England) – a very prestigious appointment as they were charged with looking after all the land in England, making decisions on new towns and developments. The board members were all land people, and it was big business, billion-pound business, including projects such as the Millennium Dome. In their hands lay the power to decide, for example, where the flyover paths would be, which in turn would impact which petrol station got more customers, and which superstore would be built. The knock-on effects of their decisions were immense.

I'd applied for a role with them and after an agonising nine month wait, was finally called to interview. Funnily enough, they noticed my qualification from Imperial was BSc Hons ARCS. This simply means that I, like anyone who studies Science at Imperial, was automatically made an Associate of the Royal College of Science. The interviewers, however, had interpreted it as some kind of certified surveyor qualification, so may have been a little disappointed to learn the truth!

What probably did make the difference was not those misunderstood initials, but having Genie Turton for my reference. She was a very senior civil servant at the time and oversaw all their work. I had met her through my involvement in the committee for the Government Office for London, and she recognised my desire to do good for others. Again, here was a woman with clout standing up for me. With Genie supporting my application, they took me seriously and I was offered a position on the board and invited to serve on their audit committee.

Having enjoyed my time with them, I was delighted when the chair assured me I would be reappointed after the 2004 mayoral election. But again, I found myself blocked. The excuse used was that my experience was superfluous as there were more business people than were needed. And then they promptly went on to appoint another business person who was a loyal party supporter.

Despite these new hurdles being set on my path by the negative whispers circulating in Parliament, I kept doing whatever I could to push forward and use my skills for the greater good.

In 2005 I saw an advert in the Sunday Times for a vacancy for the Home Office Complaints Audit Committee and decided to apply. The interview committee was chaired by a secondee from the Bank of England and, this time, there was no ministerial input in the appointment. For once, there was nothing stopping me. I got the role.

During my three years serving on the CAC, among other things, I conducted a forensic analysis of their data. In 2008, my final year with them, I discovered there were hundreds of missing files without any trace or audit trail showing who the complaints referred to.

Sensing the need to dig deeper, I carried out further analysis and interviewed Border Agency officials. It became clear that several hundred of these files had been shredded without any explanation. Our report was filed with Parliament, but the press release did not get any air time with the news channels or media.

Later however, the BBC Home Affairs editor, Mark Easton, was looking for reports filed with government that might have been 'buried' to avoid negative press, and happened upon our Annual Report, submitted the previous week. He called me immediately, finding me at the CAC office in Croydon.

"This is a really impressive report Mr Gidoomal," he said "Such a thorough analysis. I'm quite surprised no reporters picked up on this."

"Well, reporting of these matters is in the hands of journalists and the media, isn't it," I ventured. "If you really think it's important, it's up to you whether it makes it onto the BBC."

I left it at that. Within half an hour, he'd called back to tell me a car was on its way to pick me up. I found myself making the familiar journey from Croydon to the BBC studios at White City, where I was interviewed for the *Ten o'clock News*. A while later, a close friend who worked as a BBC journalist called to let me know my interview would be the third story after the lead that evening. I thanked him and headed to a business dinner in Mayfair, but at around 8pm he called again to say it had been moved up the agenda. It would now be the second story.

Half an hour later he called again.

"Believe it or not Ram, your interview is going to be leading the *Ten o'clock News!*"

I was completely speechless and very excited. I made my excuses and rushed home, arriving just in time to see the live broadcast. The inevitable followed, with the Radio 4 *Today* programme inviting me to appear live at 6 am the following morning. An extract of that interview then led the news headlines every half hour. Radio 5 Live was next and there followed interviews for BBC local radio stations, while newspapers picked up the story too. The issue was rightly gaining profile across the nation. However, neither the Minister nor the Permanent Secretary were willing to be interviewed, a fact that was broadcast alongside the interview with me.

The heart of the news item was of course the shredded files that I had found out about. It highlighted the lack of accountability towards refugees and asylum seekers in the UK. As I repeated in my interviews, "Because refugees and asylum seekers do not have a vote why should MPs care?"

I referred to an undercover *Panorama* broadcast which highlighted the degrading and inhumane treatment received by refugees and asylum seekers in our detention centres. As someone who had been a refugee myself, it terrified me to learn of the ordeals these people faced. However, I was even more appalled when some of the Border Agency officials informed me that they had received sacks full of mail following that *Panorama* broadcast, not shaming them for the hideous way they treated refugees and asylum seekers but actually commending and praising them for it. How tragically sad that we as a nation are prepared to not only tolerate but compliment such behaviour.

Refugees and asylum seekers have no right to vote, of course, but it is often impossible for them even to find work. After my mayoral hustings at Toynbee Hall where I gave my 'Homeless, Jobless, Carless' speech, the CEO of the Employability Forum, Patrick Wintour, came to find me.

"Mr Gidoomal, loved what you said! And I'd love you to speak at an event I'm organising."

It was a kind of employment fair for refugees and I was tasked with leading a seminar to encourage them. At the end, Patrick invited me to meet his chairman, Patrick Pery, the 6th Earl of Limerick who was also chairman of Pirelli. He was a remarkable man, humble despite his high status and passionate about refugees having the right to work. As a result of this meeting, I was appointed to the board and then, a year before he died in 2003, Patrick Pery sent a handwritten letter to Patrick Wintour, recommending I be appointed Chairman of the Employability Forum since he needed to step down.

The events we organised as the Employability Forum brought together a number of high-powered bodies: the Trade Union Congress, the Confederation of Business Industry, the Commission for Racial Equality, and the media, along with the government ministers for immigration and employment. All of these then signed a concordat, committing to speak positively about the contribution refugees make to the UK economy.

Eventually this led to us developing a refugee employment strategy document titled: *Working to Rebuild Lives*. Our argument was that whenever a refugee was granted the Indefinite Right to Remain in the country, they then had to wait ages to get a National Insurance number, meaning they couldn't work and were forced to claim benefits. Along with the Minister of State for Work and the Minister of State for Citizenship, Immigration and Nationality, I was a co-signatory on that document, so my name featured on the front page. We campaigned for refugees to get their NI number simultaneously with the Right to Remain. When that was granted, it transformed the experience of immigrants here in the UK.

Sometime after that, Lloyds Bank invited me to speak to a group of a dozen refugees to inspire them to either seek jobs or start a business. All of them had permission to stay and a National Insurance number. I chatted to them about where they came from, their families back home and the languages they spoke. Then in my speech to them, I said, "Here are the strengths and advantages you have over the majority of the population in the UK:

- You speak languages that very very few people in the UK speak.
- You have contacts and connections in your countries of origin that many exporters and importers in this country would die for.
- You have knowledge of those local markets and market intelligence for products."

Their jaws dropped. No one had ever articulated their strengths and assets in this way before and they left the meeting encouraged and armed with information.

Over the years I sat on countless other boards, held trusteeships for charities, and served as a school governor. I recognised one of my inbuilt gifts was to speak up when others felt unable to do so. When one of the schools I helped govern was trying to decide whether to move from boys-only to co-educational, but feared losing their Muslim students because 'they prefer their boys to be educated without girls around', I was quick to mention that, as far back as the 1950s, I had attended a co-educational Muslim school. With that settled, the decision was made to open the gates to girls. But with one caveat.

"Umm, can we just keep this quiet for a while folks? We need to work out how much all the practical changes will cost – toilets, changing rooms, showers, that kind of thing. No need to mention it until that's all clear."

I felt I had to speak again. "In the meantime, we're collecting fees from parents who believe they're sending their children to a boys' school. They'll pay their non-refundable registration fee and we will knowingly accept it, but they'll find out about the change only subsequently. Is that ethical?" I knew I was in the company of top civil servants of the highest strata of society and, even with my desire to speak up, I always felt a little hesitant. On this occasion, the Bishop of Southwark – a fellow governor at this Church of England affiliated school, was absent. I was thus able to allude to his presence in spirit. "Colleagues, if the bishop were here, I wonder how he would react?"

Admittedly there was a bit of a rumble but then the chairman spoke, "Actually, Gidoomal makes a very good point." The original decision was revoked until we had all the facts in place. Agreement was unanimous. Afterwards, various people took me aside to thank me for voicing what they too had felt uncomfortable about.

Speaking up takes courage, and though I may do it confidently, there is always some trepidation. The support of others makes a huge difference, especially when you need to act with integrity at higher levels of society or government. It was in recognition of this that The Trinity Forum was first formed. President Jimmy Carter's former Chief of Staff, Alonzo McDonald, had seen first-hand the need to encourage leaders, understanding how lonely life can be at the top. He happened to meet author and social critic, Os Guinness, and together they set up the Forum in 1991 as a mechanism to support leaders in business and politics, helping them live with integrity and balance. Trinity Forum is known as a Christ-centred academy without walls, open for people of all faiths to come together and gain a shared understanding of the issues of the day. Sunita and I had the privilege of attending a Trinity Forum in Bangalore many years ago. This was an amazing event in its own merit and was further enhanced when Prabhu Guptara arranged for us to stay with the prestigious Kejriwal family. Prolific collectors of Indian artefacts, they accommodated us in an extraordinary room surrounded by historic pieces relating to Gandhi – even original letters signed by Mohandas Gandhi himself. It was at this Forum that we met Mak and Ursula Dehejia, leading not only to a deep and lasting friendship but also to Mak inviting me to be the Dehejia Fellow for 2008, in which capacity I gave a public lecture at the Sidwell Friends School in Washington DC.

Each board I sat on, each appointment, had its own flavour, its own interest. While I loved every new challenge in its own way, there were of course a couple that stood out.

Sunita's cousin Bina, was always a good friend to us and gave her support to our many charitable endeavours. Her youngest brother Sonu happened to own the Six Senses luxury hotel chain. I say 'luxury' but this does not even begin to describe it. These are 6* hotels, in the most exquisite locations, aimed at the world's elite. For a couple of years, I served on the Six Senses board for Sonu, helping to introduce new investors and to develop the global brand and, as part of my 'duties', I had the arduous task of trying out some of the hotels. Like Bina, Sonu and his wife Eva were always hugely supportive of our work. They just got it. For example, during Christmas Cracker days, they often came forward with interest-free loans. They never forgot us, despite the vast amounts of money they were making by then.

Another appointment that was particularly meaningful to me fell into my lap without my realising the significance of it. I had gone from being an RSA member to a trustee, serving on the board with Prue Leith. Prue was also on the Royal Mail Stamp Advisory Committee, but felt it was time to step down. As we talked, my fascination with the subject must have shone through.

"Would you be interested in this, Ram?" she asked.

"Would I be interested? I'd absolutely love it."

Before I knew it the Department of Trade and Industry had called me for interview. They could see my genuine interest and were looking for diversity on the board. I was an obvious choice and was delighted when they asked me to join them.

Every stamp that is ever issued in Great Britain has to have the Queen's approval, but it also goes through this committee. It was exciting to be presented with various possible designs knowing that our opinions would influence which ones ended up being popped on the corners of envelopes up and down the country.

The stamps are planned three years in advance, and obviously we had to consider any commemorations and important events which would need to be featured. We gave our opinions but ultimately the Queen had the last word. Every single stamp with her imprimatur goes to her for final approval.

Interestingly, there was one time when stamps were being planned featuring the Queen and the Duke together. The images had been chosen and were ready to send on to the Queen, but I wasn't happy.

"You know, I just think these pictures aren't 'family' enough."

I knew I was outnumbered – everyone else was unanimous in their positivity – but, still, I needed to voice my disappointment. I just didn't really like them. Meanwhile, another image had been suggested that had more of a family atmosphere to it. I was sure this was better and tried to get them to consider it.

Again, everyone disagreed with me, and the images approved by the majority were sent on to the Palace for the Queen's input. When we heard back, I had to bite my tongue and refrain from saying "I told you so" – it turned out that the Queen was of the same opinion as me!

I served on the Stamps Advisory Committee from 2002 to 2010. Of course, this was an incredible experience on its own, but for me it had a deeper significance. All those years ago when my uncle introduced me to stamp collecting, it was a connection with the father I had never known. All those break-times trading stamps at school and Saturday afternoons poring over the albums, meticulously arranging and annotating them – it was all a link with something my father had loved too. Stamp collecting was a passion of mine but, when we left Kenya, I did not get to bring the albums with me, even though they had been my father's. They were left in someone else's safe keeping and never made their way back to me.

Through this committee, in some way, all the hard work I had put into my childhood stamp albums came full circle. That love of stamps was returned to me as I rekindled my enthusiasm for philately and enjoyed that connection once more. It was almost as if my father's lost stamp albums were being returned to me.

Things like this never cease to amaze me, how the seeds sown in younger days can bring a harvest many years later. For me, it has happened time and again. At a formal dinner for the Health Foundation, I was chatting with Elizabeth Vallance's husband, Sir Iain Vallance. He began to tell me how he had recently invested in a small local business in a Kent village, funnily enough with the name of Sutton Valence.

"It's a Post Office," he said.

"Ah, well," I smiled, "I know a thing or two about small shops,"

I went on to tell him about the corner shop where I'd begun my life in London, sharing all the tricks of the trade with him.

"Well, you know what Ram? I'd love you to join that board, because frankly you can look after my investment there far better than I can."

Another door had opened and, once again, I remembered that no matter how humble our experience, it can always lead to something more. We can never know how much our small actions and hard work are preparing us for the future. A schoolboy's good deed led to a place on a prestigious board. A childhood hobby paved the way for a fascinating opportunity helping select stamps for the nation. And now, my family's lowly beginnings, building up a little corner shop in Shepherd's Bush, were being recognised as hugely valuable. When we came to London, everything was a struggle. There was nothing exciting or glamorous about our business, selling sweets and newspapers. But by persevering, working hard, and never despising the humility of the experience, I found I was able to overcome what had previously appeared to me to be insurmountable barriers – time and again.

Chapter Sixteen
Songs of the Kingdom

The heady scent of perfume. That's what I remember. The air thick with fragrances mingling together and my tiny five-year-old hand clutching my mother's as we crept up the sloping walkway, our feet padding over the floor's geometric patterns. The Arab women wore full bui buis but Mummy was dressed in her white sari, the widow's uniform she wore for the rest of her days.

The owner of the Naaz, our local Indian cinema, was a close friend of the family and it always felt like a treat to sneak in for free with my mother on 'Zenana' showings – i.e., ladies' afternoons. Each of us found our seats and settled down with the bag of *bhajias* or *pakoras* we'd bought from the stall outside to nibble on during the performance.

Finally, the old ruffled curtain lifted, and a long ray of light cut through the darkness, projecting images onto the huge screen. The lively chatter of an auditorium full of women hushed in anticipation, and I let the magic of the moment carry me away.

These were the good days. As I became caught up in plots I barely understood, the soundtrack and dialogue floated over me, the Hindi words both foreign and familiar to my Sindhi ears.

Some years later I joined the family's Sunday evening outings, cramming as many as we could into the car to get to the drive-in cinema. Gazing up at the wide open-air screens we would see a mixture of local and international films, prefixed by the inevitable British newsreel and National Anthem (for which we all had to stand, or face arrest!). Paying 10 shillings a carload was a good motivation to squeeze up. With our estate car, I think the record was 12 in one sitting!

However, while cinema was high on our list of favourites, nothing topped our love of music. Whenever an Indian boat docked in Mombasa port, word would get around. Daddy and Dada Roopa always managed to find some connection, perhaps with the captain or the ship's doctor. They would stop by Daddy's shop to let him know of any musicians on board, whom he then gathered together to perform an impromptu concert before their boat moved on again, either at our home or at Dada Roopa's beautiful mansion in the affluent suburb of Tudor. Friends, family, and neighbours would crowd into our living room, sometimes applauding and singing along to golden oldies and well-known tunes, sometimes silenced, awestruck by the music. We children would stay up late, beaming with joy as the soundtracks of our homelands filled the night. This was where I fell in love with Indian music. We listened to classical ragas and songs from films, even before the term 'Bollywood' had been invented. So deep did the melodies embed themselves in my subconscious that even 50 years on I only have to hear the opening few notes of a song for the words, musical arrangements and memories, to come flooding back. When you're a refugee, such things are precious. Much is forgotten during those in-between days when all you can think of is survival. To hear those ragas again is a sweet breath of childhood air.

Perhaps it was that mixture of foreignness and familiarity that inspired my nine-year-old son Ricki's voice, nearly 40 years later, at an Asian fellowship service in Streatham. As I sang along to songs in Hindi and Urdu, languages Ricki had never needed to learn, I noticed him trying to join in, confidently repeating the word "now" at the end of the line, finding English words that fit with the flow of the music.

What we were actually singing was:

Khushi khushi manao
Khushi khushi manao
Bolo bolo masiha ki jai jai jai
Bolo bolo masiha ki jai jai jai

I realised that he was picking out that final syllable of 'manao' which sounded like 'now'. I explained that the song could be roughly translated as:

Come and celebrate now
Come and celebrate now
Sing your praises to Jesus with joy joy joy
Sing your praises to Jesus with joy joy joy

Happy to be able to add a few more words, Ricki began singing along in English to my Hindi. I was immediately struck, even amazed, that we could sing it together. The same timing. The same speed. The same rhythm.

We sang our quirky duet the whole way home and, by the time we pulled up outside our house, I'd had an idea. Even though it was a Sunday evening, I was too excited to wait. I called our friend June George. June was a musician who had done some work at South Asian Concern. I had a feeling she would understand.

"June, something incredible just happened! I was singing *'Khushi khushi'* in Hindi, and Ricki was able to join in in English!"

June immediately understood why this meant so much to me. It was the perfect way to marry up my following Jesus with my love of Indian culture. With his spontaneous singing, Ricki had unknowingly sparked a new kind of fusion music into life.

"What if we could do this with other songs too?" I suggested.

We agreed to speak again the following day. After hanging up, I thought about it more and decided that songs in E minor might work best. This was where my effort to learn guitar for my children back during our Geneva days paid off. I had learnt the basic chords and the one I found easiest and loved the most was always E minor. I knew a lot of Jewish music used this too and that was enough to get me flicking through the music edition of *Songs of Fellowship* where I chose a couple of well-known songs in that key. As they were songs that were popular in our churches at the time, I knew the music would be familiar to people. I worked into the night, translating the words and then making a basic recording on cassette ready to give to June in the morning.

June was as excited as I was. It was beginning to look like this might really work. We sat together and made a list of songs which could work on an album, then I called Jacob Ambrose, a singer I'd heard at Streatham Baptist Church. I shared my ideas about fusion music and the potential to sing simultaneously across cultures with ease. Jacob immediately caught the vision and agreed to come on board. Every week, Jacob and his wife, Rose, drove to our home in Sutton from Slough with their family, their daughter-in-law Katherine managing to swap her shifts in order to join in. The involvement of his family was an example of the sacrificial input of so many people in the projects which I initiated, led, or assisted: the Ambrose family did not accept compensation even for their car expenses, and actually took time out of paid work!

Similarly, had it not been for the hard work of June George, I don't know how we would have managed. With June leading the project, we were in good hands also from a technical point of view. Every Saturday afternoon, she took us through singing lessons to ensure we were all in good voice.

Finally, after several months of practice, we felt ready. We had agreed which songs we wanted to record, and I had managed to negotiate a studio within our limited budget. It was the ICC studio in Eastbourne and, for £2000, we had three weeks of their time, recording and mixing from 9–5 every day. The studio had promised a sound engineer, but on arriving that first morning they greeted us with some news.

"We're so sorry. Mr Pont's sick. We've found someone else to cover for him though – Martin Smith."

"Martin Smith? That's absolutely fine!"

For us, it was more than fine. It was a huge bonus to have Martin Smith – subsequently of *Delirious?* fame – producing our album, not just for his wide recognition or musical expertise, but because we knew Martin and his family of old. His father Eddie was a fellow elder at Chiltern Church, where Martin had once belonged to our house group. It was his first time taking the lead in producing an album, but we trusted him completely.

Every morning that week we set off as the sun was rising in order to get from London to Eastbourne by 9, not wishing to waste a precious minute of studio time. Our budget would not stretch to extending the rental. However, on the first day there was already a challenge and a delay. Before we could even begin, one of the studio managers raised their concern about the instruments we were using. They had never had a sitar or tabla in their studios before and were worried about the implications of using such instruments in a Christian setting. We mulled this over and decided that we would start with prayer and a short ceremony to dedicate and bless the space and the instruments before we began. This reassured them and, after a short time of Bible reading and prayer-walking around the studio and musical instruments, it was full steam ahead.

The first few notes were strummed on the sitar. The tabla added its beat, and we raised our voices to complete the joyful sound. The *Songs of the Kingdom* recording had begun.

As the week progressed, we sang those songs over and again, recording and rerecording until we had it just right. Sometime afterwards, I learnt that Martin and June stayed late – until 11 or 12 every night - going the extra mile to give their absolute best for the production of the album. Martin seemed to genuinely love the novelty of the project. And he wasn't alone. In the more expensive studio next door, professional session musicians were working on a new album; musicians who played backing tracks for big household names, Cliff Richard's drummer being just one. When they strolled out for a tea break, they were intrigued to see the foreign instruments and hear our unusual sounds. On learning more, they were quick to offer support, saying they'd happily give an hour here and there to play on some of the tracks. This was a gift beyond all imagining. We could never have afforded musicians like these and to have their top-quality professional input free of charge enhanced the final product immeasurably as well as encouraging us over the course of that demanding week.

Songs of the Kingdom was released in 1992. I had committed to my fellow trustees that I would ensure any project we engaged in would pay for itself. I was therefore acutely aware of the need to market and sell the album to fully recover the costs incurred. I pleaded with Kingsway to be able to use their imprimatur, paid for of course, but at no cost to them as they would be getting any royalties given - we had used songs for which they were managing the copyrights. I then spent the next six months absolutely flat out on sales, scooting between radio stations, magazines and television, anything to get a little more coverage and exposure. I knew that if people heard it, they would be intrigued and drawn in. I was right and the hard work paid off. The impact was astounding. Stories kept flooding back to us. The album was so well received everywhere that Kingsway decided to commission and fully pay for a second album, *Asia Worships* which we released in 1993. Interestingly, this time around they requested South

Asian Concern to allow them to use our imprimatur, hoping this would help them to sell the album to a wider and more diverse Christian community.

For me, this was deeply significant. Beyond my love of music, beyond just a nostalgic nod to my Indian roots, this music represented my life with its roots in Asia, in Christ, and in music. A means of bringing them all together in a way that glorifies God.

Having struggled so badly with church culture as a new follower of Christ, not even knowing if I was Catholic or Protestant, I was eager to bridge this chasm for other Asians who might have an interest. Gradually, we became more involved in encouraging the setting up of Asian church services, with the BBC *Sunday Worship* inviting me to lead an Asian worship event for Radio 4's prestigious Sunday morning service. Then came the opportunity to be involved in the BBC TV *Sunday Worship* Advent series. I suggested that we use Streatham Baptist Church as they had a regular Asian congregation and as it was there that the seeds for *Songs of the Kingdom* were first sown. It was the second Advent Sunday morning service live on BBC 1, with June George leading the music, and Martin and other celebrity artists commissioned to be a part of the service.

The response to the live broadcast was incredible. People were so taken by the beauty of the mingled cultures that they started travelling across the country, wanting to be part of this wonderful Asian Church! More than once we had to explain to slightly disappointed visitors that, although there was a regular Asian service, this special BBC event had been a one-off event with a specially invited audience from many different fellowships and churches.

Back then, Asian churches found it hard to have their own premises. Often, they had to squeeze into the gaps in mainstream church schedules. Many churches would lend their building to the Asian community on a Sunday afternoon (although one Oxfordshire church famously refused because they were worried it would smell of curry afterwards!). Elsewhere, a South Asian

Fellowship tried to rent a church that was closing down only to be told they'd been outbid by the local kennel. Every week, Asian Christians would have the heart-breaking experience of walking past this church and seeing dogs jumping around the pews.

Overwhelmed by the injustice of this situation, I made contact with the UK Evangelisation Trust and spoke to their chairman.

"Can you help us? We've got all these churches shutting down in areas with a high South Asian population. Would it be possible to share some of them with South Asian Christians who are desperate for somewhere to meet?"

"I would genuinely love that," he told me, "but the resistance from local leaders is too strong."

I suggested we visit one of the underused buildings. We chose a Brethren church in Southall, right in the middle of Little India.

"How many come to worship here?" I asked.

"None."

"But isn't there a clause in the Constitution of every Brethren church that says bread must be broken once a week?"

"Yes. Two elders come here every Sunday morning. They unlock the gates, take communion and then they just leave and shut the church. That's it."

I found the whole situation devastating and so unfair. Even in places where the church buildings weren't being used at all, they were unwilling to let the Asian church use their premises or, if they did, it would only be at very limited times.

I would keep fighting for Asian Christians to have their share of opportunities. Later, when I became a Lambeth Partner, I was very excited at my first meeting to hear Archbishop George Carey talking about a new initiative that would, for example, include black churches in Birmingham. This was great. I kept waiting to hear the word 'Asian' too but it never came. Finally, I went up and asked him, a little tongue in cheek, "Your Grace, will there be any space for Asians in heaven?"

He looked confused, "But I mentioned the black churches," he began, not understanding that this was something different.

We talked briefly and our conversation inspired me to write the book *Chapatis for Tea* with Margaret Wardell. In fairness to Archbishop Carey, although he wouldn't give me any credit for it, he did take the time to hear me out. Later, when the Lambeth Partnership organised an initiative called *Cardiff Alive*, he invited me to go and work with the Asian community in that city, to meet with the local Hindu priests and Imams and to reassure them that we were simply there to share good news and build bridges of understanding between the different communities in Cardiff. Through Viram Jasani, my sitar-playing friend from Imperial, whose relative Anand Jasani worked for the BBC, I managed to get radio airtime on her Sunday programme to talk about Asian Christians and to reassure listeners on what the Archbishops *Cardiff Alive* initiative was all about.

The Asian communities reacted very positively, and I learnt so much from the people there. One Gujarati girl who had become a Christian during her teenage years had been thrown out by her family. She was taken in and adopted by a local Welsh couple, giving her stability and hope, but even with this I could imagine how hard it must have been to lose the wide warm embrace of her family and community. Once again, I remembered the man who had told me, "When I became a Christian, I lost my family and gained lots of meetings!" He had gone on to say how much he missed his family. Of course, times like Diwali were particularly hard for Asian Christians like these.

Suddenly I had an idea.

"Why can't we have an Christian Diwali celebration?"

Diwali is the Indian festival of light, and Jesus is the light of the world. I sensed that if we held a Christian church service on the theme of light with a genuinely Asian flavour, it could fill the aching hole of cultural loneliness these converts were suffering.

So, we organised a national Christian Diwali festival at Kensington Temple, a big church in Notting Hill. The service was featured on the church notice board, announcing with large letters:

KENSINGTON TEMPLE
DIWALI CELEBRATION
SPEAKER: RAM GIDOOMAL

It was clearly a Christian event, but with the words 'Temple', 'Diwali' and 'Ram' (who is the Hindu god of Diwali) it did draw in others too. Two Indian women staying at a hotel in Marble Arch turned up not realising the situation but, when we explained that it was going to be a Christian Diwali, they were still happy to stay.

The service was covered by ITV and broadcast to the nation. Some Christians did react against it, accusing us of syncretism, but it really wasn't. The whole event proclaimed Jesus as the light of the world. In the same way that Christmas and Easter have pagan roots but have been adapted to celebrate Christian truths, we were simply using the Diwali light to celebrate our trust in Jesus the Lord. Diwali means nothing to some people in the West, so they see only syncretism. But Diwali means a lot to us from Indian backgrounds, with memories of the event going back to childhood. Organising the national Christian Diwali festival filled a need for many Asian Christians who were struggling with the need to express our love for Jesus in our way.

The same young girl came from Wales with a couple of carloads of others. She admitted "It's one of the loneliest times of year for us because we don't get to see our brothers, sisters and the wider family."

For Christians like her, this was a chance to celebrate a beloved festival again but differently, remembering and using her old traditions to celebrate Jesus. These Christian Diwali services caught on, grew, and became popular nationwide, often using the songs from our albums but also being inspired to create new music.

So Ricki's childlike attempt to sing along to Indian music in English inadvertently triggered a chain reaction, a fusion of music and cultures, not just for our own enjoyment but with national and even international reach. For example, many years later, in 2010, when John Pacalubo and Les Moir of Integrity Music (formerly Kingsway) travelled to India in search of new musical talent, they received a fairly frosty reception. No one was particularly interested in their mission to find Indian artists. However, just as their meeting was drawing to a close, they happened to mention their involvement in producing *Songs of the Kingdom* and *Asia Worships*, using the typical shorthand for both albums, 'Mukti Dilaye', which means 'He (Jesus) brings salvation' (this was one of the most popular songs we'd produced). Ears pricked up and the mood lifted in an instant. Instead of ushering John and Les out of the door as they had come to expect, their hosts were suddenly asking if they could extend the meeting. There was now a more positive atmosphere and Integrity Music found an open and receptive atmosphere resulting in Indian artists being prepared to work with them. I agreed to join the Word & Worship Trust as a trustee given its vision and mission to search for global talent in order to produce worship music across all cultures. It is all part of a move away from western-centric music, with our biggest, almost miraculous success being the discovery of Sinach and her song 'Waymaker' in Lagos, Nigeria.

Music is evocative and powerful. Even back in pre-1947 India, music communicated a depth of strength and determination, with leading Indian musicians publicising songs loaded with symbolism. There was one about caged birds, poetically urging them to burn their cages and be set free, referring to the fight for Indian independence. Such nuances may have been missed by the British intelligence agencies, but clearly understood by those who were suffering. It should come as no surprise that music continues to break through the darkness of our world.

For me, this new music was also loaded with meaning, like a microcosm of my own life, blending Christ, community, and my love of Indian culture. And, being from the lowly caste of funeral singers, it felt particularly poignant. The label that had once defined my family as 'untouchable' had come back to lift us up. God brings treasure out of the dust – our family's heritage of Indian music was being fulfilled in a way I could never have imagined.

Chapter Seventeen
Healing the Wounds: The Power of Listening

"You've got to help us, Ram."

I looked around at my friends, representatives of a community who had lent me their unwavering support during the mayoral race. Although I had not succeeded in becoming mayor, the word I had given during the campaign was that I would help minorities. It was not an empty promise but something I genuinely longed to do. I could not turn back on that now.

It was 2002 and there was tension in the air. In India's Gujarat state, around a thousand Muslims had been massacred. People were reeling with the horror of it. Prior to this however, a group of 58 Hindu pilgrims had been killed when the train they travelled on was set on fire, apparently by Muslims. Meanwhile Muslims were blaming Hindus for the consequent massacre. It doesn't take much for things like this to escalate, and soon a mood of hostility and conflict had rippled out to Britain, thousands of miles from the original incidents. Across the UK, relations between Hindus and Muslims became strained. Emotions were high and the seeds of violence were being sown, rival communities throwing bricks into mosques and temples respectively.

The Asian business community approached me, fearful and self-conscious.

"This isn't right. We should all be able to get on. What we need to do is to bring everyone together to talk. Just talk it all over and listen to each other, rather than fighting."

They went on to outline their idea for a conference where everyone would have a voice. A conference where there could be some hope of building mutual understanding and respect between these rival communities. A forum where simply communicating would be top of the agenda. I nodded enthusiastically. They would have my full backing.

"And we want you to chair it."

"Me?"

Had I misheard? They wanted me, a Christian, to chair a group of people looking at bringing peace between Hindus and Muslims here in the UK? I was taken aback but honoured to be asked and could not think of refusing. It was such essential work, crucial to the well-being and balance of the UK's Asian population. Of course, if I was surprised to be asked, that was nothing compared to the hue and cry that erupted when the news was made public.

"Why have a Christian speaking up for Hindus and Muslims?"

But perhaps it was precisely because I was neither Hindu nor Muslim that they saw me as the right person for the job. I was neither Hindu nor Muslim, yet, thanks to my background, I had an affinity with both. And the Asian business community knew me and trusted me – they had seen my values in action during the mayoral race.

Of course, it was not the first time SAC & SADP had been involved in strengthening the bonds between these communities. Back during the Kosovo crisis, when we had mobilised Indian doctors to serve in the Balkans, many found the idea of Hindus giving to Muslims via Christians powerfully moving. Here, once again, we wanted to remind both communities that we are all just human beings, looking for hope.

As well as chairing, I was roped into the organisation of the conference, which was planned for 15th August 2002: Indian Independence Day. The choice of date was significant and perhaps a little unfortunate. In direct competition with the Indian High Commission's Independence Day celebrations, the Asian community would now have to decide which event to attend.

We chose the title *'Healing the Wounds: Human Rights and Minorities in India'* with the subtitle *'Indian Independence?'*. Speakers included high profile professionals such as Maya Daruwala, the director of the Commonwealth Human Rights Initiative in Delhi; Lord Parekh; Lord Meghnad Desai of the London School of Economics; Harsh Mander, the director of ActionAid India; Shrikumar Poddar from the Vaishnava Center for Enlightenment and Center for South Asian Studies in Michigan, along with many other prominent Asians – business leaders, journalists, and a film maker. We flew in the most outstanding people in their field.

The conference itself was held at the Indian YMCA, in Fitzroy Square, and was funded completely by the same business community that requested it. It was a powerful achievement and one that I'm very proud of, because of its importance in bringing two warring factions together. Getting to the day in one piece might also have been considered a bit of an achievement, in the light of the intimidation aimed at me by 'the Saffron gang' – the code name for Hindu fundamentalists. There were threats on my life, and comments such as 'Gidoomal must face the Saffron underground" and "We're going to break his legs."

One of the business leaders got wind of this, and quickly stepped in, "Well, it seems Brezhnev's bodyguard is freelancing in London at the moment. We'll get him for you for 24 hours." So that day, I travelled to the venue accompanied by a paid Russian bodyguard. On arrival he took me around the building to check that every exit was properly sealed and chained, making sure there was only one entrance and exit in operation. Meanwhile, I had also had to inform the police who immediately confirmed that they were aware of the threat. They gave me a special code reference number to quote should there be any trouble, adding that they were on standby in case anything happened.

I was determined not be intimidated. If anything, those threats highlighted the need for the forum all the more. Instead of backing off, I extended a special invitation to those who disagreed. We needed to understand them. So I wrote a public note to all the fundamentalists saying, "Please come! You are welcome. There is no charge. You must just come and have your say. You must speak." This was the whole point, for everyone to have a voice. For everyone to be heard.

And they came. People from both sides of the divide. And there, in a functional sports hall marked with badminton court lines for more light-hearted occasions, we prepared for a day full of raw and ragged honesty. A day when people would openly vent their anger, pain, and convictions. At one point, a fundamentalist leader stood up and began to shout and rant. You could feel the friction in the air as emotions began to rise. But Brezhnev's bodyguard didn't bat an eyelid. He simply walked over, stood right next to the man and looked at him. Now, this bodyguard was absolutely huge. One look was all it took. The man quietened down immediately. No one touched anyone and the crisis was averted. Then later in the proceedings, I gave this same man a platform to speak. That was why we were there. Of course, he shouted and ranted again, but I just said, "Fine, we hear you. You've said your bit." Then someone else stood up and I said, "Yes, speak." And so it carried on, with anyone who had something to say, getting the opportunity.

As respite or reward, during the breaks, we enjoyed the delights of Indian food in the hostel restaurant. Perhaps there was little communication between the dissenting groups, but sharing meals is always a good starting point for human contact.

Before the conference took place, we struggled with negative press. All the Asian newspapers were printing letters saying "This conference shouldn't be allowed to happen!" Twenty-four hours later, however, in the very same newspapers, the comments had changed to "Why haven't we done this before?" The turnaround in opinion was incredible. People felt listened to. They had been able to vent their anger and frustration in a safe public place and had their worries and fears acknowledged.

In addition to the Asian and Indian media, the story was covered by the *Financial Times* and others. As my brother-in-law, Deepak, commented at the time "This was a high-level conference that followed the violations of human rights in Gujarat and featured leading speakers offering challenging addresses. SADP has credibility with the Asian community and media and, as a result of the conference, some policies have been changed in terms of addressing the issue of Hindu nationalist violence in India."

Around the same time, the late Andrew Rowe MP invited me to deliver a lecture for Wyndham Place Charlemagne Trust (the 26th Corbishley Lecture 2002) on "Sustaining dialogue: Multicultural Societies under pressure". Andrew was a lovely Christian man who had encouraged me during the mayoral campaign, always giving me sound advice.

The lecture was delivered at SOAS, the School of Oriental and African Studies, with a very high-level audience of MPs and diplomats. I suspected that at least one of them was there because they were a candidate for the role of Chair of a significant public board, and they'd learnt I'd been appointed as an independent member on the interview panel! The lecture itself was well received and was later published in the journal, *Futures*.

Later, SADP organised other peace-making events led by one of our patrons Dr Prem Sharma, our trustee, Deepak Mahtani, and our advisor, Robin Thomson. Amongst these were events such as *7/7 and Beyond* – a conference that brought a South Asian perspective on the July bombings in London, which itself had been carried out by British Asians. Once again, the participants represented all the South Asian faith communities as well as other groups. That conference was followed by others from 2006–2008 and resulted in a highly successful educational resource: a DVD discussion starter called *Friends, Strangers, Citizens? Life in Britain post 7/7*, widely used in schools and community groups.

But all that was for the future. At that time, we had to write up the findings of the 2002 conference, digging up the roots of the differing communities' hostilities, and looking for solutions that would bring reconciliation and healing. After a lot of thought, discussion and collating of materials and minutes, we produced a report that did justice to what had been achieved that day. A report that could pave the way to a better future.

It was one thing to organise the conference and deal with the harsh backlash and threats on my life and safety. It was another to manage emotions on the day, fulfilling my priority to give everyone from every background the opportunity to speak. And it was yet another to put this all together in a report. However, now we were faced with a further challenge: getting the report 'out there'. It needed endorsements and circulation. It needed to be seen and taken on board.

I had managed to get letters of endorsement from various British MPs and members of the House of Lords, commendations on what we had achieved, but the Indian Embassy was a little disgruntled that we had held the event on Independence Day and wasn't overly interested in it at the time.

Two things changed this, and both were through genuine relationships and interactions with others. On a trip to Delhi later in the year, I was able to meet with Sonia Gandhi, the leader of the Indian National Congress party which was in the opposition at that time. She was the widow of Rajiv Gandhi, who had previously been Prime Minister and was President of the Congress party until his assassination in 1991. Through an amazing set of circumstances and the help of my good friend Mohan Philip, I managed to get a half-hour one-to-to audience with Sonia Gandhi in her stately apartment. I walked through the immaculate whitewashed arches of 10 Janpath, Delhi, and was ushered into a waiting room dotted with officials all dressed in traditional white Indian sherwanis.

After a while I was called into her private office, a simple room cluttered with files and paperwork. Dressed in a white sari, Sonia Gandhi sat on the sofa and signalled for me to take one of the armchairs.

As I made myself comfortable, I mentioned how sad I was to see the way the media was treating her. She was preparing for elections and the newspapers were giving her a hard time for being Italian.

"I'm actually ashamed of what's going on," I told her, "You're being branded as a foreigner and not a patriot; but you married a former Prime Minister. You're part of the family. Not to mention that you speak better Hindi than I do! You're more part of the country than I am!"

Then I asked if she would allow me to pray for her as the elections were approaching. She covered her head, bowed it down just as I did, and we prayed.

After we prayed, I reminded her of the cassette version of *Songs of the Kingdom* I'd given her at a function in Kensington Palace a couple of years earlier. On the album there was one track called *My Beloved Country* which had been dedicated to her late mother-in-law, Indira Gandhi who, tragically, had been assassinated in 1984 by her own bodyguards following the stand-off at the Golden Temple in Amritsar. Because the song had been written by June George's father, it was June who had been asked to sing it at the memorial service held in honour of Rajiv Gandhi – Indira Gandhi's son and Sonia Gandhi's late husband – following his death. I explained that all of this was mentioned in the album, adding, "I'd love you to have this CD."

It felt significant to be able to hand Sonia Gandhi this copy in person now that we'd been able to produce it on CD. Throughout our meeting she was so welcoming, hospitable, and gracious, listening carefully to my account of the *Healing the Wounds* conference and my request for an endorsement from her to include in our final report. I had asked the Indian government officially but hadn't had any response (the representatives at the High Commission in London were still upset). She, however, was delighted and instantly agreed to send an endorsement. When it came, it surpassed all expectations: an incredible commendation on heavy duty notepaper from the leader of the opposition.

So now I had endorsements but desperately needed more attention for the report. Having ruffled the Indian Embassy's feathers, I was blocked any time I tried to make contact there, so there was minimal coverage in the UK. We kept pushing in different ways, with some degree of success, but it was when I attended the US President's Prayer Breakfast at the Washington Hilton the following February that the big break came. Although 'Breakfast' in name, this event is in fact a week-long series of meetings, seminars, discussion groups and panels, attended by ambassadors, prime ministers and presidents from all over the world. While it certainly does include several breakfasts (as well as lunches and dinners), there is far more to it than that. One lunchtime I was seated next to the former President of Bangladesh, another day next to the Kuwaiti ambassador. However, despite the high level and calibre of delegates, discussions were always very relaxed, with everyone respecting each other as peers. At one lunchtime meeting, I happened to be on a table with Congressman Pitts of Pennsylvania and, as we chatted, our conversation turned to the conference I'd chaired and its subsequent report. He was immediately interested and said he would do whatever he could to support me. As a Christian himself, he understood the significance of what I was trying to achieve.

"If you give me your report," he said, "I'd be happy to do a three-minute statement in the house."

"Really? That would be so helpful. I can't thank you enough."

"Don't mention it. And while we're at it, if you come to my office after this, we can see what else we can do."

So once the meal had drawn to a close, he drove me to his office in the Capitol building, explaining that I would need to enter through a different gate to him, but that he would send his assistant to collect me. I followed his instructions and waited to be met and escorted to the office. Shortly afterwards a young lady began walking up to me. To my delight, I realised I knew her.

Her mouth dropped open as she exclaimed, "You!" and I replied, equally astonished, "You!"

Congressman Pitts was equally amused and surprised to find that I already knew his assistant. She had been my student at the cross-cultural course I had run at the London Institute of Contemporary Christianity a couple of years earlier. The course was about understanding people of other faiths.

"I loved it," she said as we walked to the office, "It's been such a help in my work here." Then, as I handed over my press release, she told me that Congressman Pitts had asked her to prepare a fax blast.

"That sounds great… but um, what exactly is a fax blast?"

I'd never heard of such a thing, but she explained that my press release would go to several thousand contacts by fax, including 1000 media channels, all at the push of a button. This was before mass mailings by email – and was far more publicity than I could have dreamed of.

So together we organised this fax blast and, sure enough, by the time I got back to my hotel room half an hour later, several messages awaited me from media outlets asking for interviews.

As promised, Pitts also gave a three-minute presentation about my report to Congress, something that would be recorded in their equivalent of Hansard and then get picked up by other governments. Later, we booked a room at the Press Association opposite Capitol Hill and did a press launch there. Once it hit the wires, there was no longer any concern about lack of exposure! On returning to England, I had a call from a very upset Indian High Commissioner demanding to see me immediately.

"Why didn't you come to see me here?" he asked, "We could have handled this. Now I've had a call from Delhi telling me that some British citizen has gone to the US and stirred up negative publicity."

I explained that when I had organised the London conference, there had been strong opposition from his officials.

"I tried, I really did." I assured him, "Every time I planned to come and see you, I was blocked, but I'm delighted we've made a connection now, and next time I promise I will call your office directly and come through you."

So, my relationship with the Indian Embassy was smoothed over. Most importantly, the message from the conference was now out there, all thanks to the goodwill of those I had met along the way. The way things came together was serendipitous. It was not something I had achieved in my own strength. Finding myself in the right place, at the right time, with the right people was a mixture of God opening doors and the power of relational networking. Real friendships. It is vital to make sure that our relationships with others are deep and authentic. We cannot simply use them to achieve our own means. Instead, it is crucial to truly value others and form genuine bonds.

Allowing God to work and having true relationships: these two things have gone hand in hand throughout my life. It is as if one unlocks a door and the other holds it open. When we follow this way, we find opportunities previously closed by discrimination and prejudice miraculously open up before us. As with the conference for healing and reconciliation, it's about power of genuine communication.

The power of listening.

Chapter Eighteen

The Far Pavilions, Close to My Heart

"So, what do you think about this Far Pavilions idea then?"

Amidst the hum of conversation in the Royal Society of Arts hall, where hundreds of voices joined in lively but indiscernible chatter, those words jumped out at me with astounding clarity. I looked around to see who had spoken and turned to join them.

"I'm sorry, I couldn't help overhearing… You were talking about *The Far Pavilions*? The M.M. Kaye novel?"

"Yes. You know it then?"

Did I know it? My memory of the book is inextricably linked not just to the exquisite descriptions of India where it is set, but also to the family vineyard in the south of France, owned by Sunita's uncle as a business asset and one of many holiday homes. Domaine du Galoupet sits a stone's throw from the French President's Provençal summer palace at Le Lavandou. Every year the extended family would gather there for a happy reunion, organised by Sunita's Aunty Lakshmi and her daughter, Contessa

Bina Sella. It was a time for the adults to relax and catch up with each other, while children and grandchildren ran wild and free in the huge gardens. The property itself was sheer luxury: a ten bedroomed château with plenty of space for everyone – including a big barn where the teenagers slept and enjoyed late night parties. What always made us smile was that Aunty Lakshmi, who generally travelled First Class, was happy to take a Ryan Air flight to Hyères as you could almost see the planes landing and then send a driver to pick up any new arrivals.

Although Domaine du Galoupet has now been sold to the LVMH Group, for the years that the property was in the family, those family gatherings were incredible, and the memories that remain are of warmth, sunshine, and joy. One thing I always loved to do there was to catch up on my reading and there was one year when it was difficult to get much sense out of me, so engrossed was I in the book I was reading.

That book was *The Far Pavilions* by M.M.Kaye and, once I had picked it up, it practically had to be prised out of my hands if anyone wanted my attention. The hero of the story is an Englishman, Ashton Pelham-Martyn, who is brought up in India as a Hindu and struggles to reconcile the culture-clash at the heart of his existence. It is, of course, a romance, with Ashton falling passionately in love with an Indian princess, but the undercurrents and backdrop of the book are pure 19th century Indian history. And that is what I loved about it.

Bringing myself back down to earth, I turned to my RSA companions and nodded enthusiastically.

"Oh yes, I know it well. It's one of my favourites."

"Ah, well we were just discussing the possibility of staging a West End musical."

"Really? That would be incredible."

Immediately I could visualise it, the colours and sounds of my motherland splashed across the stage, breathing the story alive. And, quite aside from all the artistic scope, it felt like the perfect time to run a show like this. The culture-clash experienced by the main character was echoed in the current British-Asian identity crisis, something I knew all too well. On an emotional level I wouldn't have needed asking twice. However, even with my more rational business head on, I could see that there was a new openness and interest in South Asian culture here in the UK. With the popularity of Bollywood films, fashion, and Indian cuisine, I could envision a big take up on a mainstream Anglo-Indian production. I felt a frisson of excitement at the thought.

So, while I didn't exactly agree to be involved on the spot, I was certainly keen and, once I'd had time to study the business plan and work out the investment credibility, I got back in touch with them to lend my support. I was fully on board and happily committed to investing and helping raise funds towards the £4 million needed to stage it. Backing a West End show had never even crossed my mind before this, but *The Far Pavilions* felt of deep personal importance to me. If I could be part of sharing that with the world, why would I say no?

Although no one in my direct family had ever worked in theatre, we are related by marriage to the Bachchans – one of the most famous Bollywood families in India. The actor Amitabh Bachchan, in particular, could fill Wembley Stadium several times over, such is his popularity. Meanwhile, in the same family, the broadcaster Ramola Bachchan had often given me invaluable airtime on her channel, TV Asia, most notably during the mayoral campaign, but also at other times in my career.

However, family contacts and relationships are one thing. Staging a musical was something else entirely. While I wasn't involved in the artistic or performance elements, I was on the board and had a say in the overall management of the show. As well as my own financial support, I managed to persuade others to put their hands in their pockets too. Of course, everyone is aware that a stage play is fairly high-risk, but we were hopeful that our confidence would pay off in this case. That said, just to break even, the musical would need to come close to filling the house for nine months. After that it might start to make money. It was a tall order, but one we were happy to reach for. M.M. Kaye is an institution in her own right, and we felt her novel was worth the effort and risk.

When the opening night rolled around, the sights and sounds were everything I had imagined. It was a joyous blast of colour and life. With beautiful sets and breathtaking colourful costumes which were both intricately detailed and authentic, the show managed to tell the story I loved so much in an engaging manner.

There were many positive comments from critics, especially about the Indian music, by the composer Kuljit Bhamra, which one reviewer described as 'captivating and energetic'. In fact, it was generally agreed that the Indian influences brought a buzz to the production. Of course, there were others who were less favourable in their reviews, giving backhanded compliments about the lavishness of the show. Pretty much all of them, however, recognised the high level of musicianship, skill, and performance.

Sadly, as it turned out, the show did not go on. It ran at the Shaftesbury Theatre from April to September 2005. Not long enough to fill the coffers. Not long enough to pay back investors like me. It simply didn't draw enough audiences to refund the initial outlay. I lost my money as did many others.

Do I regret it? Not at all. It's never nice to lose money, but the whole experience was the most delightful fun and gave credit to a book which had brought me so much joy. Rather like the CDs we had recorded some years earlier, it felt like an expression of my mixed cultural heritage. But perhaps even more significant was a love story within the story. Way back before the opening night, the theatre had contacted me about the pre-launch shows.

"Ram, you've been allocated 50 tickets. How many do you need?"

A sudden memory from my corner shop days sprang to mind. A regular customer would occasionally drop by and give us a wad of 25-30 free tickets for West End theatre shows. We never really understood where they came from or why he gave them to us, but now I realised these were the review shows. Before the official launch, they wanted people to come and watch the performance to give feedback. Back in my school days I usually donated at least half a dozen to the drama teacher at school so they could be used by other students. This time, I had another idea.

Sunita & I weren't able to use those tickets but our daughter Nina was studying at the London School of Theology at the time. We decided to give her as many tickets as she needed so she could take along a group of college friends.

One of those friends was a young Swedish man called Jonas Kurlberg, who came along with his sister Frida. The show was finishing late, and because Frida and Jonas were due to be in Sutton the next day, we had invited them to stay at our home overnight. As we chatted over breakfast the subject of food came up, particularly mangoes and Indian food, and we realised just how much we had in common.

"Oh, we love spicy food!" Jonas grinned, "We grew up in Nepal."

I knew instantly that our curries would not bother him in the slightest. Nepalese food trumps Indian for heat any day. Up in the Himalayas they need all the warmth they can get!

Jonas went on to explain that his parents had been missionaries in Nepal, where he and his siblings had grown up, before moving back to Sweden. Jonas had therefore lived far more authentically as a South Asian than we ever had. And, as he and Nina's relationship deepened and blossomed into a happy marriage, we couldn't help thinking what a wonderful dovetail of cultures this was, how perfectly their backgrounds complemented one another: the girl with South Asian roots who had grown up in Europe marrying the boy with European roots who grew up in South Asia.

On their wedding day in 2006, we celebrated in the garden with fresh Indian food for our 300 guests. And, in memory of their first outing together, we surprised their guests by hiring some of the same traditional musicians who had performed at the show that first night. Before the main wedding celebration, we had a recital from the tabla and the shehnai – a rather mournful classical instrument always played at Indian weddings (perhaps to grieve the fact that a daughter is leaving home). So, while *The Far Pavilions* might not have taken off as a musical, it will always have a place in our hearts.

Nina's wasn't the only family wedding that year. Just four weeks before she and Jonas tied the knot, our son Ricki got married in Bournemouth to Natanya, a Hungarian-Jewish girl whose parents pastored a church there taking care of asylum seekers and refugees. Again, here was a connection with our family's past. Here were good people who were helping others in the difficult situation I had once found myself in.

Then, a while later, our eldest son, Ravi married Ruth, an English girl. Even here there was a cross-cultural element. Ruth's parents were living in Normandy, France. Not only that, but her maternal grandparents had been missionaries with the Afghan Border Crusade, meaning that Ravi's mother-in-law had spent her early childhood in Pakistan.

One surprising thing that has linked us all is mangoes. We always look out for Alphonso mangoes in early April. It is our family's favourite and is only available for about six weeks. The family tradition was for my mother-in-law to buy dozens of boxes of these Alphonso mangoes when they reached London and distribute them to the extended family. Sunita and I have continued with that tradition for our three children.

One year we sent a few Alphonso mangoes to Ravi's mother-in-law in France, much to her delight. Now, I grew up with a rather specific way of eating mangoes and I was amused to learn that not only Ravi's, but also Nina's mother-in-law both eat mangoes in exactly the same way. Having cut off all the flesh and shared it out, only the kernel is left. At this point, you unashamedly suck the stone dry. I realise this isn't a very British thing to do in the company of others, but for us it is the best part. The thing that most people throw away is absolutely full of goodness. The grandchildren have been quick to cotton onto this however, and now there is a bit of competition for who gets the stone. A family tradition continues to a new generation.

With such a mix of nationalities in the family now, our seven wonderful grandchildren are growing up with a rich cultural heritage and understanding. In fact, it has kept me on my toes linguistically as I need to know enough Swedish and Hebrew to be able to keep up with some of them. I also love watching the way our children have thrown themselves into parenthood, giving their time to their children through coaching sports and developing their gifts.

Sunita often comments that between the last child leaving for university and the birth of the first grandchild, we had a kind of second honeymoon. It was a time for us, when she could join me on business trips and other travels. We have many incredible memories from this time, plus a couple of more harrowing ones.

For instance, there was one time we were in Washington for an International Justice Mission (IJM) Board meeting and went for dinner at the home of some good friends there. We travelled to them by metro, buying a return ticket in the expectation of going back to our hotel that way too. However, our friend insisted on driving us back.

It was dark and the lighting on the roads wasn't that good. Our friend took a turning to get on the highway, but as he drove on we noticed the cars on the other side of the highway were driving in the same direction as our car.

"Hang on, surely they should be going in the opposite direction?" I thought out loud. My friend looked first a little puzzled, then horrified. As I turned my gaze to look straight ahead I realised to my terror that there were cars in the fast lane approaching our car at speed, flashing their headlights. The terrible realisation hit us that we had not only taken the wrong turn but had somehow managed to join the highway using the exit rather than the entry slipway and were now in the fast lane, travelling in the opposite direction to the flow of traffic. A constant stream of cars hurtled towards us, only just managing to swerve out of our way, each one narrowly missing crashing into us.

It wasn't long before flashing blue lights appeared on the central reservation along with the wail of a siren. A police car approached from the hard shoulder and pulled up in front of us. My friend looked thoroughly petrified as the traffic cop came over to speak to him.

"I'm so sorry Officer. We don't know this part of DC and I think we got lost."

This seemed like rather an understatement. The traffic cop replied "You certainly are lost, but my priority is to ensure you come through this alive!"

Our friend was sheepish and more than a little embarrassed having realised what he had just done – a moment's misunderstanding that put all of us in so much danger. Thankfully, the police were able to direct us safely off the road and away from the risk of death. After some questioning, he accepted our friend had made a genuine mistake and, somehow, let him off scot free. Sunita and I were both very shaken and were relieved to get back to the hotel in one piece that night after rather more excitement than we'd bargained for.

Another near miss came on one of our regular visits to our son Ricki in Israel. Having loved swimming since those childhood Saturdays in the Indian Ocean, one of the highlights when we visit Israel is the opportunity to go for a swim in the sea near their home. Normally we go to a beach which is fairly safe and sheltered but on this occasion we went to Caesarea, a lovely setting in an historic place. I began to swim gently along the shore not realising that a current was moving me steadily out and away from where I started. It did not seem very far to me... until I tried to make my way back and found the current getting stronger, carrying me steadily further away. I tried returning to my starting point but there was no way I could fight the strength of the sea.

I decided instead to aim for the nearest point of shore, but by now I was further out, heading to a rockier area further west. Making a quick assessment, I aimed for a large rock. However, the waves kept threatening to knock me against the same rocks I'd been hoping would save me. I had to carefully follow the rhythm of the waves, hoping to grasp the rock with both hands and hold tight. When I did eventually manage to get hold of it, the rock was so slippery I couldn't get any grip on it. The receding waves kept pulling me back, then buffeting me against the rock. Eventually, however, I managed to hold tight and started shouting for help.

Thankfully someone was fishing nearby. He scrambled down from his ledge and held out his hand to pull me up. Even now I wasn't out of danger. I was too heavy and, with every ebb, the waves pulled me back. Eventually his friend saw and rushed over to help. Together they managed to haul me out of the water. After thanking them profusely, I staggered back to the family, disoriented and weak.

"Papa! What happened? You're covered in blood!"

I hadn't realised that my chest and legs were bleeding, though that did explain the strange looks I'd been getting as I'd made my way back. Strange looks I could cope with, however, knowing how many swimmers were swept offshore and did not make it back alive, I simply felt grateful and relieved to be back on dry land.

These brushes with unwanted adventure were the exceptions, however. Most of our travels were incident-free and simply gave us a wonderful opportunity to discover the beauty and diversity of our world. Being able to share these times with Sunita made them all the better, adding to the joy, and it wasn't just me who missed her when she stopped being able to come. Other board members would always ask where Sunita was.

Our 'second honeymoon' had come to an end with the arrival of grandchildren. However, once they burst into our lives, they brought so much joy, love and delight, there could be no question of wishing it otherwise. It was a new season, one full of hope. Looking to the future.

Chapter Nineteen

May You See Your Children's Children

The clatter of 40 knives and forks mingles with animated chatter and occasional bursts of laughter. Someone calls for second helpings and a chair scrapes with the fidget of a grandchild.

I take a moment to let it all soak in, for the wave of gratitude to fully sweep over me once more.

Family. It has always been at the heart of Indian culture, and I have been so blessed with mine. Looking around the dining room in the Oast house where we were staying, I could see children, grandchildren, cousins, and in-laws, all reunited in one place and enjoying each other's company.

After all the years of early parenthood, taking our children on travels and holidays, this time it was them doing the organising. It was 2019 and our children and their cousins, with the initiative and under the leadership of our eldest son, Ravi, put their heads together to come up with a spiritual retreat for the whole extended family at The Oasts, a luxurious Christian centre lost in the East

Sussex countryside. We had the whole place to ourselves and were able to enjoy a flexible programme of daily prayer, worship and a Bible message, balanced with free time for walks and shopping, and then games in the evening. The centre had a pool with a steam room and sauna, as well as a tennis court, and we never lacked things to do. All this, plus some truly amazing meals.

On the final day, I found out that the Oasts' owner was Sir Christopher Wates. He had been one of the earliest supporters of Citylife-Allia, which I chaired. As we were leaving, I had the chance to meet him and was able to share how from a challenging start 20 years previously, when he had invested in the vision, we had now been able to issue several hundred million pounds' worth of Bonds.

The Oasts was just one of many memorable holidays we took together after our family grew a new generation. Little did we know it would be the last for a long time, with Covid and lockdowns hidden just beyond the horizon. It was painful not being together during those times, missing seeing the grandchildren change and grow. And, when I turned 70 at the end of 2020, there was of course no family party. However, we were able to celebrate virtually – the children and grandchildren having worked hard to prepare videos and to source messages from friends and relatives across the globe.

I, perhaps more than anyone, understand the strength that comes from the crossover between generations, sharing our time and experience. Back when my mind was young, curious, and growing, I loved to stay up late joining in with the adults and their visitors as they discussed life, or to sit listening to my uncles' debates about politics and work during those long family lunches in Mombasa. So many of my skills, so much wisdom has come from sitting at the feet of my elders and, if I can pass even a fraction of that on to another generation, I will be satisfied. Perhaps that is one reason I love being a grandfather.

I remember vividly the moment Ricki told us we were to become grandparents. He and Natanya were living in Oxford at the time but came down to London to share the good news with us. It is incredible how a third party can change your status in this way, from father to grandfather. Of course, that first time felt particularly special but the delight and happiness we took in hearing the news was equal with each subsequent grandchild. Each new life. All seven of them are unique and precious to us and we are grateful for the way our family has grown. When I think back to those days in my twenties, when I wasn't even sure if I would be able to marry the woman I loved, let alone have children and grandchildren with her, I know I have been blessed beyond compare. The story could have ended very differently but somehow, I have come through this, surrounded by those I love.

As Natanya's pregnancy progressed, we waited eagerly for news, keeping in touch perhaps rather more than usual. Just before the due date we visited them, going on a long walk and encouraging Natanya to eat curry to hurry the birth along. One week later, little Izak appeared in the world. The early morning phone call from Ricki was all that was needed to make us hop into our car and take a brisk drive to the John Radcliffe hospital. There we met Natanya's parents, who were equally excited as this was also their first grandchild. Seeing Izak for the first time – holding him and hearing him cry – was such a moving moment. He was a strong healthy baby, and I was astonished to find him pushing his tiny legs as if to stand up just hours after his birth.

Later, when he was 18 months old, I recall having what felt like a very meaningful telephone call with him, despite the fact that his language of choice was gibberish. Each time I spoke, Izak would reply in an intelligent sounding babble. It was almost as if he understood what I was saying and was responding accordingly. We must have 'chatted' for quite some time, much to everyone's surprise and amusement.

Izak's arrival in 2008 was closely followed by his sister, Anjali, the following year. Then, Ravi's son, Rohan, and Nina's daughter, Eliora, were both born in 2010. Nina and Jonas were staying with us at the time while Jonas finished his Masters at

LSE and Nina worked on disaster risk reduction with Tearfund. I will never forget the day Eliora was born. I was due to fly to Cape Town for a Lausanne conference but managed to drive Nina to hospital at 6 am and then, later that afternoon, to visit her and the newly born Eliora, just before my flight. I returned from the same conference in Cape Town just in time to see Ruth and Ravi with their new son, Rohan, who had been born 10 days later than Eliora, but in Kent.

Then in 2012, all three couples each had another baby: Ravi and Ruth bringing us a third granddaughter, India, while Nina and Jonas, by this time in Norway, had a son, Silas, and Ricki and Natanya, now in Israel, another son whom they named Ezra.

Sunita and I happily took on our new identity: Mama and Papa to Ravi and Ricki's children while Nina's children call us Nani (Sunita) and Nana (me). Of course, the latter has at times caused eyebrows to raise here in England. On a train once, an English lady overheard Eliora asking for 'Nana' – clearly talking about me. "But surely your wife, her 'Nana', is with her?" she asked, very concerned. I realised the confusion and had to explain that according to Indian tradition, my daughter's children refer to their grandparents as 'Nani' (maternal grandmother) and 'Nana' (maternal grandfather). At first, even the grandchildren found these terms a little puzzling, though they have all got used to them as they've grown older. Admittedly, it does leave me open to some teasing and more than once they've called me 'Nana Banana'!

We love to spend time with them all, one trademark of this during their early years was when I would make up 'Shoko loko bango shay' stories for them. 'Shoko loko bango shay' was a folkloric character in my junior school textbook in Mombasa, but when I told the stories I would adapt them to include the children's names and characteristics. So, for example, there would be stories about Izaklokobangoshay for my grandson Izak and then about Indialookybangoshe for my granddaughter India and so on for all the others. I veered significantly off piste from the original African stories by adding in elements of their own lives, perhaps what they were having for dinner to encourage them to eat up, and I'd drop in all sorts of characters from their favourite films and TV shows for good measure.

When Sunita and I had said goodbye to the carefree travels of our 'second honeymoon', it was by no means the end of our adventures. Quite the opposite! Before the get-together at The Oasts, many other big family holidays had taken us far and wide, the generations mingling happily. The role of grandparents is a happy mix of fun, complicity with the grandchildren, and support for the parents. Although it is not without moments of hard work, the rewards are great. It is a true joy and an honour to be involved in each of these young lives.

Our family is rather far flung now, Ricki and Natanya having moved to Israel in 2010 (living first in Haifa before settling in Binyamina, near Caesarea, in 2013). However, we try to meet as often as we can. This usually works out with us having at least one meet up a year in the UK and then alternate years, a gathering abroad too. In 2014 we met in Ludlow on the Welsh border where we shared a rambling farmhouse which had a large kitchen – perfect for noisy family meals – and an Aga where we dried our clothes after the inevitable rain showers. The grandchildren loved the garden with its pirate ship climbing frame as well as the working farm where they spent time with the animals, rode horses, and watched chickens lay eggs.

Then, in 2016, we went to Cyprus where we rented a large villa with a pool, just a rocky cliff-walk away from the beach. Every mealtime, there would be the universal struggle to get all the children to eat up. This was when my 'Shoko loko bango shay' storytelling came into its own.

"No spoonful, no story," I announced.

Seven pairs of wide eyes stared at me, taking this in. Then, each of them picked up their cutlery and shovelled in a mouthful, waiting expectantly for the next line of the story as they chewed. Two years later, in Sri Lanka we used the same approach, though admittedly the hotel buffet there was so bountiful and varied that feeding the children was not really a problem. This time, as I told the stories, even the waiters listened in, wanting to know what happened next. I was always thankful that the grandchildren remembered where I'd got to in the fast-developing storyline because I had usually forgotten what I'd made up during the previous meal!

Sri Lanka was a memorable holiday for so many reasons, not least because Nina and Jonas had lived and worked there from 2007 to 2009, some ten years earlier, Nina having served with Tearfund on a Tsunami housing project in partnership with the UN, while Jonas was a lecturer at Colombo Theological seminary.

We spent our first night in Colombo at the Mt Lavinia, a hotel with all the atmosphere of an old British Colonial residence, and guards dressed accordingly. Waiting for lunch that first day, I couldn't resist the lure of the pool. I dived in with the grandchildren and swam several lengths before realising that my phone was in the pocket of my swimming trunks, now rather the worse for wear. As well as the pool, the beach was mere metres from our bedroom. A few short steps took us down to a sheltered cove where, phone-free this time, we swam in the warm clear waters of the Indian Ocean, watching Water Monitors that looked like large lizards sunning themselves on nearby rocks.

Moving on, we travelled south to stay at the beach, where the grandchildren all took turns to scare their parents by rope-swinging from a coconut tree on the sand right across the sea in a long arc. In the afternoons, huge fast-moving turtles would come out to play. The grandchildren and their parents donned snorkels, and swam alongside, trying to keep up.

But perhaps the most magical moment came early one morning when the owner of the hotel called us.

"The turtles are hatching! Do the children want to come and watch?"

Quickly and quietly we all made our way to the beach where the baby turtles were beginning to poke their sandy heads out of the nest. It was the most extraordinary sight, especially seeing the grandchildren holding the hatchlings in their hands, cradling them gently and carefully before lovingly placing them on the sand and following their onward journey to the sea. To share such moments has been a privilege I will never forget.

Though learning from my elders has always been important to me, I recognise too the wisdom of youth, their positive, open-minded take on life and their new insights into old ways, not to mention the fact that sometimes they genuinely know more than me about certain things!

So, as my family has grown not only larger, but also more international, I have had the pleasure of being taught by my grandchildren. When it came to learning Hebrew in Israel, I was always glad to have Izak, Anjali and Ezra there to help me pronounce the words correctly – "'No Papa, it is KHHHH – KHHH KHHH KHHH, from the back of your throat. Try again Papa, and again.' Then eventually, there was the feeling of satisfaction (and relief) as they praised me, "Yup, you've got it Papa!" It was in the pool in Colombo during that same Sri Lanka trip that the three of them realised the secret pleasure of knowing another language. They whispered to me with delighted complicity, "We've got our own coded communication here Papa! We can say what we like in Hebrew and nobody else will understand!"

Similarly, on a family holiday in Sweden, Eliora and Silas had been wonderful at helping me with my Swedish, although with one small hiccup. When out for a walk, I used the Swedish words I'd learnt for 'right' and 'left'. Both of them were convinced I had learnt these the wrong way around. There followed a serious discussion in which Eliora and Silas insisted I had been wrongly taught, to the extent that I began to doubt myself... until they spoke with their dad and found, much to their dismay, that on this occasion I was right!

Meanwhile, Rohan and India both have their own interests. Rohan's love for cricket is a constant source of conversation during our walks in the park. Although, I hope, it won't get him into the same trouble it landed me in on my honeymoon.

Despite having given up playing cricket as a teenager because of my propensity to minor injuries, I still loved to follow it, avidly listening to test match specials in Mombasa on our short-wave radio receiver. Even without my own radio, it would have been no problem keeping up – every Indian trader there had the radio commentary blaring out onto the streets of Mombasa.

When Sunita and I married in July 1976, the week of our wedding happened to coincide with the 4th Test Match between the West Indies and England in Leeds. Despite all the wedding paraphernalia and activity, it was fairly easy to keep up with the progress of the match. After the wedding and two further days of family celebrations, we finally set off on our honeymoon, flying out to Alderney in the Channel Islands on a ten-seater two-engine plane from Southampton. By then, the match was quite evenly balanced, and I was desperate to know what would happen, so decided to smuggle my tiny red transistor radio into the pocket of my blue denim jacket, sneaking a listen whenever circumstances allowed. However, on Tuesday 27th, the final day of the test match, we had planned a long romantic walk. Much as I was enjoying it, it was hard to resist taking the occasional opportunity to hang back and put the transistor to my ear for an update. Walking slightly behind Sunita every now and then, I managed to keep up with progress without being found out. It was only when we sat down to enjoy the picnic lunch laid on by our hotel that temptation got the better of me. The match was so close, and England was battling to survive. I had to have a quick listen. That did it! Sunita cottoned on and my game was up.

"This was meant to be a long romantic walk!" she cried.

After all that, the West Indies won, if only by 55 runs. As for me, I was well and truly in the doghouse with my new wife. So you could say both England and I lost on that occasion!

This disgrace aside, my love of cricket has never wavered, and it has been wonderful to see my son Ravi become an accredited cricket coach with Rohan's club, passing down his skills to the next generation. Watching Rohan play, I was pleased to be able to capture on video the moment when he scored a four off a reverse sweep shot, even if I sadly missed getting his 'caught and bowled' action immortalised on camera when he switched from batting to bowling. Rohan's love of cricket is equalled by his sister India's love of nature. She would probably have been a better companion for Sunita, on that long Alderney walk! When we do go walking with India, however much we enjoy her love for all things wildlife, it can be a little disconcerting when we suddenly realise she's vanished into thin air.

"Where's India?"

"I have no idea. She was right here a minute ago!"

Panic stations ensue and Sunita rushes around setting up search parties, only to find that India is happily chatting to insects hidden behind some copse of dense bushes or another, wondering what all the fuss is about. Of course, every parent and grandparent has a story like this.

Because where there are children there will always be stories: the ones we tell them and the ones they live themselves. Of course, my own 'Shoko loko bango shay' stories were a bit of fun, made-up tales to make the children smile. But as my grandchildren grow, I will continue to tell them stories: stories of truth and courage. In many ways, all the stories I'm telling here are for them. I want my grandchildren and their contemporaries to grow up knowing both their value and their values, knowing to stand up for what is right. And most of all, knowing they can push through difficulties and overcome any obstacles that are put in their way. Because that is my story.

Chapter Twenty
All the Lost Things

Daddy's shop smelled of haberdashery and thick earthy leather. As a boy, I would watch him unfurl a spool of silk, the billowing clouds of soft material suspended momentarily in mid-air before settling in gentle waves upon the counter. Then that rhythmic, metallic scrape of blades, the gentle rip of cloth and the final click of the scissors before he folded and packaged it up for a waiting customer.

The family shops of my childhood sold silk, traded honestly but at great financial gain. We were negotiators, always astute and looking for the best price, no matter what. Not that Daddy and the uncles weren't good, hard-working men. Of course they were. But having lost everything during the Partition and with such a large family to support – not to mention daughters' dowries to save for – their main concern was profit.

Of course, back then, the term Fair Trade hadn't even been invented. No one was talking about such things, but years later as it rightly hit the agenda, I educated myself. I had seen first-hand the hope-shattering inequalities faced by those in low-income countries. However gifted we might be, any one of us placed in their shoes simply would not find prosperity, because the whole system is skewed against them. Over the years, as I immersed myself in different charity ventures, I became convinced that Fair Trade was a key of colossal importance in easing poverty.

Having grown up in a family of silk traders, perhaps it is not surprising that the cloth trade has once again become part of my life in later years. As my journey unfolded and my values evolved, I became aware of the injustices and by-products of the textile industry. Not silk this time, but cotton. I was shocked to learn that 24% of the world's insecticides and 11% of pesticides are used in cotton production, with the fashion industry as a whole responsible for 10% of annual global carbon emissions. Chemicals used on the ground shorten the lives of cotton farmers and their families; the infected water and insecticides in the air make children sick. Meanwhile, the land becomes virtually unusable. I see nothing fair about a trade that impacts others so badly.

I decided I had to get involved in counteracting this by promoting organic sustainable cotton and thus became the Chair of CottonConnect, a social enterprise founded by Textile Exchange (USA) and C&A Foundation. CottonConnect helps companies ensure their supply chain is clean. Business can, and should, be powerfully involved in changing society for the better. Working with clients including big names such as Primark, C&A Europe, Tesco, and Carrefour we are able to make a real difference to the lives of farmers and their families. Organic textiles are, of course, not just about the health of the consumer, but also, and perhaps far more so, about the health of the workers. Companies come to us wanting their supply chain to be organic, but responsible business means more than that. They need to be acting justly on a growing number of levels. Are they paying their workers a fair price? Are they gender-empowering? Are they environmentally sustainable? Are they respecting human dignity? These are all important questions that need addressing to provide assurance of a clean supply chain.

Cotton is of course just one area. Long before this, I had thrown myself into the Fair Trade movement, supporting Traidcraft from its early days and putting my money where my mouth was (or perhaps vice versa), even back when their coffee was barely drinkable! Nowadays, it easily stands up to the best in the market. For many years, I was Chairman of Traidcraft, only stepping down in 2020. During my penultimate year there, trading became so bad that the organisation was staring bankruptcy in the face. I found myself with 72 hours to save the situation. We desperately needed a six-month loan of £300,000, but after trying several Christian millionaires with no success, things were looking hopeless. At the time I was also Chairman of Stewardship, and decided to call my predecessor there who I knew had managed to rescue Lion Publishing a while before. He gave me one more name, a man who lived in the Isle of Man and who turned out to be someone I had met. He was also one of Traidcraft's biggest shareholders! With just hours to go, he offered us an interest-free loan not needing any security or repayment until the January, when we would have our Christmas profits in place. It was, as the Bible tells us – God is able to do immeasurably more than we ask or imagine, exceeding all our expectations. The following day, instead of announcing bankruptcy as many had feared, I was able to give everyone this wonderful news.

I won't pretend it was always easy, but these, the pioneers of Fair Trade, proved time and again that it is possible to make a profit and still treat everyone with the respect and justice they deserve. Along with Oxfam and other bodies, Traidcraft had formed the Fair Trade Foundation back in 1992, long before my own involvement. This is something hugely valuable, but it has become a little more challenging since bigger businesses have started gathering around the table, paying significant membership fees but wanting the Fair Trade kitemark for a lesser 'cost'.

"Look," one of them said at a meeting, "I know we're saying we have to use 100% Fair Trade ingredients to get the kitemark, but surely if it's 90% that's fine, isn't it?" Traidcraft had to speak up, because where exactly do you draw the line. Is it half Fair Trade? Part Fair Trade? It is still possible to make a profit, but the commitment to those in need must be our priority and there is a cost involved. To empower the disadvantaged will always be a mixture of trade and aid in my opinion. However much money we raise – whether pennies from cake sales and car washing or millions from high level TV campaigns, in the long run, those funds will run out if we don't help the disadvantaged find ways of working and making sufficient money with dignity. Ways like the sewing business Christmas Cracker teenagers set up to help women in Dharavi escape prostitution; or the little bakery we helped get going in the Fortaleza slum. Good business can change lives.

Business is rarely the first thing people think of when they want to help others, but business was my speciality, my gifting, my expertise. When I first sensed that unignorable call to live life differently, I assumed it would mean moving out of commerce and taking a completely different path, but on the contrary, my gifts were there to be used. Gradually it became clear that business didn't have to be all about profit, I could use my know-how to bring good to the world – much more good than I could have dreamed of. Whether through promoting justice and Fair Trade, helping charities raise and use their funds wisely or speaking up for good business practice, morals and integrity in my role as a Vice-President of the Institute of Business Ethics International Advisory Council (IBE), the second part of my working life is testimony to the value of business skills in bringing positive social change.

Other challenges came in different packages. As Vice-Chairman of Lausanne, I was attending a debrief on the 2010 Lausanne conference (the one I had famously fit in between two of my grandchildren's births). On the first morning, the Chairman Doug Birdsall, called and asked to see me.

"Ram, I'm not well. I'd like to request that you chair the meetings and chair the board". The meetings were scheduled to last a few days beginning later that morning.

He had done incredible fundraising work, raising the substantial sum of money required for the meetings in Cape Town, but there was a significant deficit, made up of two loans, both accruing interest. I suggested some other candidates who would be more suited to take on the role of chair, well known American Christian philanthropists, but seemingly no one wanted to take on the challenge of an organisation with such a large deficit.

Standing there, I remembered an evening over twenty years beforehand. Our friend, Tim Amies, had invited Sunita and me to a dinner at London's Guildhall in 1989. On arrival, we looked over the programme. Our eyes widened. There was an opportunity to meet someone quite extraordinary after the formal dinner. We crept down to the allotted place in the Crypt, expecting to see throngs of people surrounding the great man, but it was strangely quiet. Billy Graham looked over at us and smiled.

"Ah, I was beginning to think no one was coming!"

Here was a chance to meet one of the giants of the Christian faith, and everyone else had somehow missed the memo! For us, it was incredible. That time just to talk with him, quietly, one to one and without a crowd nearby.

Twenty years on, I was being asked to take the mantle for the movement he co-founded with John Stott. The memory jogged me, reminded me of my belief in the genuine value of this movement which was aptly described to me by Richard Bewes as 'a network of truth and trust'. Finally, I stopped protesting and agreed to take on the role of chair. I'm happy to say that when I handed over responsibility to the new chairman, Bob Doll, 6 years later, it was with a healthy bank balance. The credit for this dramatic turnaround goes to the fundraising committee to whom I delegated the task. The committee included the incoming Chairman, Bob Doll, the newly appointed CEO, Michael Oh, the Chair of the Audit

Committee Jerry White, the Vice-Chair Grace Matthew, and Doug Birdsall who, even as he was recovering, opened up to the committee his incredibly wide network of donors, and deep and trusted relationships.

For me, using my business skills is my Christian service to others, as is speaking up for truth whenever necessary. All the numerous boards I have served on have been focussed on bringing justice and a fairer society. The most recent example is my involvement on the Parliamentary and Health Services Ombudsman (PHSO) board, outstandingly chaired by Rob Behrens, a man of great integrity with whom I had already worked during my time as Chairman of the Office of Independent Adjudicator for Higher Education in England and Wales many years previously.

Even longer ago, various members of the wider family – not wanting me to leave my high earning career – had suggested I should simply keep working, get that seven-figure-salary, and donate a chunk of it to the disadvantaged. Surely that way I would be doing more than my fair share? No doubt that may be the Call for some people. However, God used me differently, giving me the privilege of generating a ten-figure sum for good causes through Allia, Christmas Cracker, and other charity ventures. What I have helped create in charity revenue far exceeds anything I could have donated from my own salary.

This is the point that Charles Handy made in his acclaimed 2006 book, *The New Philanthropists*. With photographs taken by his wife Elizabeth, he featured prominent entrepreneurs who chose to involve themselves in real tangible charity ventures rather than just giving away chunks of their wealth. It was exactly what I had been trying to do all those years since my Dharavi experience, and I was both humbled and delighted when Sunita and I were included in the publication.

While my main charity concern was always SAC, I loved getting involved in other causes too. In 2005, my good friend Lord McColl (who many years earlier had helped me bring an Indian child with leukaemia to Great Ormond Street for treatment) nominated me as Vice President for The Leprosy Mission in England and Wales (TLMEW). Having been involved with The Leprosy Mission's vital work back in Christmas Cracker days, it was a joy and a great honour to be able to contribute to their great work. It is a cause I am deeply committed to and now, even as I shed responsibilities elsewhere, I have chosen to become one of their trustees.

Ironically, I only met Lord McColl in the first place because I was desperately trying to help someone in need. As was so often the case, my one relatively small act of kindness repaid me with countless wonderful opportunities. Our compassionate actions show others who we are deep down. We become entrusted with more. It is a theme I have seen over and over; how both the good we've done and the pain we've suffered finally come back to us, full circle. Or, as the Bible puts it, "… in all things, God works for the good of those who love him."

There is another verse in the Bible that springs to mind too: one which speaks of God restoring to us the years the locusts have eaten (Joel 2:25). It has been so true for me. When we first moved to London, my charmed life seemed to be over. All I could see was the back of the tapestry – the mess, the broken threads and frayed edges, all the things that had gone wrong. But gradually, all these things came back to me in different, even better ways. Yes, I had to keep going, I had to persevere, constantly repeating my mantra of 'Focus on what you can do, not what you can't'. Nothing happened quickly. There were years, years of wondering if things would ever come good. But later, all the lost things were returned to me in ways that exceeded my imagination. And the same can be true for anyone. It is too easy to focus on the messy back of the tapestry but later, if you don't give up, you will see how those threads have been looping into a pattern, making something beautiful. When those threads come full circle, you will gasp in wonder at how there was always a plan, how the potential was there all along.

Grant Colfax Tuller describes this eloquently in his poem, *The Weaver*:

My life is but a weaving
Between my God and me.
I cannot choose the colors
He weaveth steadily.

Oft' times He weaveth sorrow;
And I in foolish pride
Forget he sees the upper
And I the underside.

Not 'til the loom is silent
And the shuttles cease to fly
Will God unroll the canvas
And reveal the reason why.

The dark threads are as needful
In the weaver's skillful hand
As the threads of gold and silver
In the pattern He has planned.

He knows, He loves, He cares;
Nothing this truth can dim.
He gives the very best to those
Who leave the choice to Him.

We may lose things which are deeply and immensely valuable to us, or we may choose to give things up for others, but eventually these find us again in different ways. For me, there have been so many examples.

How, as a young boy, I shared my tuck money out of a deeply engrained sense of equality and justice, and decades later, was rewarded with a place on a prestigious board.

How, at 16, I went from a having a privileged school position and status as Head Boy to a much humbler experience, having to start again and catch up on missed time in a school where my accent was laughed at, any time I opened my mouth. But through hard work and the support of others, I not only achieved a high level of education, but became an A-level Cambridge examiner and governor of several schools.

How I left behind my friends in Kenya and thought I had lost them, but found that true friendship lives on. My Kenyan classmates still keep in touch to this day and, even now, though we rarely see each other, I still consider Jack one of my closest and most trusted friends. On top of this, despite the difficulties when first moving to London, there have been new friendships at every turn in the road, the most notable and significant being one that grew out of a visit to family friends Chatru and Jyoti in Tenerife many decades ago, dinner and chess blossoming into a deep and true friendship which has continued to this day.

How, also when leaving Kenya, I was devastated to lose my father's precious stamp collection, the one I had worked on for so many years. My one physical connection with him. But decades later, I was appointed onto the Royal Mail Stamp Advisory Committee, helping select stamps for the approval of Her Majesty the Queen.

And how I would probably never have met Sunita, my life partner and best friend, without the upheaval of losing everything and moving to London.

How, to pursue my chance at a marriage of love rather than arrangement, I postponed my PhD, eventually having to let go of that dream altogether – yet, through my service to others, I was later awarded numerous honorary doctorates and a Fellowship of Imperial College, not to mention being appointed as an honorary member of the Cambridge University Faculty of Divinity.

How I let go of the chance to live in India but always felt the influence of my homeland permeating my life's decisions.

Seeing myself featured in *High Flyers 50* in 2021 was a moving confirmation of that ongoing, unbreakable bond.

How, my family's original ranking as lowest-of-the-low funeral singers flourished into a deep appreciation of music that led me to record two CDs and become part of a team searching for new artists from diverse communities across the globe.

How we lost everything, not just the wealth but the ease and security it brings. The respect of others. The dent in reputation when you fall. We lost it all, but taking every opportunity, my family rebuilt a thriving business, and I took flight with a career in finance and trade, only leaving it later of my own choice.

And finally, how I lost two fathers but gained a heavenly one.

Every broken thread, all the lost things, each one was restored to me or came full circle in some way, looping back into the tapestry, whether through my own actions and perseverance or through some seemingly coincidental gift.

Every one of these things felt lost to me at some point, yet nothing really was. And how did these things come back to me? Not by some stroke of luck but through perseverance, ongoing hard work, and pushing at doors. Even when things seemed impossible, I kept doing whatever I could. What was always there, however, was that potential for change. Once I'd done the groundwork and made the connections, things did finally fall into place. Sometimes it was seemingly miraculous, other times through sheer determination. And very often, breakthroughs came thanks to the genuine relationships I had built up with others, never seeking to use them for my own purposes, but valuing them as fellow human beings and looking for ways to help and support them. So many times, it was my own passion for equality and justice for others that in turn, brought good things to me.

If I had to write a letter to my younger self, and perhaps in a way that's what this is, I would tell him: these are the things that will save you. You must never give up. You must never let obstacles grow so high they seem insurmountable. Instead, always think about what you can do, rather than what you can't. I would tell him about the importance of creative thinking, diplomacy, and determination. Those things alone, however, suggest that we can do it all without help. I would be lying if I said that was so. Help came from the love and support of family. It came from principles rooted in my Indian heritage. It came from learning from my elders. It came through 'relational networking' which is genuine friendship and compassion for others. And yes, because I follow Christ, I also believe that many of my breakthroughs came through study of the Bible, and through discussing things with God.

But there is another, perhaps more surprising layer to this. I learned the real secret – that I didn't need all the riches and recognition in the first place. Letting go of this false need for wealth has allowed me to live freely and generously, always having more than enough for a good life, without any sense of envy towards those who have more. Overwhelmed by the huge needs of those less fortunate than myself, I found I had lost my taste for success and acclaim. But ironically, letting go of this and throwing myself wholeheartedly into serving others, I have received more blessings and recognition than I could have ever imagined.

I will never forget an incident from my teenage years in Kenya when the Aga Khan visited our school. There was a tremendous fanfare and excitement around this. It was a huge honour that he should visit and, as Head Boy, I was offered the even greater honour of a face-to-face meeting with him. However, as plans were made and arrangements put into place, I somehow knew I needed to forego this, to give this wonderful opportunity to someone else. An African boy had recently joined my class, the first African Kenyan student to be admitted to this school. He was asked to sit next to me so I could help him settle in and make friends with the other students. I suddenly realised this would mean the world to him and would also be a significant moment for the school. Not only that, it would also demonstrate to the

Aga Khan an aspect of integration that the school was engaging in following the Independence of Kenya in 1963.

It seems to mirror the way that later in life, when I'd reached that much strived for success and respect, I realised I needed to let it go and prioritise the needs of others. Remembering myself as that 16-year-old Head Boy with all the dreams and expectations – and yes, perhaps some sense of entitlement – I am finally thankful that my rich idyllic lifestyle was whipped away from me. I am thankful for the life of learning from experience and struggle, understanding the difficulties and obstacles of others and recognising discrimination and injustice.

As a refugee from a family who were twice-migrants, I had to watch my beautiful life unravel like the threads and offcuts of silk on the floor of Daddy's shop. Threads to be swept up and thrown away, scraps to be sold off cheaply. Sometimes it felt that way. But instead, we picked up those threads and wove them into something more precious than ever. Far better than the life I had planned for back in Kenya.

All this has left me with a legacy to pass onto anyone facing the same seemingly insurmountable obstacles and a confidence that such things can be overcome, often with results more precious than anything we could plan.

All the lost things coming full circle to reward us in the most unexpected ways.

All the love and hard work returning to me tenfold.

Over the course of my life, there were some roads I did not choose, some I did. But whether or not we have chosen the path we're on, we can always choose how we walk it. As for me, I chose to simplify my lifestyle, to find a different road, one which ironically led me to riches of greater worth than I could have imagined. A road where the obstacles were many but never insurmountable. A road of compassion that left me with a peaceful heart.

A road that led me far and wide but took me right where I belonged. My chosen path.

My silk road.

PIPPA RANN BOOKS & MEDIA
and GLOBAL RESILIENCE PUBLISHING
imprints of
SALT DESERT MEDIA GROUP LTD., U.K.
Working in collaboration with international distributors
from the whole of the English-speaking world.

Salt Desert Media Group Ltd. (est. 2019) is a member of the Independent Publishers Guild. At present, the company has two imprints, **Global Resilience Publishing** and **Pippa Rann Books & Media (PRBM).**

PRBM was launched on August the 17th, 2020, with the first title published in Autumn 2020 – Avay Shukla's *PolyTicks, DeMocKrazy & MumboJumbo: Babus, Mantris and Netas (Un) Making Our Nation.*

Since then, we have published:

- Sudhakar Menon's *Seeking God, Seeking Moksha*;
- Sudeep Sen's *Anthropocene: Climate Change, Contagion, Consolation*;

- Brijraj Singh's *In Arden: A Memoir of Four Years in Shillong, 1974 to 1978*;
- Valson Thampu's *Beyond Religion: Imaging a New Humanity*; and
- *Mantras for Positive Ageing*, edited by Padma Shri Dr V. Mohini Giri and Meera Khanna, with a Foreword by H. H. The Dalai Lama.

If there is no further significant disruption by pandemics and wars, PRBM plans to release, in the near future, Jyoti Guptara's *Business Storytelling From Hype to Hack*, Varghese Mathai's *The Village Maestro and 100 Other Stories*, Rashmi Narzary's *An Unfinished Search*, and Anthony P. Stone's *Hindu Astrology: Myths, Symbols and Realities*.

In addition, there are two books especially commissioned for the 75th anniversary of India's independence: Catherine Ann Jones's *East or West: Stories of India*, and *Converse*, an anthology of Indian poetry in English, especially chosen by the international prize-winning poet, Sudeep Sen.

We are always open to first class ideas for books, provided complete manuscripts can be turned in on time.

Please note that Pippa Rann Books & Media focuses entirely and exclusively on publishing material that nurtures, among Indians as well as among others who love India, the values of democracy, justice, liberty, equality, and fraternity.

That means we publish:
- Books and media by authors of Indian origin, on any subject that broadly serves the purpose mentioned above.
- Books and media by non-Indians on any subject connected with India or with the Indian diaspora, which serves the purpose mentioned above - again, broadly interpreted.

* * *

By contrast with PRBM, Global Resilience Publishing began operations in Autumn 2021, with the first publications being released from Summer 2022. As the name suggests, the imprint focuses on subjects such as:

- Climate Change
- The Global Financial System
- Multilateral Governance (e.g., the United Nations)
- Public-Private Partnership
- Leadership around the World
- International System Change
- International Corporate Governance
- Family Firms around the World
- Global Values
- Global Philanthropy
- Commercial Sponsorship
- New Technologies including Artificial Intelligence

Two things make GRP unique as an imprint:
1. Our books take a global perspective (not the perspective of a particular nation);
2. GRP focuses exclusively on such global challenges.

* * *

Global Resilience Publishing and **Pippa Rann Books & Media** are only two of several imprints that are conceived of, and will be launched, God willing, by Salt Desert Media Group Ltd., U. K. The imprints will cover different regions of the globe, different themes, and so on. And if you have an idea for a new imprint that you would like to establish, please get in touch.

Prabhu Guptara, the Publisher of Salt Desert Media Group, says, "For all our imprints, and for the attainment of our incredibly high vision, we need your support. Whatever your gifts and abilities, you are welcome to support us with the most precious gift of your time. The *seva* you do is not for us but is for the sake of our nation, and for the world as a whole. Please email me with your email, location, and phone contact details on *publisher@pipparannbooks.com*, letting me know what you feel you can do. Could you be an organiser or greeter at our events? Could you ring people on our behalf? Write to people? Write guest blogs or articles? Write a regular column? Do interviews? Help with electronic media, social media, or general marketing? Connect us with people you know who might be willing to help in some way or other?"

He adds, "I am one man, so I do not and cannot keep up with everything that is happening in India, let alone in the world. There are many challenges and numerous opportunities – help me to understand what these are. Pass information on to me that could be useful to me. Put your ideas to me. Any and all insights from you are most welcome, as they will multiply our joint effectiveness. It is only as we work together that we can contribute effectively to changing our nation and our world for the better".

* * *

Join our mailing list to discover Pippa Rann Books which will inform you on a wide range of topics, and inspire as well as equip you as an individual, as a member of your family, and as someone who loves India.

www.pipparannbooks.com